Facts On File Encyclopedia of

IN AMERICA

Law and Government

Encyclopedia of Black Women
in America

Facts On File Encyclopedia of

Black Women

IN AMERICA

Law and Government

Darlene Clark Hine, Editor

Kathleen Thompson, Associate Editor

☑® Facts On File, Inc.

Facts On File Encyclopedia of Black Women in America: Law and Government

Facts On File, Inc.
11 Penn Plaza
New York, NY 10001

Library of Congress Cataloging-in-Publication Data

Facts on File encyclopedia of Black women in America / Darlene Clark
Hine, editor : Kathleen Thompson, associate editor.
p. cm.
Includes bibliographical references and index.
Contents: v. 1. The early years, 1619–1899—v. 2. Literature—
v. 3. Dance, sports and visual arts—v. 4. Business and professions—
v. 5. Music—v. 6. Education—v. 7. Religion and community—
v. 8. Law and government—v. 9. Theater arts and
entertainment—v. 10. Social activism—v. 11. Science, health,
and medicine.
ISBN 0-8160-3424-9 (set: alk, paper)
ISBN 0-8160-3429-X (Law and Government)
1. Afro-American women—Biography—Encyclopedias.   I. Hine,
Darlene Clark.   II. Thompson, Kathleen.
E185.96.F2   1997
920.72′08996073—dc20   96-33268

Text design by Cathy Rincon

Cover design by Smart Graphics

RRD FOF 10 9 8 7 6 5 4 3 2 1

This book is printed on acid-free paper.

CH 7/97

Contents

How to Use This Volume

SCOPE OF THE VOLUME

Law and Government includes entries on individuals and organizations in the following subject areas: attorneys, judges, elected and appointed officials, and law enforcement officers.

RELATED OCCUPATIONS

Professionals in related occupations covered in other volumes of this encyclopedia include the following: social activists (*Social Activism*), community leaders (*Religion and Community*), and educators (*Education*).

HOW TO USE THIS VOLUME

The introduction to this volume presents an overview of the history of United States law as it has affected and been affected by black women. A chronology at the end of the book lists important events in that history.

Individuals and organizations are covered in alphabetically arranged entries. If you are looking for an individual or organization that does not have an entry in this volume, please check the alphabetically arranged list of the entries for all eleven volumes of this encyclopedia that appears at the end of this book, in addition to the tables of contents of each of the other volumes in the series.

Names of individuals and organizations for which there are entries in this or other volumes of the encyclopedia are printed in **boldface.** Check the contents list at the end of this book to find the volume where a particular entry can be found.

Introduction

" 'We the people'—it is a very eloquent beginning. But when the
Constitution of the United States was completed on the seventeenth of September in 1787, I was not included in that 'We the
people.' I felt for many years that somehow George Washington
and Alexander Hamilton just left me out by mistake. But through
the process of amendment, interpretation, and court decision, I
have finally been included in 'We the People.' "

Barbara Jordan, statement at the impeachment
proceedings of Richard M. Nixon

It was July 22, 1993, and a black
woman stood on the floor of the United
States Senate. She was the first black
woman who had ever served in the Senate,
and she hadn't been there long. But one
day, an amendment was proposed to a
bill. What the bill was isn't important. The
amendment itself wasn't earth-shattering,
not in the great scheme of things. But to
Carol Moseley-Braun, it was very important indeed.

Senator Jesse Helms had proposed that
the United States Congress renew its recognition of the insignia used by the United
Daughters of the Confederacy. That insignia included the official flag of the Confederacy. A test vote had passed the
amendment, 52 to 48. Then Senator Moseley-Braun took the floor.

"On this issue," she said, "there can be
no consensus. It is an outrage. It is an
insult." The Senator continued to talk, not

yielding the floor. She talked about the
Civil War, "fought to preserve our nation,
to keep the states from separating themselves over the issue of whether or not my
ancestors could be held as property, as
chattel, as objects of trade and commerce
in this country."

To those who said she was blowing
things out of proportion, that it was a
small matter, just the proud insignia of a
group of women, "most of them elderly,
all of them gentle souls who meet together
and work together as unpaid volunteers
at veterans' hospitals," Moseley-Braun had
an answer. "This is no small matter," she
said. "This is not a matter of little old
ladies walking around doing good deeds.
There is no reason why these little old
ladies cannot do good deeds anyway. If
they choose to wave the Confederate flag,
that is their right." However, she continued, a flag that symbolized slavery must not

1

"What did the president know and when did he know it?" This was the question raised repeatedly during the House of Representatives hearings into the impeachment of President Richard M. Nixon. Representative Barbara Jordan spoke eloquently and passionately of her belief in the Constitution during these hearings. (SCHOMBURG CENTER)

be "underwritten, underscored, adopted, approved by this United States Senate."

It was, all in all, an astonishing move for a freshman Senator. What was more astonishing still is that her speech worked. Minds, and votes, on the floor of the U.S. Senate are seldom changed by speeches. That happens only in old Frank Capra movies. But it happened here. A "daughter of slavery" spoke out, and the Senate voted down the amendment, 75 to 25.

After centuries of enslavement, disfranchisement, and oppression, the voice of black women was finally being heard in the halls of American government.

IN AMERICA, BUT NOT OF IT

There are a number of theories about how and why governments are formed. The model used by the founders of the United States was that of the Social Contract, which goes something like this.

Governments are formed by people who believe that groups have a better chance of survival than individuals. (Not everyone believes this, but the ones who don't have little effect on society, for obvious reasons.) They are formed for defense against enemies, human and otherwise, and for the orderly continuation of everyday life.

Members (citizens) of these governmental groups (countries) agree to do three things: (1) abide by the laws that form the structure of the government; (2) perform some services for the government; (3) support the government financially. In other words, they refrain from stealing or murdering, they carry guns or drive ambulances in times of war, and they pay taxes.

In exchange, citizens receive protection and the enjoyment of certain benefits, such as good roads and a postal service.

Carol Moseley-Braun was only forty-five years old when she became a United States senator, but she was not afraid to take on the "powers that be" over the issue of the Senate endorsing an insignia that included the flag of the Confederate States of America. She won. (MOSELEY-BRAUN CAMPAIGN)

That's putting the whole notion of law and government in the simplest possible terms, of course, and it's not really a simple notion. For one thing, most people don't actually take part in the forming of a country. They don't even decide, in any active way, to "join" a country that already exists. They are simply born and that's it. Still, most people consent to being citizens of the countries in which they are born and go through their lives subject to the laws of their government.

In a democracy, what makes this acceptable is one simple thing: the right to vote. People modify existing governments by voting to change laws and replace the people who make them. In that sense, all democratic governments are constantly being reformed by their citizens. Since participating in this reformation is parallel to signing the original contract, the right to participate is, in effect, what defines a citizen.

But what about people who are not full and willing participants in a government? In a democracy, there should be no such people. But in the United States, there always have been. When the founders wrote that all men were created equal, they weren't using "men" as a generic term. They really meant men. And white men at that.

Being a citizen, but not a fully participating citizen, is a role that ranges from frustrating and difficult, at one end of the scale, to dehumanizing and dangerous at the other. What is even worse is being the unwilling subject of a government you neither choose nor assent to. That position is where the history of black women and American government begins.

DEFINED BY LAW

African women were first brought to North America, by force, in 1619. At that time, slavery was not a legally recognized institution in the colonies, but it existed in one form or another, under one name or another. Between 1641 and 1717, it was legalized in every colony but Georgia. In Georgia, there was even a law passed in 1735 banning the importation and use of slaves, but that law was repealed in 1749. One year later, Georgia also legalized slavery.

Having decided that certain people were not people, but property, the colonies were faced with a legal dilemma. It was clear that they had to have laws regulating the behavior of slaves, just as they had laws regulating the behavior of citizens. But before deciding how slaves must behave, what they can do and where they can go, you have to decide who they are. What makes one person a slave and another person a citizen with rights and privileges? Slavery is fairly easy to assign in a dictatorship. Whoever is in charge just says, "You're a slave, you're not." No one argues. In a democracy, it's not easy at all.

From the middle of the 1600s until about 1800, there were literally hundreds of laws passed in all of the colonies in an attempt to define the status of slaves, former slaves, and other African Americans. Their number and their complexity make enormously clear just how difficult it is to take a person and, through legislation, turn him or her into a nonperson and then back again.

The colonists began with the assumption that white people, in general, could not be slaves. They could be indentured servants, and that status was a form of temporary slavery, but they could not be slaves. (A few laws declared exceptions to this rule, but they didn't last long.) It was also decided early on that Native Americans could not be slaves, as they were all over South America. Africans—black people—were the only people it was allowable to enslave in the North American colonies.

However, children were soon being born who were both black and white or both black and Native American. Did their "white blood" make them free, or did their "black blood" make them slaves? The various colonies passed varying laws. In 1670, for example, Virginia declared that all non-Christians imported to its territory would be slaves for life. Just a year later, Maryland decided to make it clear that slaves who converted to Christianity stayed slaves. At one point, in Maryland, English women who married slaves were enslaved, as were their children. Eighteen years later, in 1681, that law was reversed.

Even more important than the results of these laws was who made the laws and how they were made. The people who had formed the various colonial governments—or whose fathers had formed the governments—*voted* that under these governments certain other people would not be people. The people who were not included in the contract in the first place (black and white women, African-American women and men, Native American women and men, and so forth) *had no say* in the decision. After the law was made, even those who had voted against it, or who had no vote, were bound by it, so long as they lived in these colonies. And all the forces of the government were brought to bear to enforce it.

In practice, this meant that a minority of the people living in a colony could make laws governing the majority, so long as they were able to define the majority as non-people, non-citizens, or second-class citizens. Nothing could bring home more clearly the powerlessness of a people who do not participate fully in the government of a place in which they live. Nothing could make it more obvious how completely arbitrary laws involving rights and power can be . . . unless they are based on basic principles of human rights.

The evolution of the legal status of African Americans in Massachusetts from 1641 until the Civil War gives a good idea of the situation in an average Northern colony/state. In 1641, slavery was legalized. In 1670, a law was passed declaring that the children of a slave mother were slave and of a free mother, free. In 1705, interracial marriage was banned. In 1712, the importation of slaves was banned. In 1767, a bill banning slavery was introduced into the legislature but did not pass. In 1771, the bill passed and was vetoed by the governor. In 1774, the bill passed, and the governor suspended the law. In 1780, the new state constitution abolished slavery. Two years before it passed, however, free black males lost the vote.

At various times during this period, free blacks were: (1) barred from military service; (2) required to observe a 9:00 P.M. curfew; (3) forbidden to strike a white person at the risk of being severely whipped; (4) forbidden to keep hogs; (5) required to put their children into indentured servitude between the ages of four and twenty-one; (6) forbidden to entertain slaves in their homes.

It is certainly clear that the definition of *free* is open to question if a "free" person is required by law to put her four-year-old child into indentured servitude.

Virginia presents us with a model for a Southern colony/state. Slavery was legalized in 1661, twenty years later than in Massachusetts. The next year, the mother-slave, child-slave law was passed. And the year after that, interracial marriage was banned. In 1668, equality before the law was specifically denied to free blacks; in 1670, the vote was taken away from free black males. Slavery was not abolished until the Emancipation Proclamation.

At various times, free African Americans in Virginia were: (1) forbidden to attend Quaker services; (2) barred from holding civil, military, or church offices; (3) barred from serving as witnesses in a court, except against a slave accused of a capital crime; (4) required to place mulatto children into indentured servitude until they were thirty-one; (5) forbidden to carry weapons.

In addition, black women were also subject to the restrictions put on all women. They could not vote; they could not own property independent of their husband; they could be locked away in mental institutions by their husbands without a legal or medical hearing.

Clearly, then, black women have suffered in the American legal system because they are members of two groups that the laws discriminate against. Besides that, however, the law has explicitly singled out black women, as a group, for oppression.

As early as 1644, both Maryland and Virginia passed laws stating that they would tax those persons who farmed, whether they were slave or free—and that those persons included all adult men and black women. Thus, whatever protection this statute offered for white women—either not farming or not having to pay taxes—it was a benefit black women would not get.

Later on, after the Civil War, the federal government created the Freedman's Bureau, to help former slaves make the transition to productive lives as free people. The regulations of the Freedman's Bureau, however, distinguished between black men and black women who had been slaves. In the wage labor agreements for employers who wanted to hire former slaves, the government recommended that black adult men receive $10–12 per month, but that black women be paid only $8 per month.

The basic patterns were set early. Black women would suffer whatever black men or white women suffered. They would be slaves because they were black. They would be worth less money than men in a free economy because they were women. But there was more. In the unlikely event that black men were to get any benefit under the law, black women would not get it, for they were women. In the unlikely event that white women were to receive a legal benefit, black women would again be ignored, for they were also black.

There are many examples of these basic patterns in the early years. Many of them revolve around issues of reproduction, marriage, and rape. Three of the statutes that were in force in Virginia before the Civil War show the effect those laws might have had on the lives of black women.

The first law provided that it was legal for a white man to have sex with a black female slave. The second stated that it was *illegal* for whites to marry blacks, whether those blacks were slave or free. The third was the law previously mentioned, making the freedom of a newborn infant dependent on the legal status of the mother.

These three laws made it possible to do terrible harm to black women. The first made it clear to the white slave owner that he was completely free to exploit his black female slaves sexually. The second emphasized that his sexual relations with black women could *only* be exploitative. A black woman could be anything to him *except* his wife. The third law provided a financial incentive for white slave owners to exploit black slave women sexually, because any child born to one of these women would be another slave—another source of work and income for the master.

Even when a statute was written in a way that appeared to protect black women, it was possible for a judge to interpret the law in a way that denied protection. One example of this took place in Missouri and involved a young black slave named Celia.

Celia defended herself against rape by hitting her master with a stick twice. He died, and she was tried for murder. At the time of the attack, Celia was pregnant with the man's third child, had been sick for four months, and had warned him that she would hurt him if he forced himself upon her again.

In Missouri, at this time, the law stated that it was unlawful for a man to force sex upon "any woman." The law also provided that, if a woman killed a man who was trying to rape her, that would be considered a legitimate act of self-defense, not a crime. Celia's lawyer used the law as it was written on the books. He argued that because the law protected "any woman" in this situation, the legislators must have meant to protect slave women too.

The judge disagreed. Because Celia was a slave, that statute could not apply to her. She was not included in the phrase "any woman." A slave woman had no rights over her body and could not legally resist her master's sexual assaults. Celia was sentenced to death and hanged.

Black women, slave or free, had no legal protection from rape, even from rape by other slaves. In 1859, the Mississippi Supreme Court held that a slave woman held no rights to her body and so could not be violated by rape. If another slave raped her, that was simply not a crime.

In other words, the law has discriminated against this one group of Americans for being black, for being women, and for being black women. Three different categories have produced three different forms of oppression.

Does all of this mean that the only relationship black women had with the law at this time was a passive one? Were they only being defined and limited by it? Or, on the other hand, does a person deprived of the rights of citizenship have any way to affect the government under which she lives?

The answer, of course, is that she does, and black women did.

RESISTING THE LAW

There were three basic ways black women could try to change their situation: civil disobedience, legal challenge, and influence. They had the choice of disobeying the laws they had no say in making. They could try to challenge those laws in court.

They could influence the people who did have a say in an attempt to get the laws changed.

Many, many black women broke the laws of slavery. A slave revolt in 1708, which included black women, killed seven whites in Long Island, New York. In 1712, in New York City, another revolt of slave men and women resulted in the deaths of nine white men.

Many women, as well as men, ran away. About 10 percent of fugitive slaves in the colonies were women. Of the 562 runaway slaves for whom owners advertised in the Huntsville, Alabama, newspapers between 1820 and 1860, 15 percent were women. Fewer women ran away than men, of course, because, for women, running away usually meant leaving children behind. (Men were most often already separated from their children.)

Harriet Tubman, a slave woman from Maryland, ran away. And then she went back into the South, not once, but nineteen times. Each time, she brought others out to freedom. She broke the law—and risked her life—to help approximately 300 other slaves find their way to safety and freedom.

Slave women also broke the law by refusing to obey their masters. They talked back to authority figures, stole food, met secretly with other slaves, plotted against masters, and physically harmed whites. In 1777, for example, Jenny, a slave woman to John Lewis, was condemned and executed for conspiracy. The following year, Rachel, a slave of Lockey Collier, was executed for murder. Between 1819 and 1831, seventeen female slaves in the state of Virginia were found guilty of crimes such as stealing and suspected arson. Six were found guilty of capital crimes such as mur-

Harriet Tubman broke the law not only by "stealing herself" (that is, running away from her master), but also by returning to the South nineteen times to help other slaves escape.

der, conspiracy, and arson and were executed.

Slave women also resisted their enslavement and that of future generations by refusing to have children. Slave women used crude contraceptive methods in order to maintain control over their procreation. Owners suspected them of using contracep-tives and inducing miscarriage but rarely were able to find them out.

All of these instances of disobeying laws were ways of denying the legal definition "slave." They were, in their way, attempts to make unworkable a set of laws which African Americans had not made and which they did not feel bound by.

More than one black woman also directly challenged the slave laws in court. **Jenny Slew** went to court in 1765 to sue for kidnapping and unlawful enslavement. Because her mother was white, she argued, she was born free, according to the law of the land. Her "master" claimed that she had no legal right to take him to court. Slew won. She was awarded her freedom, four pounds, and court costs.

Another woman, **Elizabeth Freeman**, also known as Mum Bett, went to court in 1780. She insisted that, since the Massachusetts state constitution declared all men free and equal, slavery was illegal. Illiterate herself, she found a lawyer who would present her case and filed a writ. She, too, was granted her freedom. It was a landmark case in American law.

Freeman's case is particularly important because she was not seeking only her own freedom. She believed that a verdict in her favor ought to free all slaves in the state of Massachusetts. Logically, it should have. The fact that it didn't takes nothing away from Freeman's courage or her political insight. She offered herself as a "test case," establishing a model that would be followed by the **National Association for the Advancement of Colored People** (NAACP) many times in the twentieth century.

Finally, black women and men crusaded to influence the leaders of government, the makers of laws—white men.

ABOLITION

Throughout the history of the United States, black people have again and again been forced to use their voices instead of their votes to influence government. The crusade for the abolition of slavery, led by free blacks and by white reformers, was the first major political movement in black America.

The number of free African Americans in the half century before the Civil War grew substantially. In fact, there were 108,435 free blacks in the United States in 1800, 233,634 in 1820, and 386,293 in 1840. By 1860, there were almost half a million. Most were located in cities and towns in the Northeast. It was in these urban centers that the abolitionist movement began.

Before the Revolutionary War, most antislavery activity focused only on the conditions of slavery, bringing to public attention, for example, the physical abuse of slaves. It also emphasized the gradual elimination of slavery. Northern colonies began to ban slavery without forcing slave owners to give up their slaves. The children of slaves were born free. Selling slaves was outlawed.

After the war, however, the mood was different. During the break from England, a great deal had been said about the natural rights of man, about equality and justice. In the South, slavery had become such a crucial part of the plantation economy that radical notions about black people having rights were not welcome. In the North, however, where economic conditions did not particularly favor slavery, these ideas fell on more fertile soil. The emphasis in liberal political circles shifted from gradual emancipation to immediate abolition of the institution of slavery.

Among the earliest opponents of slavery were the Quakers, the Society of Friends. The Quakers took a public stand against slavery from the beginning. Many individual members supported slavery and even owned slaves during the early eighteenth century, but by 1750, the church was punishing such members. By 1780, Northern Quakers were forcing church members to free their slaves. Many Congregational and Methodist churches joined in this effort.

What we usually think of as the abolition movement began to grow during the 1820s, when there was no longer any significant number of slaves in the North. But it was not, as some have portrayed it, a Northern phenomenon. By 1827, there were about 130 antislavery societies in the United States, and 106 of them were in the South.

The abolition movement was long dominated by its white members. It was also, and always, dominated by its male members, black and white. But black women were extremely active, if often unrecognized. In 1832, a landmark organization dedicated to the elimination of slavery was founded. It was called the Female Anti-Slavery Society of Salem, Massachusetts, and its founders were free black women. The next year, an interracial group, the **Philadelphia Female Anti-Slavery Society,** was founded. Among its charter members were some of the most important women in the abolition movement.

Of the forty-two women whose names were on the charter, nine of them were black. The white women included Lucretia Mott, who would later be a leader in the suffrage movement. The black women included Charlotte **Forten** and her three daughters—Harriet Purvis, Sarah Louisa Forten, and Margaretta Forten—Grace Douglass, Mary Woods, Lydia White, Margaret Bowser, and Sarah McCrummel. **Sarah Mapps Douglass,** Grace Douglass' daughter, joined the organization a little later.

The Philadelphia group continued in existence for thirty-six years, until the Civil War and the Emancipation Proclamation had removed its reason for being. At all times, black women were dynamic members of the group.

In other parts of the country, as well, black women were in the forefront of the struggle. The great orator **Sojourner Truth** traveled around the country speaking against slavery and for women's rights. **Sarah Parker Remond** toured the Midwest and, later, England, speaking out against slavery. **Frances E. W. Harper,** later to be an important black woman novelist, began her career writing and lecturing for the Maine Anti-Slavery Society.

While all of these attempts to influence lawmakers were going on, black women continued to strike on the other two fronts, breaking the law and challenging the law. **Mary Ellen Pleasant,** later to make her fortune as an entrepreneur in San Francisco, helped finance John Brown's raid on Harpers Ferry. In 1836, a group of free black women rushed a Boston courtroom and carried away to freedom two fugitive slave women before they could be returned to the men claiming to be their masters. Black women in New York performed a similar rescue. In 1851, armed black men and women went to the defense of four escaped slaves in Christiana, Pennsylvania, in defiance of the Fugitive Slave Law.

Thirty-six of them were accused of treason, but they were later acquitted in court.

Challenging the law directly again, Elizabeth Jennings brought a suit against the Third Avenue Railroad Company in New York City in 1854. She won $225 in damages and the ruling that "colored persons, if sober, well-behaved and free from disease" could ride the horsecars unsegregated by color.

Almost all of these women remained active in the fight for black rights long past the end of the Civil War. While still functioning in American society as virtual noncitizens, they were influencing law and government policy. But they were also seeking the status they had so long been denied.

THE VOTE

Although the demand for women's rights began even before the founding of this country, it was the abolition movement that brought the issue to the fore. White women as well as black committed themselves to that movement. Both were consistently denied the right to speak, forced to take a back seat to male leaders, and confronted by the reality that they were not considered equals by men who talked eloquently about equality. The result was a movement for their rights as women.

Black women were active in the movement from the early days. Sojourner Truth was on the women's rights lecture circuit, as well as the antislavery circuit, as early as 1849. She often spoke on the same platform with white feminists such as Susan B. Anthony. **Sarah Jane Woodson Early** was active in the fledgling women's movement, as were Harriet Forten Purvis, Margaretta

Black women fought long and hard for their right to vote. The August 1915 issue of The Crisis *included a special section entitled "Votes for Women: A Symposium by Leading Thinkers of Colored America," with essays by such luminaries as Nannie Helen Burroughs and Robert H. Terrell. This photograph of suffragists opens the section.* (THE CRISIS)

Forten, and Sarah Remond. **Nancy Gardner Prince** was a participant in the 1854 National Woman's Rights Convention.

After the Civil War, there came a crisis for the movement, which had by now focused on suffrage, or the right to vote. The vast majority of suffragists had also been abolitionists. The Thirteenth Amendment to the U.S. Constitution prohibited slavery in 1865. When the Fourteenth Amendment was passed in 1868, saying that no citizen could be denied the rights guaranteed by the Constitution, black and white suffragists challenged the unwritten assumption that all citizens were male. Just as Susan B. Anthony attempted to vote in New York State, Sojourner Truth tested the law in Michigan and **Mary Ann Shadd Cary** in the District of Columbia.

However, there were other women— black and white—who believed that all attempts to gain the vote for women— black or white—should be shelved until it

had been guaranteed to black men. This issue of priorities has come up repeatedly for black women. Not an easy issue to decide, it split the woman's suffrage movement right down the middle in the nineteenth century.

The women who fought to make the Fifteenth Amendment cover women as well as black men joined the National Woman Suffrage Association—which counted among its members Sojourner Truth, Mary Ann Shadd Cary, Susan B. Anthony, and Harriet Forten Purvis. Those who suspended their agitation for woman's suffrage until black male suffrage was won joined the American Woman Suffrage Association—which attracted Frances Harper, Caroline Remond Putnam, and Lottie Rollin, under the presidency of white abolitionist Henry Ward Beecher.

When the battle was over and the Fifteenth Amendment was passed in 1870, it said that the right to vote could not be denied to any citizen on the basis of race, color, or previous condition of servitude. Gender was not mentioned. It would take women of all races another fifty years to win the same right.

During that fifty years, relations between black and white women in the suffrage movement deteriorated. By the last decades of the nineteenth century, there were few white suffragists who had fought next to black women for abolition. Susan B. Anthony, in her seventies and eighties, remembered her African-American allies and recognized publicly the important contributions of **Ida B. Wells-Barnett,** the women of the black women's club movement, and others. But she was in the minority, and even she sometimes sacrificed the respect black women were due in favor of what she believed was the best chance for getting the Nineteenth Amendment passed.

Most white suffragists ignored the fact that black men in the South were being deprived of their right to vote by Jim Crow laws and that black women would be equally deprived, regardless of a constitutional amendment. Others among them counted on that fact. They secretly and not-so-secretly assured potential Southern supporters that they would not challenge legal restrictions on black voters. By the time the Nineteenth Amendment was passed in 1920, granting women the right to vote, relations between black and white feminists were seriously damaged.

In the meantime, black men were able to exercise their right to vote for a very limited time. During Reconstruction, the period immediately following the Civil War, federal troops were stationed in the South to see that white Southerners followed the new law of the land. African-American men began to register and vote and to be elected to office.

Black women did not share in this political activity. They did, however, show great interest in political concerns. In her article "In Quest of African American Political Women," political scientist **Jewel L. Prestage** writes, "According to one state politician and former state senator, they followed their men from morning to night telling them how to vote, formed a large segment of the audiences at political meetings, and evidenced a deep interest 'in all that pertained to' politics."

However, when President Rutherford B. Hayes withdrew the troops in 1877, the progress that African Americans had made began to unravel. In 1881, the first of the Jim Crow laws was passed in Tennessee.

Named after a figure from minstrel shows, Jim Crow laws were designed to shut African Americans out of the mainstream of American life. In addition to holding voters to requirements that virtually no black man could meet, they forced black citizens to use separate facilities of all kinds, public and private. These laws went against the Civil Rights Act of 1875, which stated that there could be no discrimination in public places or on means of transportation within the United States. And, at first, that Act offered some protection against Jim Crow.

However, in 1896, in the *Plessy* v. *Ferguson* case, the United States Supreme Court declared that separate but equal facilities in interstate railroad transportation were legal. This set a precedent that would be used in court cases concerning everything from public washrooms to public schools. From that ruling until the 1954 *Brown* v. *Board of Education* ruling, "separate but equal" prevailed, and the definition of "equal" was pretty much up to whatever white sheriff, mayor, or school board was in charge.

In 1913, the Supreme Court officially approved this form of discrimination when it ruled that the Civil Rights Act of 1875 was unconstitutional. The test case was that of Emma Butts, a black woman who sued a steamship company for denying her accommodations equal to those it provided for white passengers. She lost, and so did all other black Americans.

The ruling led to the development of two separate societies, which were far from equal. There were segregated hospitals, schools, restaurants, and neighborhoods. There were signs all over the South that said "whites only" or "colored only." They hung over water fountains, bathrooms, and doorways. They were posted on vending machines. Black citizens were denied the right to enter amusement parks and swimming pools, concert halls and zoos. In the courtroom, they were sworn in on a separate Bible.

The law no longer defined black people as inferior. Because of the "separate but equal" ruling, it did not have to. Isolated from mainstream society in every way—politically, socially, and economically—African Americans were robbed of power. It is astonishing, then, to see what black women managed to accomplish during this time.

OFFICERS OF THE COURT

In 1872, women did not have the vote. Opposition to educating women was at its height as some universities began to be-come timidly coeducational. The idea of a woman lawyer was, to most people, inconceivable. And yet, in that year, **Charlotte E. Ray,** an African-American woman, graduated from **Howard University** Law School and was admitted to the bar of the District of Columbia.

A few white women had been admitted to the bar in one state or another—none in the District of Columbia—but hardly any of them had attended law school. Usually, they were wives of attorneys who studied with their husbands, in their husbands' offices, and then took the bar examination. Even fewer of them practiced. The most prominent white woman lawyer of the time was Myra Bradwell, who edited the *Chicago Legal News* instead of practicing law.

Charlotte Ray opened a law office in Washington, D.C., and proved herself an able attorney. But discrimination against both African Americans and women was too strong, and she was unable to make a living. However, Ray was a strong feminist and became active in the suffrage movement, attending the annual convention of the National Woman Suffrage Association in New York City in 1876.

In 1883, Mary Ann Shadd Cary became the second black woman to earn a law degree, also graduating from Howard University Law School. She could have been the first, having attended Howard's law school in 1869, but she was "refused graduation on account of her sex," according to a letter she wrote in 1890.

Both Ray and Cary were legally able to argue in the nation's courts before they were able to vote in the nation's elections. In fact, neither of them lived to see the day that women in this country would be allowed to enter voting booths.

Mary Ann Shadd Cary was the second black woman in the United States to earn a law degree, graduating from Howard University Law School in 1883. (SCHOMBURG CENTER)

The next wave of black women attorneys came just after the Nineteenth Amendment gave women the greatest right of citizenship, the vote. In 1920, **Violette N. Anderson** became the first black woman to practice law in the state of Illinois. She later became the first black woman to argue a case before the United States Supreme Court. She was also the first woman prosecutor in Chicago.

In 1925, **L. Marian Fleming Poe** became probably the first black woman to practice law in a Southern state when she was admitted to the Virginia bar. She went into practice for herself in Newport News and had a distinguished career that stretched into the 1960s, when she was twice the Virginia delegate to the multiracial National Association of Woman Lawyers.

In 1927, **Sadie Tanner Mossell Alexander** became the first black woman to be admitted to the bar and to practice law in Pennsylvania. She went into partnership with her husband, Raymond Pace Alexander, until he became a judge in 1959. Together, the husband-wife legal team helped draft the 1935 Pennsylvania law banning segregated public accommodations and, after it was passed, tested it regularly. When one theater manager repeatedly refused to admit them, they had him arrested. He went to jail, where he decided that the Alexanders wouldn't be such bad patrons, after all. The Alexanders were also among the founders of the National Bar Association, which is the professional organization for African-American lawyers.

Sadie Alexander is an extraordinary example of black women lawyers participating in the political process. In the early years of her practice, she was appointed assistant city solicitor of Philadelphia, a position she held from 1928 to 1930 and from 1934 to 1938. In 1946, she was appointed to the United States Commission to Study the Civil Rights of All Races and Faiths. In 1963, President John F. Kennedy appointed her to the Lawyers' Committee for Civil Rights under Law. And she was chair of the White House Conference on Aging in 1979 and 1980.

Notice that all of Alexander's positions were appointments. For decades after black women were legally able to hold political office, appointed positions remained their primary access to power in government. For example, **Jane Bolin,** the first black woman judge, was appointed Justice of the Domestic Relations Court in New York by Mayor Fiorello La Guardia in 1939. The first black woman to be *elected* a judge would be **Juanita Kidd Stout,** two full decades later, in 1959.

Black women lawyers frequently found that government agencies offered greater opportunities than private practice. **Eunice Hunton Carter,** the first black woman district attorney in New York, joined the New York County district attorney's office shortly after she graduated from Fordham Law School in 1934. She was given the unpopular job of handling low-level

Eunice Hunton Carter was the first black woman district attorney in New York City (1934), eventually becoming head of the Special Sessions Bureau, responsible for more than fourteen thousand criminal cases a year. (SCHOMBURG CENTER)

prosecutions for such crimes as prostitution.

Carter didn't get many convictions in the corrupt New York courts, but she noticed something. Virtually all of the prostitutes who took the stand were represented by the same law firm, told the same story, and had the same bondsman if they were found guilty. Carter believed they were controlled by a large criminal organization, and she took her suspicions to her boss, William C. Dodge. Dodge jeered. So Carter went to Thomas E. Dewey, a special prosecutor assigned to investigate corruption in New York. Dewey hired her away from Dodge.

At Carter's urging, Dewey shifted the focus of his investigation from loan sharks to prostitution. A raid netted a hundred prostitutes and madams, three of whom were willing to talk to Carter. She put together enough evidence to convict Charles "Lucky" Luciano and put him in prison. Dewey became New York County district attorney, and Eunice Carter became chief of his Special Sessions Bureau, responsible for more than fourteen thousand criminal cases every year.

Another lawyer whose political appointments made her a force to be reckoned with was **Edith Sampson.** A Chicago attorney who had been the first woman to graduate from Loyola University Law School in Chicago, she came to public attention through the **National Council of Negro Women.** That group chose her, in 1949, to be their representative in a program called America's Town Meeting of the Air. This group traveled to twelve countries, debating issues of interest worldwide.

Sampson's work with the Town Meeting led President Harry S. Truman to appoint her an alternate delegate to the United Nations General Assembly in 1950. Later, she became a member-at-large of the North Atlantic Treaty Organization (NATO) and of the United Nations Education, Scientific, and Cultural Organization (UNESCO). Back in Chicago, she was an assistant corporation counsel, associate judge of the Municipal Court, and judge of the Cook County Circuit Court.

There was another woman who came to prominence through the National Council of Negro Women. She was not a lawyer, but she took "power by appointment" to new heights.

MARY MCLEOD BETHUNE

Mary McLeod Bethune was the most powerful black woman in the history of American government—and she never held an elected public office.

Bethune came into government from the black women's club movement, a remarkable phenomenon that resulted from the history of black women and from their lack of official political power. The club movement can trace its origins to the mutual benefit societies and the literary groups of the 1800s. Then, in the last decades of the nineteenth century, it began to develop a character of its own. It consisted of groups of determined, educated black women committed to using their education, and even their ambition, in the service of the African-American people.

Many of these women came out of a middle class that had its roots in free black society before the Civil War. But the black middle class was not defined primarily by money or family background. In a society

Mary McLeod Bethune first came to national attention as the director of the Negro Division of the National Youth Administration. She is pictured here (in 1938) in the famous "Black Cabinet" portrait of the black members of Franklin Delano Roosevelt's administration. (SCURLOCK STUDIO)

where economic opportunities were so limited for African Americans, that was hardly possible. Instead, social status was based largely on behavior, on upholding extremely strict standards of respectability and morality. A washerwoman could easily be considered middle class, so long as she had the appropriate values and manners.

The club movement developed in Northern cities such as Boston and Philadelphia. In these cities, black women were enthusiastic participants in the many church and community groups formed to provide the services they could not expect from a white government. They were also aware of their position as the black elite. Often coming from families that had been free for generations, they had many more resources, financial and educational, than the average black woman in the United States.

Some of these women were the wives of prosperous business and professional men, but a great many were not. They were not idle women trying to find ways to spend their time; they were busy women trying to find ways to improve the status of black women and black people in general in this country.

The clubs founded schools and raised funds for hospitals, orphanages, and homes for the aged just as their white counterparts did. But there was a special consciousness behind their efforts, an awareness that they were serving their own people—and a knowledge that no one else was going to.

Boston, New York, and Washington, D.C., were the hub of what would become the national club movement. Washington, in particular, was the home of many of the black elite. Its Bethel Literary and Historical Society provided a forum, as well, for the intellectual elite. The great women leaders and speakers of the day spoke to its members. In 1892, members of the Bethel group came together with others in Washington to form the Colored Woman's League of Washington, D.C.

In that same year, New York and Boston clubs were formed after a testimonial dinner held in New York to honor Ida B. Wells-Barnett, the great crusader for equal rights and against lynching, which brought women leaders together. New York women, including **Victoria Earle Matthews** and Maritcha Lyons, formed the **Woman's Loyal Union.** Boston women, including **Josephine St. Pierre Ruffin,** her daughter **Florida Ruffin Ridley,** and **Maria Baldwin,** formed the Woman's Era Club.

Two major efforts were made in the next few years to consolidate the ever-growing black women's club movement. Two "national" organizations were formed. In fact, they both held their national conventions in Washington, D.C., in July of 1896. As a result, a committee was formed to work out the differences between the two groups and, that same year, they merged to form the **National Association of Colored Women** (NACW).

This was the first strong, unified national black organization, preceding the **National Association for the Advancement of Colored People** (NAACP) by almost fifteen years. It would help the community for four decades.

In service to the community, the black women's club movement was unparalleled, but it was equally as important as a training ground for black women as well as a source of political talent. Mary McLeod Bethune was the prime, though by no means the only, example of this. A woman with vision and a sense of mission, she believed she could be a great leader of her people. She also fiercely believed that it was time for black women to have participation and power in American society. And she needed a power base.

Bethune became president of the NACW in 1924. She immediately began to expand its influence. To begin with, she used the primarily white National Council of Women (NCW) of the United States. In this council of thirty-eight national women's organizations, only one, the NACW, was black. In 1925, the conference of the International Council of Women, which met every five years, took place in Washington, D.C. Thirty-five countries were represented. Bethune went into the conference with a plan.

First, she enlisted black women of the NACW from around the country as delegates to the conference. Then, she insisted on a policy of desegregated seating at all conference events. And then, when the policy was violated, she and all the other black Americans at the conference walked out, straight into the arms of the waiting press. Bethune then, in one of her typically brilliant moves, appealed to American patriotism. It was humiliating, she said, for black Americans to be segregated in the presence of women from countries around the world.

Bethune won. The black delegates were assured that they would be seated properly if they would return to the conference, and they did. It was one of many times that Bethune's keen political sense would lead her to just the right words and actions at just the right time.

After four successful years in office, Bethune was barred by the NACW's constitution from reelection. This did not stop her

for long. If the NACW could no longer be the base from which she would realize her vision, she would create another.

In 1935, with the help of **Charlotte Hawkins Brown** and other women from both inside and outside the NACW, Bethune founded the National Council of Negro Women (NCNW). This new organization was different from the NACW in that it admitted as members only national organizations. These organizations, fourteen of which were represented at the founding meeting, were diverse. They included sororities, Christian women's societies of different denominations, and academic organizations. The only requirements were that the groups represent black women and that they have national memberships.

Bethune was elected president and at one stroke became the executive officer of a group representing 500,000 women. When she spoke, she spoke with the power of those numbers behind her. She had never run for office, much less been elected, but she had a constituency of half a million people. And she had put herself in the perfect position to be appointed to public office. In 1936, the year after the founding of the NCNW, she was.

Bethune, who was founder and president of **Bethune-Cookman College,** was appointed to a post in the National Youth Administration (NYA) by President Franklin Delano Roosevelt. She quickly persuaded Roosevelt, largely through his wife Eleanor, that a Negro Division of the NYA was needed to ensure some equality in the administration of benefits. In 1939, she became official director of the Negro Division. This was the highest federal appointment ever held by a black woman.

After President Franklin Roosevelt's death, Mary McLeod Bethune continued to be actively involved in the affairs of national government. She is shown here with President Harry Truman and other black leaders. (BETHUNE MUSEUM AND ARCHIVES)

Her directorship gave her status in the Roosevelt government. Her friendship with the president's wife gave her tremendous influence. She became leader of the Black Cabinet, a group of twenty-seven men and three women who worked for racial justice within the administration's multitude of public service agencies.

Bethune rose to such a position of power and influence in the Roosevelt administration that she and her Black Cabinet were directly or indirectly responsible for the establishment of the Fair Employment Practices Commission, the admission of black women into the Women's Army Corps (WAC), and the training of black pilots in the Civilian Pilot Training Program, among many other accomplishments. During the 1930s and 1940s, she was generally considered to be the most important black leader in the country.

Bethune continued to be active in government after Roosevelt's death, during the administration of President Harry

Truman. Others, however, were working toward that critical next step in the forward progress of women in general, and black women in particular, toward full citizenship.

THE VOTE AND BEYOND

Sadly, when black women officially gained the right to vote, it was little more than a gesture. Black men had been granted that right by the Constitution fifty years before, and Jim Crow laws had robbed them of practicing it. Black women had to live with those same laws. Jewel Prestage cites Louisiana records to show how painfully unrepresented African Americans were in the South as late as 1940. "There the number of African Americans registered to vote was only 886," she writes, "while the adult African American population was estimated at 473,562." And this example was the rule, not the exception.

Nonetheless, black women were active. In 1917, when women had gained the vote in Texas, they organized Negro Women Voter Leagues. In 1918, the Women's Political Association of Harlem was one of the first African-American organizations to advocate birth control. In 1924, the National League of Republican Colored Women was organized, and **Mary Montgomery Booze** was the first black woman elected to the Republican National Committee. In 1927, Minnie Buckingham-Harper became the first black woman to serve in a United States legislative body when she was appointed to fill her husband's unexpired term in the West Virginia legislature after his death. She wasn't elected, but she did serve in an elective office.

In 1935, Crystal Bird Fauset became director of Negro women's activities of the Democratic National Committee. Three years later, she became the first black woman elected to major public office in the United States when she was elected to the Pennsylvania State Assembly. (SCHOMBURG CENTER)

In 1935, **Crystal Bird Fauset** became director of Negro women's activities of the Democratic National Committee. Three years later, she became the first black woman elected to major public office in the United States when she was elected to the Pennsylvania State Assembly.

Then, in 1952, a black woman was nominated for vice president of the United

States. She was not a Republican or a Democrat; she was on a third-party ticket, but it was an important one. **Charlotta Spears Bass** was a candidate of the Progressive Party.

The Progressive Party was formed in 1948 to promote the candidacy of Henry Wallace. Bass was one of its founders. Its platform called for peace and an end to government corruption, discrimination and segregation, and unemployment. When Bass was nominated as its candidate for vice president in 1952, it was not her first race. A California newspaper editor, she had been politically active for years. In 1940, she was western regional director of Wendell Willkie's presidential campaign. In 1943, she was the first black grand jury member for the Los Angeles County Court. In 1945, she ran as a people's candidate for city council in Los Angeles. In 1950, she ran for the congressional seat from the fourteenth legislative district.

Her bid for the vice presidency was an opportunity to have an impact. "Win or lose," she said again and again during her candidacy, "we win by raising the issues." She fiercely attacked Richard Nixon and stressed the need for more women to run for political office.

However, before black women could be elected in any numbers, black women and men had to be able to vote. And so, in the 1950s, the civil rights movement became the focus of most black political activity. Social activism, rather than conventional electoral politics, took center stage.

Theoretically, black Americans had all the rights of citizenship. They should no longer have had to resort to the methods of the disfranchised—lawbreaking, legal challenges, and influence—but in fact,

those were the three tools of the civil rights movement.

CONSTANCE BAKER MOTLEY AND OTHERS

In 1921, the year after the Nineteenth Amendment gave women the right to vote, Constance Baker was born in New Haven, Connecticut. In 1946, she graduated from Columbia Law School and married Joel Wilson Motley. That same year, she got a job with the NAACP's Legal Defense and Education Fund, under the leadership of the legendary Thurgood Marshall. In 1949, she and John Lynch, another NAACP lawyer, represented a group of black teachers who were being paid considerably less than white teachers in the same school district. "When the word got out," she says, "that there was not only a 'nigra lawyer' but a 'nigra woman lawyer' as well, it seemed as though the whole town decided to see what was going on. They had to keep the huge oak doors open because of all the spectators."

By 1950, Motley was an assistant counsel. One of her most important early cases was *Sipuel* v. *Board of Regents* of the University of Oklahoma. Under Oklahoma law, it was a misdemeanor—not a serious crime, but a crime nonetheless—for school officials to admit "colored" students to white schools or to teach classes of mixed races. The Oklahoma NAACP convention in 1945 decided to attack segregated education by trying to enroll black students in the graduate schools and professional schools at the University of Oklahoma and Oklahoma State University. One of the students was **Ada Lois Sipuel [Fisher]**.

In 1946, Sipuel applied for admission to the University of Oklahoma School of Law. At the time, it was the only law school in the state. The university, as was its policy, rejected her application solely on the basis of her race. Motley represented Sipuel as two Oklahoma courts upheld the university's decision. (The university claimed it was planning to open a "substantially equal" law school for Negroes.)

The NAACP took the case to the U.S. Supreme Court. Thurgood Marshall argued the case, with able assistance from Motley. In 1948, the court reversed the Oklahoma court decision. Relying on a precedent set in *Missouri* ex rel. *Gaines* v. *Canada,* a 1938 case involving the University of Missouri School of Law in which the higher court reversed the Missouri courts, the Supreme Court ordered the University of Oklahoma School of Law to admit Sipuel.

After the Sipuel case, states could not require African Americans to wait until they established separate graduate or professional schools. This was one of dozens of cases the NAACP sponsored that attacked the "separate but equal" doctrine. As each court's decision came in, it became more and more clear that the doctrine was becoming legally indefensible. Finally, the Legal Defense Fund team decided to attack the situation head on.

Marshall, Motley, and the other lawyers prepared *Brown* v. *Board of Education* in Topeka, Kansas, the landmark school desegregation case. The Supreme Court ruled that there really was no such thing as "separate but equal" in education. Schools had to desegregate.

The 1954 case was the catalyst for civil rights activity around the country, and not just in schools. Inspired by the court's decision, African Americans began to desegregate lunch counters and buses, swimming pools and parks. Every "whites only" sign in the South became a target.

In the years that followed, Motley became the NAACP Legal Defense Fund's principal trial lawyer. She argued ten cases before the Supreme Court and won nine of them. She helped James Meredith gain entrance to the University of Mississippi, was Martin Luther King's lawyer in Birmingham, Alabama, and went up against Lester Maddox in Atlanta, Georgia.

Motley was not the only woman active in civil rights law. **Juanita Jackson Mitchell** was the NAACP's first national youth director before she decided to return to school to get her law degree. In 1950, she became the first black woman admitted to practice law in Maryland and immediately began to work on discrimination suits. She was counsel in a successful suit to desegregate Maryland state and municipal beaches and swimming pools. Because of a case she initiated in 1953, Baltimore was the first Southern city to desegregate public schools after the 1954 *Brown* v. *Board of Education* ruling. She successfully defended student activists and represented home owners whose residences had been invaded by police without warrants. Mitchell remained active in the NAACP throughout her life.

Also active in civil rights law was **Marian Wright Edelman**. Her involvement in civil rights actions at **Spelman College** in Atlanta in 1960 led her to take up the law. When she graduated from Yale University Law School, she became an NAACP Legal Defense and Education Fund intern and the first black woman to pass the bar in Mississippi. Her private practice was devoted to the defense of civil rights demonstrators and to bringing school desegregation cases before the courts. Later, Edelman would found the Children's Defense Fund.

While these attorneys were in court directly challenging the laws of the South, other black women were outside in the streets disobeying these laws and exerting every ounce of influence they could muster on the people who made them.

REJECTING THE LAW

In one sense, a legal challenge was at the heart of it. When **Rosa Parks** sat down and refused to yield her seat on a Montgomery, Alabama, bus, she was arrested. She went into her trial with the NAACP lawyers at her side. But that event mushroomed to include demonstrations, protests, and massive civil disobedience. And women were involved in every part of it.

In recent years, historians have re-evaluated the civil rights movement and the position of black women in it. In an article entitled "Men Led, but Women Organized," Charles Payne states that, in the years before the summer of 1964, women considerably outnumbered men in the civil rights movement. Although the genders were relatively balanced among young people and old people, women between about thirty and fifty outnumbered men three or four to one.

Their participation was not just a matter of numbers, either. Payne quotes Lawrence Guyot, a member of the **Student Nonviolent Coordinating Committee** (SNCC), say-

ing, "It's no secret that young people and women led organizationally." The question is why? Historically, women have always been less active in politics than men. Why were black women the exception?

The answer, according to Payne, lies in the strength of religion and community action among black women. From the earliest years of slavery, the black church has been a crucial part of the black support system. And black women have made up between 60 and 90 percent of black congregations. In the churches, they have learned to organize, to raise funds, and to work together as a team. They have also had a similar

Rosa Parks was not just another tired seamstress who didn't want to give up her seat on a bus. She had behind her "a life history of being rebellious against being mistreated because of my color." (SCHOMBURG CENTER)

experience in the black women's club movement that led to Mary McLeod Bethune's prominence.

The difference between black women in the 1950s and 1960s and other women in other times and places in history, then, is that black women knew how to organize, were accustomed to working together, and cared deeply about members of the community outside their immediate families. They also believed that God would take care of them.

Black women were major participants in the event that started the wildfire of demonstrations and protests—the Montgomery Bus Boycott. Montgomery, Alabama, had racially segregated buses since the city bus line began operation in the mid-1930s. In the early 1950s, the **Women's Political Council** (WPC) of Montgomery decided to make the bus issue its prime concern. They met regularly with city officials to discuss the segregation policy, without success. They also looked for a test case that would be suitable to take to court.

When Rosa Parks refused to give up her seat to a white man, they had their case. Although Parks had not planned her calm protest, she recalled that she had "a life history of being rebellious against being mistreated because of my color." The time had come "when I had been pushed as far as I could stand to be pushed. . . . I had decided that I would have to know once and for all what rights I had as a human being and a citizen."

When **Jo Ann Robinson,** president of the WPC, learned of Parks' arrest, she decided to begin a boycott. For the next year, the women of the WPC passed out flyers, raised funds, and ran a car pool. They also worked with twenty-six-year-old Dr. Martin Luther King, Jr., whose charismatic personality drew interest to the boycott and who became its spokesperson.

The female leadership network was crucial to the boycott's success, but the backbone of the long protest was several thousand working class women who, in the face of intimidation and threats, rode in the car pools or walked as far as twelve miles a day, even in the rain, to participate in the boycott.

The Montgomery Bus Boycott was not an isolated case. Women were leaders in the movement everywhere and at every moment. **Ella Josephine Baker** had been organizing people for a long time before she connected with the NAACP. In 1930, at the age of twenty-seven, she joined the Young Negroes Cooperative League in Harlem. She was soon elected national director. During this time, she also worked with the Women's Day Workers and Industrial League, the Harlem Housewives Cooperative, and the YWCA. By the time she joined the NAACP in 1940, she was an experienced organizer, committed to involving black people of all social, educational, and economic levels.

Baker started as a field secretary and later became director of branches. Her fieldwork took her to small black communities throughout the South. Before long, she had contacts everywhere, a network of friends and supporters. But, by 1946 she was fed up; she could no longer work in the NAACP bureaucracy nor believe in the legal strategy. She resigned. However, she remained a volunteer for the organization and was president of the New York branch, the first woman in that position.

After the Montgomery Bus Boycott, when King and others formed the Southern

Christian Leadership Conference (SCLC), that group called on Baker to head their Crusade for Citizenship. She agreed to take over this voter rights campaign, but she soon found the same problems she had encountered in the NAACP. Much as she admired King, she felt the movement was depending too much on his charismatic personality. She also believed that too many decisions were made by a small group of leaders, without enough participation by the mass of black people.

After the student-led sit-ins at Greensboro, North Carolina, Baker quit the SCLC. The new student movement was much more what she believed was needed. She went to work for the **Young Women's Christian Association** (YWCA) in order to have a base from which to work with the young people. In April of 1960, she called a conference of sit-in leaders at Shaw University in Raleigh, North Carolina. Out of this conference came SNCC.

From the beginning, Baker encouraged the students to abide by the principles she had always valued. These were grass-roots democracy, group-centered decision-making, and the involvement of all members of the community. SNCC opened its leadership circles to youth, poor people, and women in a way that was unusual in the civil rights movement.

SNCC organizers went into the rural areas of the Deep South, using the contacts that Baker had formed there over the previous two decades. They emphasized direct action over court battles. The focus of a great deal of this organizing was voters' rights. Black women and men were still seeking full citizenship in their own country. In 1964, with Baker's participation, SNCC members **Annie Devine**, Victoria Gray, and **Fannie Lou Hamer** were among the founders of the **Mississippi Freedom Democratic Party** (MFDP).

Fannie Lou Hamer was a sharecropper who worked the fields from the time she was six years old until 1962, when she was forty-five. In that year, she tried unsuccessfully to register to vote. Soon thereafter, she became a member of SNCC. In 1964, she became a fieldworker. She faced violence again and again as she worked to register black voters. When the idea of the MFDP came up, she was ready.

The purpose of the MFDP was to challenge Mississippi's all-white Democratic Party leadership. In the year of its founding, the MFDP registered 80,000 voters in its Freedom Ballot campaign. Those voters elected a delegation to the 1964 Democratic convention, an alternative to the regular delegation that was elected by white voters. Not legally recognized, the Freedom Ballot election was the only one in Mississippi that year that was run in accordance with the U.S. Constitution and the policies of the Democratic Party.

At the 1964 Democratic convention, the group challenged national Democratic Party leaders to seat them instead of the regular Mississippi delegation, whose election was the result of a discriminatory process. In the course of the action that followed, Fannie Lou Hamer stood before the convention and spoke. She told about a people who had been disfranchised. She also told about what happened to civil rights workers and black people who tried to vote. In painful detail, she described the beating she and five others received in jail. That speech became one of the historic documents of the civil rights movement.

The MFDP wasn't seated. However, the MFDP won from the Democratic Party a vow that no delegation would be seated at the 1968 convention which had benefitted from discriminatory practices in its election, and that promise was carried out.

Many other women were active in SNCC. **Diane Nash** and **Ruby Doris Smith** were among the Freedom Riders who went to jail in Jackson, Mississippi. Nash later became leader of the direct-action wing of the organization. Smith (later Smith-Robinson) eventually became executive secretary of the organization. Victoria Jackson Gray ran for Congress on the MFDP ticket. There were dozens of other black women in positions of leadership, and thousands more who worked with dedication.

During Freedom Summer, in 1964, the SNCC members registered voters at the risk of their lives. They, along with women and men from SCLC and the Congress of Racial Equality (CORE), started on a march from Selma to Montgomery in March of 1965, only to be clubbed and teargassed by police on horseback. Two weeks later, they started out again. Five months later, Lyndon Johnson signed the Voting Rights Act into law.

THE AGE OF THE VOTE

Between 1964 and 1968, registration of black voters in Mississippi went from 8 percent to 62 percent. Think about that for a moment. In 1964, fewer than one out of every ten adult African Americans in Mississippi was legally able to cast a ballot, to have a say in the laws that governed him or her. Four years later, six out of ten had registered and could help decide the political future of their state and the nation. The statistics are similar for other Southern states. There can be few political changes, short of armed revolution, that have had a greater impact.

For black women, it meant that being elected to public office, not just appointed, was a real possibility for the first time. In 1963, **Constance Baker Motley** had been appointed to fill the unexpired term of a New York state senator, and the next year she was elected to that office. She was the first black woman in the New York Senate. It was a great victory for a distinguished woman. And in the years that followed, there were many more such victories. Indeed, just seven years after the Voting Rights Act had guaranteed African Americans the right to vote, a black woman ran for president.

Shirley Chisholm's career in politics began in the 1940s when she became involved in her neighborhood political organization, the Seventeenth Assembly District Democratic Club. There she learned two hard lessons: black issues weren't important, and women were supposed to stick to fundraising. Eventually, exasperated by the white male politicians, she turned to the Bedford-Stuyvesant Political League, which was led by a black man, Mac Holder. Chisholm didn't find what she was looking for there, either, and dropped out of politics for a time. Then, in 1960, Chisholm helped found the Unity Democratic Club. The purpose of the organization was to run black candidates for virtually all offices.

In 1964, running from the Unity Democratic Club, Shirley Chisholm was elected

Unbought and unbossed, Shirley Chisholm made political history in 1972 when she made the first serious bid by a woman for the presidential nomination of a major party. She is shown here with National Council of Negro Women president Dorothy Height. (BETHUNE MUSEUM AND ARCHIVES)

to the New York State Assembly. For four years she was the only woman and one of four African Americans in the assembly. In 1968, she became the first black woman in the U.S. House of Representatives. She ran on the slogan "Unbought and Unbossed," which later became the title of her first autobiography.

In addition to being a strong advocate for the rights of black people in general, Chisholm was also a feminist. She was a founder of the National Women's Political Caucus. With the support of the women's

movement and the African-American people, Chisholm had a potentially powerful political bloc. She made a serious, significant bid for the Democratic nomination for the presidency of the United States. She ran in the primaries, stayed in the race until the convention, and won more than 150 votes on the first ballot.

Chisholm was disappointed in the outcome of the race; she believed that both white women and black men failed to give her needed support. Still, for that moment in history, hers was a stunning achievement. In the meantime, other black women were setting the scene for the triumphs of the 1990s.

In 1966, **Barbara Charline Jordan** was elected to the Texas state senate. She was the first African American to serve in that state's senate since 1883. In 1972, she was elected to the United States House of Representatives. Her first major impact on the national political scene came in 1974, at the impeachment hearings of President Richard Nixon. She spoke with tremendous intensity and eloquence about her belief in the United States Constitution. An orator of exceptional power, she caught the attention of her colleagues and of a national television audience.

Two years later, Jordan delivered the keynote address at the 1976 Democratic National Convention. Again, her power as a speaker inspired the nation as she rose above politics to statesmanship. Although she retired from public office in 1978, she was again called upon by the Democratic Party in 1992 for her image and her leadership. She gave the keynote address at that year's national convention and proved as strong a voice for courage, integrity, and justice as she had been sixteen years before.

Yvonne Braithwaite Burke came to national attention when she cochaired the Democratic National Convention in 1972. It was the first time an African American had chaired a major party's national political convention. That year, Burke was also elected to the House of Representatives from California. She was the first black woman to represent California in Congress and, in 1976, became the first woman to chair the Congressional Black Caucus.

On a local level, too, black women were making inroads. In 1961, Helene Hillyer Hale had become a county chairperson in Hawaii, a position equivalent to mayor. Twelve years later, Lelia K. Smith Foley became the first African-American woman to be mayor in the continental United States. The town of Taft, Oklahoma, was not a large one, but her victory there was. And there were many more in store for black women at this level of government.

In 1976, **Unita Blackwell** was elected mayor of Mayersville, Mississippi, making her the first African-American mayor in that state. Her political career had begun, as it had for so many black women, with the struggle to be allowed to vote.

By 1988, the numbers of black women mayors had grown to the point that they formed their own caucus, the **Black Women Mayors' Caucus** (BWMC), at the National Conference of Black Mayors. As of 1992, sixty-seven black women mayors were members of the BWMC.

As black political power grew, not all the victories came in elections. The highest offices held by black women continued to be appointed ones. In 1977, for example, President Jimmy Carter named **Patricia Roberts Harris** the Secretary of Housing and Urban Development (HUD), making her the first black woman in a U.S. cabinet. **Eleanor Holmes Norton** became the first woman to chair the Equal Employment Opportunity Commission (EEOC). **Mary Frances Berry** became assistant secretary for education in the Department of Health, Education and Welfare (HEW). In 1979, Patricia Roberts Harris became Secretary of HEW. In 1993, **Hazel O'Leary** became the first woman and the first African American to serve as Secretary of Energy, and **Joycelyn Elders** was confirmed as Surgeon General of the United States.

Black women were making consistent political progress. A report from the Joint Center for Political Studies (JCPS) showed that in 1973 there were 337 black women holding public office in the United States. In 1989, there were 1,814. In addition, there have been inroads in political parties. Again according to the JCPS, *50 to 60 percent* of all Democratic Party state officials are African-American women.

However, the struggle that would trigger the 1992 election of the first black woman in the U.S. Senate, as well as three white woman senators and five new black congresswomen, was being fought in a completely different arena—the U.S. courts.

The Civil Rights Act of 1964 was on its way into history when one section of it stopped just long enough to pick up an entire gender. That section was Title VII, which was designed to prevent discrimination in employment. Just as in the nineteenth century with the Fifteenth Amendment, black men were the proposed beneficiaries of the law. Although it would have theoretically protected black women as well, there is little doubt they would have continued to be deprived of employment and advancement, with gender used as an excuse, if nothing else.

Again paralleling the nineteenth-century situation, there were women who felt that Title VII should apply to them as well as to men. However, before those women got a chance to add the word *sex* to the bill, somebody else did.

That somebody else was Representative Howard Smith of Virginia. It was his idea that adding women to those covered by the bill would make it so ridiculous no one would vote for it. However, as **Paula Gid-**dings relates it in *When and Where I Enter,* "There *was* much ribaldry in the Congress; the day Smith made his proposal was called 'Ladies Day' in the House. But evidently the good ol' boys were laughing so hard they missed a step. Some of their colleagues, particularly Representative Martha Griffiths of Michigan, were able to marshal forces sufficient to pass the bill—with the sex provision."

Title VII, and its enforcement arm, the Equal Employment Opportunity Commission, changed the face of American business in many ways. With the force of the government behind them, black women were more frequently able to find jobs that suited their talents and their educations, as were black men and women of other races. All of this was the predicted outcome of the law. No one, however, could have predicted that black women would use the law to fight one of their oldest and most terrible enemies.

SEXUAL HARASSMENT

As a crime, sexual harassment did not exist. As an act, it had no name. Yet, from the time that women first entered the labor market, they suffered it, fought it, and sometimes succumbed to it.

Sexual harassment arises from disorders deep within our culture. It reflects a disrespect for women that is apparent in and caused by the longstanding practice of patriarchy. However, to provide a context for sexual harassment and its relevance in the lives of black women, it is necessary to go back to their sexual exploitation by men who considered themselves their legal owners.

The sexual exploitation of domestic servants—whether slave or free, black or white—has existed throughout Western history. Historically, women servants seldom had many options. Giving in to their employers' sexual demands kept them not only from unemployment but also from starvation or prostitution. The situation was so common that the seduced housemaid was a comic figure in fiction and on the stage. In real life, of course, her case was far from comic. If, after being abused by her employer, she became pregnant, she lost her job and often, in the end, her life. If she refused to submit, the power of her employer to deprive her of other jobs was such that being fired often meant the same thing.

In the earliest days of the American colonies, employers frequently sexually exploited servants, especially indentured servants. African women, in the years between 1619—when they first came to this country—and 1640, shared this oppression. Then, after 1640, when virtually all African servants were reduced by law to the condition of slavery, their condition became far worse.

The laws of the time gave mixed signals with regard to the sexual exploitation of slaves. In the earliest days of the colonies a white man who was convicted of having sexual relations with a black woman faced a more severe punishment than one who did so with his white neighbor. That punishment extended to sexual relations between a man and his slave. However, if he forced a woman slave to have intercourse and she bore a child, that child was, by law, his slave as well, giving his action a significant financial advantage. As Paula Giddings points out, "Being able to repro-

duce one's own labor force would be well worth the fine, even in the unlikely event that it would be imposed." Later, the laws forbidding a white man to have sexual relations with a black woman were repealed, and the situation became worse.

From the earliest years of America, then, white men were encouraged by law and custom to force sexual acts upon women who tilled their fields and cleaned their houses. However, black women did not accept this exploitation without resistance. Even though their families were hostage to the slave owner, they refused, fought, poisoned, and aborted in their determination not to lose their sexual self-respect or to participate in the breeding of new slaves. But the struggle was grossly unequal.

Some men believe that forced sex is the same act as consensual sex, in every way except its origin. For this reason, these men can exercise "conjugal rights" on women who reject them. They can pay for intercourse with women who despise them. And white men could, for two centuries in this country, force female slaves to accept them as sexual partners.

Some men are also able to get satisfaction out of using their power in the workplace to force unwanted attentions on co-workers and employees. There are other men, of course, who have no illusions about or interest in the desires of the women they exploit. It is the act of domination that satisfies.

These men often harass women who threaten their power. Harassment is a tool for keeping women in their place, by causing them embarrassment, undermining their confidence, and defining them as sexual beings in the eyes of co-workers. The behavior of all of these men is not unusual.

It has been sanctioned by society, in other forms, throughout America's history and beyond. This is one of the reasons that sexual harassment cases are difficult to prosecute.

The progress of the industrial revolution did nothing to control the problem. While domestic servants tried to fend off attack in private homes, women in factories faced the forced attentions of foremen and supervisors. One account tells of women in a broom factory who carried knives to protect themselves.

Today, the problem is huge. In a 1980 study by the U.S. Merit Systems Protection Board of federal employees, 42 percent of women reported being sexually harassed at some time in the two years covered by the study. Other studies have yielded equally discouraging figures.

Black women's position is complicated by the way white society tried long ago to justify the behavior of slave owners. A lie was told. That lie said that a black woman was so sexual no man could resist her. Therefore, no white man could be blamed for *failing* to resist her. In addition, she was immoral, so engaging in an immoral act with her was not a white man's fault. This lie has haunted black women ever since. It is certainly one of the reasons that black women have played such an important role in the legal history of sexual harassment.

Until the Civil Rights Act of 1964, sexual discrimination was not illegal in this country. And sexual harassment, as a legal form of discrimination, did not exist. A woman who was raped by a co-worker could charge him with rape and try to take him to court. A woman who was subjected to forced touching and fondling by her boss could make an attempt to charge him with sexual assault, though that would almost certainly be a fruitless act. A woman who, day in and day out, was forced to listen to sexual innuendo and humiliating remarks could do nothing at all.

Then, in 1976, things began to change. Within a very short time, a number of women brought suit charging that sexual harassment was sex discrimination. Among these were several black women. Paulette Barnes and Margaret Miller brought two of the earliest cases. These cases were unsuccessful in the lower courts, the judges ruling in Miller's case that the acts in question were not sufficiently tied to the workplace.

Barnes' case, however, tested whether sexual harassment was treatment "based on sex" within its legal meaning. The lower court said no, but Paulette Barnes appealed her case. On appeal, a three-judge panel ruled that when an employer abolishes a woman's job because she refuses his advances it is sex discrimination. The ruling was a landmark in the legal definition of sexual harassment.

Another black woman brought the case that was the turning point in sexual harassment prosecution. Diane Williams, a public information specialist in the Justice Department, refused the sexual advances of her supervisor. She was fired. After several hearings, the judge of the appeals court stated that "the conduct of the plaintiff's supervisor created an artificial barrier to employment which was placed before one gender and not the other, despite the fact that both genders were similarly situated."

Defense attorneys argued that, since either gender could be harassed, harassment was not discrimination on the basis of gender. The judge returned that, regardless of who *could* be harassed, if one gender, primarily, *was* harassed, discrimination was being practiced.

One of the greatest contributions a black woman has made to this struggle was not a court case at all. In 1991, college professor **Anita Hill** agreed to appear before a congressional committee that was hearing testimony on the confirmation of Judge Clarence Thomas to the U.S. Supreme Court. It was not her choice to make her charges against Thomas public. She had answered questions in a confidential investigation, and her answers had been leaked to the press. At that point she was asked to testify publicly and she did. During her testimony before an all-male committee, all of the cultural biases already discussed here—and more—were apparent in her questioners.

Whether they believed Hill's statements about Thomas or not, many observers were appalled by the questions that were asked her and the attitudes they revealed. There was the implication that no woman's career could be important enough to provide a plausible reason for silence about harassment. There was the insinuation that women who receive sexual attentions must in some way provoke them. Arguments were presented based on Hill's attractiveness, as judged by the male members of the committee and the press.

All of this was made worse, if not caused outright, by Hill's status as a black woman. It is possible that a white woman with Hill's professional reputation and credentials might have been subjected to the same interrogation. But to many social critics, it did not seem likely, at least not by white

men who hoped to be re-elected and not on national television.

The lack of awareness on the part of men in both the government and the media was stunning. People all over the country watched the hearings on television. They saw one woman sit in front of ranks of men who were clearly incapable of understanding her situation. They heard questions that made it painfully clear that these same men could not draw the line between appropriate behavior toward a woman and inappropriate behavior. The suspicion began to arise in many minds that the widespread sexual harassment of women in a country where 98 percent of the Senate is male might not be accidental.

No one will ever convince the women of America that the next election's results were a coincidence.

THE ELECTION OF '92

Cardiss Collins was elected to the House of Representatives from Illinois in 1973, and in 1992 she was still there. **Maxine Waters,** from California, was elected in 1990, along with **Eleanor Holmes Norton** from Washington, D.C., and **Barbara-Rose Collins** from Michigan. That's a total of four. While Anita Hill was testifying, there were four black women in the House and none in the Senate.

At the next election, for the first time in history, a black woman, Carol Moseley-Braun of Illinois, was elected to the United States Senate—along with four white women—and five more black women were elected to the House: **Carrie Meek** of Florida, **Eddie Bernice Johnson** of Texas, **Eva**

The election of 1992 brought Bill Clinton to the White House, with a substantial percentage of the black vote. He is shown here meeting with a "high level" group of black women. From left to right are: Minyon Moore, Lottie Shackelford, Dr. C. Delores Tucker, Dr. Dorothy Height (president of the National Council of Negro Women), President Clinton, Alexis Herman (special assistant to the President), Maya Angelou, and Maggie Williams (chief of staff for Hillary Clinton). (THE WHITE HOUSE)

Clayton of North Carolina, **Corrine Brown** of Florida, and **Cynthia McKinney** of Georgia. At the next election, **Sheila Jackson Lee** of Texas joined the team.

This group of black women, totaling eleven in 1994, may be new in the U.S. Congress, but they are not new to politics. Their records are impressive and their struggles have been great.

Cardiss Collins, the veteran, ran for her husband's seat after he died in 1973. Two years later, she became the first woman and the first African American to be appointed Democratic whip-at-large. In 1979, she became chair of the Congressional Black Caucus.

Maxine Waters served in the California Assembly from racially troubled South Central Los Angeles from 1976 until 1990. She battled that whole time for services for her people. When she was elected to the U.S. House of Representatives in 1990, her mission did not change. She fought an attempt to weaken laws requiring banks and savings and loans to serve minority communities. She went to bat for black soldiers and veterans of Operation Desert Storm. She also spoke out loudly for her constituents after rioting in South Central Los Angeles followed the verdict in the Rodney King case.

Eleanor Holmes Norton came out of the civil rights movement of the 1960s. She was a participant in the **Mississippi Freedom Democratic Party** and a member of the national staff of the March on Washington in 1963. She worked for the American Civil Liberties Union before becoming head of the New York City Commission on Human Rights. In 1977, she became chair of the Equal Employment Opportunities Commission. She cleared the EEOC's reputation as a mismanaged bureaucratic mess, increasing the productivity of its area offices by 65 percent. Her bid for congressional representative for the District of Columbia was her first try for elected office, and she is a knowledgeable, experienced veteran of Washington politics.

Barbara-Rose Collins served three two-year terms in the Michigan House of Representatives, starting in 1974. As a state legislator, she was responsible for the passage of bills dealing with sexual harassment, pension rights, and domestic violence. She grew up in Detroit and is personally familiar with that city's problems. As a result, she brought to the U.S. House a concern for the urban issues of African Americans that matched in intensity that of Waters.

Unlike their predecessors, all of the 1992 entries, with the exception of Moseley-Braun, are from the South. As a result, they are accustomed to dealing with opposition. "I have had to work with the same kind of people, only much meaner, *much meaner,* than you would find here," says Carrie Meek. They all also represent black-majority districts, again with the exception of Senator Moseley-Braun.

Meek spent fourteen years in the Florida house and senate before coming to Washington at the age of sixty-eight. She lobbied for and won a position on the House Appropriations Committee, the only one given to a freshman Democrat.

Eddie Bernice Johnson was the first black woman ever to be elected to any public office in Dallas, Texas. She became a representative in the Texas state legislature more than twenty years ago. She was also a regional director of HEW during the Carter administration. She has a lot of experience and it shows.

Eva Clayton was the first black woman elected to represent North Carolina in Congress. From a poor, rural district, her concerns are expected to be somewhat different from those of the two Collinses, Waters, Norton, and Moseley-Braun, all of whom represent large cities. But her attitude toward old-line members of Congress is the same. "Let's face it, this institution is male-dominated," she says. "Sometimes when I'm speaking, I know some men are thinking, 'Oh, what does she know?' I just feel they want to cut me off, but I just look them in the eye as if to say, *Don't even think about it.*"

Corrine Brown, of Florida, was first elected to the Florida state legislature in 1983. During the years since, she has gained expertise on tax policy by serving on the Finance and Taxation Committee of that legislature.

Cynthia McKinney, of Georgia, was the youngest of the new crop. A Ph.D. candidate in international relations from Tufts University's Fletcher School of Law and Diplomacy, she cowrote the plan that created three Georgia majority black House districts. She served in the Georgia Assembly from 1988 until she was elected to the U.S. House. She has shown great concern for issues of environmental racism.

Sheila Jackson Lee came to Congress through municipal government. For many years she was a strong advocate for human rights on the Houston City Council. She

Pictured here are five of the ten black women who were members of the House of Representatives in the 104th Congress. From left to right they are: Sheila Jackson Lee, Corrine Brown, Carrie P. Meek, Barbara-Rose Collins, and Eddie Bernice Johnson. (TOM HORAN)

was also director of the State Bar of Texas. Upon reaching Washington, she was elected president of the Democratic freshmen.

"Seven decades after women's suffrage," wrote Francis Wilkinson in *Rolling Stone,* "four decades after *Brown* v. *Board of Education* and three decades after the passage of the Civil Rights Act, black women are for the first time seated at the white man's table."

That is indeed one way to look at it. But the truth is that white men have never owned the table. They just believed they did, and acted as though they did. They can't get by with that anymore.

The Senate and the country were stirred when Carol Moseley-Braun went up against Jesse Helms to keep the insignia of the Daughters of the Confederacy from receiving Senate approval. But, powerful as it was, that was the action of a bold, naive, angry freshman. In September of 1995, a plan was afoot in the Senate to significantly weaken fair-housing enforcement in a housing appropriation bill. Moseley-Braun grabbed Senate Majority Leader Bob Dole and said, "You're not going to let this happen, are you? We'll be riding on the back of the bus again."

When Moseley-Braun and Dole were finished talking and negotiating, he walked over to the Republican leader of the assault, Christopher Bond, and had a talk with him. Bond withdrew from the battle, and the bill passed without the damaging modification. Of course, Moseley-Braun and her colleagues had to make certain concessions, but she indicated that she would deal with that later.

It is now crystal clear that the black women in Congress, in the cabinet, in mayors' offices, and governors' mansions are not token guests at the table. They are players. They didn't just drop by for dinner, they have moved in.

[This introduction incorporates material from the following articles in *Black Women in America: An Historical Encyclopedia:* "Abolition Movement" and "Slavery," by Brenda E. Stevenson; "Law: Oppression and Resistance," by Judy Scales-Trent; "Sexual Harassment," by Kathleen Thompson; "National Association of Colored Women," by Dorothy Salem; "Montgomery Bus Boycott," by Stewart Burns. Other sources include the "Suffrage Movement," by Rosalyn Terborg-Penn; "Jim Crow Laws," by Aferdteen B. Harrison; and "Mississippi Freedom Democratic Party," by Chana Kai Lee.]

A

Alexander, Sadie (1898–1989)

In an interview in 1981, Sadie Tanner Mossell Alexander provided this advice for young black men and women: "Don't let anything stop you. There will be times when you'll be disappointed, but you can't stop. Make yourself the best that you can make out of what you are. The very best." Alexander, the first black woman to earn a Ph.D. in economics, a lawyer, and a civil rights activist, could truthfully say that she had always been the best that she could be, and this was usually more than society wanted her and other black women to be.

Sadie Tanner Mossell was born into a prominent Philadelphia family on January 2, 1898. Her father, Aaron Mossell, was the first African American to receive a law degree from the University of Pennsylvania. Her grandfather, Benjamin Tucker Tanner, was a well-known author, a bishop in the African Methodist Episcopal Church, and editor of the country's first African-American scholarly journal, the *African Methodist Episcopal Review.* The famous painter Henry Ossawa Tanner was her uncle. At the turn of the century, the Tanner home was a gathering place and intellectual center for the black community.

Mossell was educated in the public schools of Philadelphia and Washington, D.C. In 1915, she graduated from M Street High School and was awarded a scholarship to **Howard University.** Her mother, however, was convinced that opportunities

for graduate training would be better if her daughter received a bachelor's degree from the University of Pennsylvania. Mossell went along with her mother's wishes.

Sadie Mossell found her college course work to be extremely difficult, but she graduated with a B.A. with honors in education in 1918, completing a four-year program in three years. Continuing her studies in economics, she obtained an M.A. in 1919, became a Frances Sergeant Pepper Fellow, and earned a Ph.D. on June 6, 1921. Only one day later than Georgiana Simpson, she became the second African-American woman in the United States to receive a doctoral degree and the first to receive a Ph.D. in economics.

Finding employment that measured up to her abilities and qualifications was her next challenge. Mossell found that her Ph.D. was useless in the job market and it did not enable her to secure a job at any of the large white insurance companies. Despite excellent recommendations from her professors, no one would hire an African-American woman, even in positions for which she was clearly overqualified. Her professors threatened, to no avail, not to refer any other students to the insurance companies unless she was hired. Then Mossell decided to utilize her minor in insurance and actuarial science to take a position as assistant actuary for the North Carolina Mutual Life Insurance Company, an African-American firm in Durham. She

The first black woman to receive a doctorate in economics in the United States, Sadie Tanner Mossell Alexander was also the first to be admitted to the bar and practice law in the state of Pennsylvania. She was a founder of the National Bar Association and helped to draft the 1935 Pennsylvania public accommodations law. (SCHOMBURG CENTER)

remained there for two years, until she returned to Philadelphia in 1923 to marry her college sweetheart, Raymond Pace Alexander, who had just finished Harvard University Law School.

Sadie Alexander abhorred domestic life, and after twelve months of running the house she expressed her discontent to her husband. When asked what she would

rather do, she replied that she wanted to go to law school.

In September 1924, she entered the University of Pennsylvania Law School and quickly earned honors and became a member of the Law Review Board. Upon graduation in June 1927, she became the first African-American woman to enter the bar and practice law in the State of Pennsylvania. She and her husband entered into private practice as one of the earliest husband-wife legal teams in the United States. The partnership lasted until her husband became a judge in the Philadelphia Court of Common Pleas in 1959. Alexander was appointed assistant city solicitor for Philadelphia, serving from 1928 to 1930 and from 1934 to 1938. Returning to private practice, she specialized in probate law, divorce, and domestic relations matters. In 1925, she and her husband were among the founders of the National Bar Association, the professional organization for African-American lawyers.

During the 1920s and 1930s, the Alexanders were personally responsible for ending overt discrimination against black Americans in Philadelphia hotels, restaurants, and theaters. Tired of sitting in the "Coloreds Only" sections of movie houses and theaters, they helped to draft the 1935 Pennsylvania state public accommodations law, which prohibited discrimination in public places. Following its passage, the Alexanders tested the law at a Philadelphia theater that refused to admit African Americans. They made several attempts to gain admittance but were turned away each time by the manager; they had him arrested. After several nights in jail, the manager relented. The Alexanders used the same technique to end discrimination in several of the city's hotels and restaurants.

During the 1940s, the Alexanders pressed for the hiring of African Americans on the faculty of the University of Pennsylvania and for the integration of the U.S. Armed Forces. In 1946, President Harry S. Truman appointed Alexander to the Commission to Study the Civil Rights of All Races and Faiths, on which she served until 1948. The commission's report, *To Secure These Rights* (1948), recommended the desegregation of the armed services, and this occurred in 1949. Alexander also served on President John F. Kennedy's Lawyers' Committee for Civil Rights under Law in 1963 and was chair of President Jimmy Carter's White House Conference on Aging in 1979 and 1980.

Alexander also held a number of other important professional positions throughout her distinguished career. Between 1919 and 1923, she served as the first national president of **Delta Sigma Theta Sorority.** She maintained a long association with the American Civil Liberties Union and for twenty-five years served as a national secretary for the National Urban League. Between 1950 and 1967, she was a member of the Philadelphia Commission on Human Relations and for a time she served as the chair. For several years she served as chair of, and the only female on, the Philadelphia Bar Association's subcommittee on human rights.

Alexander received many awards and honors. She was elected to Phi Beta Kappa at the University of Pennsylvania in 1970. She received honorary degrees from the University of Pennsylvania, Swarthmore College, Drexel University, Lincoln University, and the Medical College of Pennsylvania. On April 15, 1980, she received the Distinguished Service Award from the University of Pennsylvania. In 1987, the Philadelphia Bar Association named its public service center in her honor.

Alexander practiced law in Philadelphia until she was eighty-five years old. She died on November 6, 1989, of complications from Alzheimer's disease, Parkinson's disease, and pneumonia. She died in her home in the Roxborough section of Philadelphia, where she had lived since 1983.

In her 1981 interview, Alexander summarized her career and approach to life by declaring, "I haven't worked for the money. There's only so much you can eat, and you can only sleep in one bed—but I always wanted to do something where you can contribute something."

V. P. FRANKLIN

Anderson, Violette N.   (1882–1937)

Born in 1882 in London, England, Violette Anderson was the first black woman to practice law in the state of Illinois. Anderson was a graduate of the University of Chicago Law School in 1920. She attended the Chicago Athenaeum and the Chicago Seminar of Sciences. Anderson further distinguished herself by becoming, in 1926, the first black woman to practice law in the U.S. Supreme Court, in the U.S. District Court in the Eastern District of Illinois, and in Chicago as the Assistant City Prosecutor.

Anderson was a member of the Federation of Colored Women's Clubs, president of the Friendly Big Sisters' League of Chicago, first vice president of the Cook County Bar Association, an executive board member of the Chicago Council of

In the 1920s, Violette Anderson made legal history when she became the first black woman to practice law in Illinois and then the first to argue a case before the U.S. Supreme Court. (SCHOMBURG CENTER)

Social Agencies, and a member of the Zeta Zeta Chapter of the Zeta Phi Beta Sorority. Anderson died in 1937.

WENDY BROWN

Atkins, Hannah Diggs (1923–)

Hannah Diggs Atkins, Oklahoma state legislator, 1969–80, traces her interest in po-litical involvement to watching her father coming home late at night bloody and beaten for trying to vote during her childhood in North Carolina. She has had a long, distinguished career in politics and government, ranging from work in voter registration drives to membership on the Democratic National Committee. Describing herself as a "gadfly to prick the moral conscience of legislators," she worked for reform legislation in education, civil rights, mental health, employment, criminal justice, housing, women's rights and child care as an Oklahoma lawmaker.

Born in Winston-Salem, North Carolina, November 1, 1923, to James Thackeray Diggs and Mabel Kennedy Diggs, Hannah Diggs received her B.A. from Saint Augustine's College (1943), her B.L.S. from the University of Chicago (1949), and later studied at Oklahoma City University Law School and the University of Oklahoma (where she received an M.P.A. in 1989). Professionally she worked as a news reporter, teacher, biochemical researcher, school librarian, law librarian, and chief of the general reference division, Oklahoma state legislature. After leaving the legislature she served as the assistant director of human services for Oklahoma, 1983–87. From 1987 to 1991, as both secretary of human resources and secretary of state, she was the highest-ranking woman in Oklahoma state government. In 1980, President Jimmy Carter named her delegate to the United Nations, Thirty-fifth Assembly.

She married Charles N. Atkins, and they have three children: Edmund Earl, Charles N., and Valerie Ann.

JEWEL LIMAR PRESTAGE

B

Barrett, Jacquelyn H. (1950?–)

In 1992, Fulton County, Georgia, made history by electing Jacquelyn Barrett sheriff. She was the first black woman sheriff in the United States.

Jacquelyn H. Barrett grew up on the campus of Johnson C. Smith University in Charleston, North Carolina. Her mother, Ocie P. Harrison, was secretary to the university president. Her father was Cornelius Harrison, Sr. She attended Beaver College in Glenside, Pennsylvania. There, she became interested in the field of criminal justice. "I was also somewhat afraid of it at first," she told an *Ebony* interviewer in 1995, "because you are dealing with an element that has obviously shown you that they don't abide by the rules."

Later, Barrett received a master's degree in sociology from Clark-Atlanta University. Before she became sheriff of Fulton County, she worked for ten years with the Georgia Peace Officer Standards and Training Council and five years as director of the Fulton County Public Safety Training Center. She also married and had two children.

Barrett was elected sheriff after the deputies' union "literally put their jobs on the line" by voting to pay her qualifying fee so that she could run. She is now in charge of a budget of more than $40 million and a staff of more than 800 people.

"I am a particular advocate of a sense of community," Barrett says of her work in law enforcement, "caring about each other as members of the community, acting like neighbors."

Fulton County includes Atlanta, and the police chief there, **Beverly Harvard,** is also a black woman.

KATHLEEN THOMPSON

Bass, Charlotta Spears (1880–1969)

"We offer these candidates as peace candidates," said the candidates committee of the Progressive Party in 1952. "We offer them as new hope to an America sick and tired of the corruption, the militarism, the segregations of and discrimination against the Negro people, and the growing unemployment that has been brought about by both Democrats and Republicans." One of the candidates offered was Charlotta Spears Bass, the first black woman to run for vice president of the United States.

Charlotta Spears was born in October 1880 in South Carolina. She was the sixth of the eleven children of Hiram and Kate Spears. The details of her childhood and education are not known, but in 1900, at age twenty, she left South Carolina to live and work in Providence, Rhode Island. She moved in with her oldest brother and took a job working for the *Providence Watchman*. She remained there for ten years. At the end of that time, she was suffering from exhaustion.

41

At the suggestion of her doctor, she moved to California to rest. It was to have been a two-year stay, but shortly after arriving, she ignored her doctor's advice and took a part-time job at a newspaper, the *Eagle*. Before her two years in California were over, she had taken over the paper, renaming it the *California Eagle*. A new editor arrived, Joseph Bass, one of the founders of the *Topeka Plaindealer*, and soon the two were married. As managing editor and editor, respectively, Charlotta Spears Bass and her husband set their paper firmly on a course of social and political activism. They vehemently attacked the racial stereotypes and the glorification of the Ku Klux Klan in D. W. Griffith's *The Birth of a Nation*. They defended the black soldiers of the Twenty-fourth Infantry who were unjustly sentenced in the Houston riot of 1917. They supported the defendants in the Scottsboro trials.

In 1930, Charlotta Bass helped found the Industrial Business Council, which encouraged black people to go into business and fought discrimination in hiring and employment practices. She also formed a group to attack housing covenants that denied the right of black Americans to live wherever they chose.

Joseph Bass died in 1934, and Charlotta Bass continued to run the *California Eagle*. In the years that followed, she became more and more active politically. In 1940, she was western regional director of the political campaign of Wendell Willkie. Three years later, she became the first black grand jury member for the Los Angeles County Court. In 1945, she ran in the seventh district as a people's candidate for city council. Her platform was progressive,

and her campaign united black organizations in the district. She received wholehearted support from the community, and though her bid was unsuccessful, it was a landmark campaign.

In the postwar United States, there was a plague of oppressive activity in the South, including an increase in Klan activities and, horrifyingly, an outbreak of lynchings. Bass was in the forefront of the battle against these and other outrages. She supported the Hollywood Ten and, during the years of McCarthyism, was accused of un-American activities.

Bass was one of the founders of the Progressive Party. She believed that neither of the two traditional parties was committed to working for black people, so she supported Henry Wallace's candidacy for president in 1948. Although she was now approaching seventy, she began to travel extensively in the service of her growing political concerns. In Prague, she supported the Stockholm Appeal to ban the bomb at the peace committee of the World Congress. She traveled in the Soviet Union and praised its lack of racial discrimination.

In 1950, Bass ran on the Progressive Party ticket for the congressional seat from the fourteenth legislative district in California. Again she was unsuccessful, but again she brought attention to important political issues. Her most important campaign came in 1952, when the Progressive Party nominated her for vice president of the United States. She campaigned fiercely, reserving her hardest attacks for Republican vice presidential candidate Richard Nixon. Her refrain during the campaign was, "Win or lose, we win by raising the issues." In addition to civil rights and peace, Bass stressed the issue of women's rights, encouraging women to run for political office.

In 1960, Bass published her autobiography, *Forty Years: Memoirs from the Pages of a Newspaper*. She died in Los Angeles in 1969. The causes for which she had fought so hard were now at the forefront in the United States; the issues she had raised were being addressed. She had won.

KATHLEEN THOMPSON

Belton, Sharon Sayles (1951–)

She was not only the first black but the first female mayor of Minneapolis. Having spent her life committed to bettering the community of her hometown Minneapolis, Sharon Sayles Belton was well-equipped to take over the leadership of this prosperous, middle class—and primarily white—city.

Belton grew up in Minneapolis and graduated from Minneapolis Central High School. She attended college across the Mississippi River in neighboring St. Paul, at Macalester College. She had to go on welfare during her senior year, but she graduated from the small liberal arts college.

After graduation, Belton became a parole officer for the Minneapolis Department of Corrections. She also worked in a variety of posts devoted to improving the lives of women and children who had been subjected to violence. She was assistant director of the Minneapolis Program for Victims of Sexual Abuse, and cofounder and president of the Harriet Tubman Shelter for Battered Women.

From 1983 to 1993, Belton was city council member from the eighth ward. For her last four years in the city council, she

Sharon Sayles Belton was elected mayor of Minneapolis, Minnesota, in 1994, the first black and the first woman to have the job. In her campaign she stressed the importance of communities working together. She won with 60 percent of the city vote. (OFFICE OF MAYOR BELTON)

was voted president. Increasingly, Belton became recognized for her progressive leadership and her ability to build bridges between communities and factions.

Belton worked on a wide range of civic projects, all focused on getting people to work together to build the community. Her organizations include the United Way, the Greater Minneapolis Food Bank, Affordable Housing Coalition, the Affordable

Day Care Coalition, and the Minneapolis Initiative Against Racism.

In 1994, Belton decided to run for mayor as a Democrat. Many people told her she could never win: Minneapolis was 78 percent white. It had never elected a woman or an African-American mayor; she was a Democrat, and her party was losing elections right and left to conservative Republicans.

Belton took little notice of any of this. She had a broad-based appeal to women, blacks, and a variety of other local groups, and she based her approach on old-fashioned grass-roots campaigning. She ran on a platform for education, city growth, and city unity, and against crime. She continually stressed the importance of residents working together. Her long record demonstrated that she could make good things happen under her leadership.

Unlike many candidates of the 1990s, Belton did not depend on big money interests. Instead, she focused on local, human concerns. She deeply cared about the city and maintaining the quality of urban life. Minneapolis is considered one of the most liveable cities in America, and Belton presented herself as the candidate best able to maintain quality within the communities. Belton won the election with 60 percent of the vote.

As Belton said after her victory, "We emphasized throughout the campaign that the citizens of Minneapolis were capable of setting aside the issues of race and gender and voting for the candidate that was best-suited to keep the city a viable community and they did that."

Apart from being mayor, Belton has considerable home responsibilities. Married to a lawyer, she cares for a physically disabled daughter and two young sons. Sixty-hour workweeks are normal for her—she just uses the same team approach with her family that has worked so well in politics.

ANDRA MEDEA

Berry, Mary Frances (1938–)

Mary Frances Berry is a scholar trained in history and law, a public servant, and a political activist of international renown. She has to her credit impressive firsts, such as being the first African-American woman to serve as chancellor of a major research university and the first African-American woman to hold the post of the nation's chief educational officer. She has taken numerous stands on the basis of principle, but her 1984 suit against President Ronald Reagan to reaffirm the independence of the U.S. Commission on Civil Rights, as well as her sit-in, arrest, and incarceration to protest racial injustice in South Africa, established a place for her in the national and international press. Her place in history, however, has been created not only by prestigious appointments and political activism but also by her contributions as a historian. Berry both writes and makes history.

Mary Frances Berry was born on February 17, 1938, in Nashville, Tennessee, to Frances Southall Berry and George Ford Berry. Throughout her childhood and youth in Tennessee, with her brother, George, Jr., her mother, and later with a stepfather and younger brother, Troy, Berry experienced hardships occasioned by poverty and racial discrimination. Nevertheless, her extraordinary intellect was recognized by Nashville teachers, particularly Minerva Hawkins, who challenged her to overcome obstacles and excel academically.

Berry graduated from Nashville's Pearl High School with honors in 1956. Thereafter she worked her way through college and graduate school as a laboratory technician at **Howard University** in Washington, D.C. She went on to earn a Ph.D. in U.S. constitutional history at the University of Michigan in Ann Arbor. Upon receiving her doctorate in 1966, Berry taught history at Central Michigan University in Mt. Pleasant while seeking admission to the University of Michigan Law School in order to obtain a J.D. She also taught history at Eastern Michigan University and at the University of Maryland until she earned her law degree. Concurrently she engaged in antiwar and pro–civil rights activities. In 1970, she accepted an appointment as an adjunct associate professor of history at the University of Michigan in Ann Arbor as well as a full-time appointment as the acting director of Afro-American Studies at the University of Maryland in College Park. She moved to the Maryland-Washington, D.C., area, where she has made her home.

Mary Frances Berry's deep personal interest and involvement in the cause of racial justice and the creation of new historical scholarship found expression in her decision to become a member of the bar in the District of Columbia, in her political activity, in her teaching of African-American and legal history, and in her research and writing of the 1970s. While demonstrating for the rights of African Americans and lobbying for federal enforcement of laws affecting African Americans, Berry maintained high standards of academic excellence and established an impressive scholarly record. She published *Black Resistance/White Law: A History of Constitutional Racism* in 1971, "Reparations for Freedmen, 1890–1919" in 1972, *Military Necessity and Civil Rights Policy* in 1977, and *Stability, Security, and Continuity: Mr. Justice Burton and Decision-making in the Supreme Court, 1945–1958* in 1978.

Berry also excelled during the 1970s in educational administration. At the University of Maryland she rose from one position of responsibility to another, becoming the director of Afro-American Studies, the interim chairman of the Division of Behavioral and Social Sciences, and the provost

Mary Frances Berry became known as "the woman the president couldn't fire" when she successfully sued President Ronald Reagan to retain her position on the U.S. Commission on Civil Rights. (MOORLAND-SPINGARN)

of that division. As provost from 1974 to 1976, she became the highest-ranking African-American woman on the College Park campus. When, in 1976, Berry accepted the invitation of the Board of Regents of the University of Colorado to become chancellor of the University of Colorado at Boulder, as well as professor of history and law, she became the first African-American woman to head a major research university, presiding over a student body of 21,000, a faculty of 2,000, and an annual budget of more than $100 million. Berry took a leave of absence from her professorship as well as her chancellorship at Colorado, however, in order to respond to the call of the recently elected President Jimmy Carter. From 1977 to 1980, Berry distinguished herself as assistant secretary for education in the Department of Health, Education and Welfare (HEW), becoming the first African-American woman to serve as the nation's chief educational officer.

Since leaving government, Berry has accomplished much as a scholar, continued her public service, and intensified her political activism. Leaving her posts in the Carter administration and at the University of Colorado, she returned in 1980 to her alma mater, Howard University, for a time teaching legal history in its history department and serving as a senior fellow at the Institute for the Study of Educational Policy. With John Wesley Blassingame, she coauthored *Long Memory,* a history of African Americans, in 1982. In 1986, she published *Why the ERA Failed: Politics, Women's Rights, and the Amending Process,* which became the subject of many reviews and debates regarding the Equal Rights Amendment and the women's movement. National recognition of her talents and her

contributions to the field of history led to Berry's receiving the University of Pennsylvania's distinguished Geraldine R. Segal Professorship in Social Thought in 1987 as well as a professorship in history. In terms of her professional affiliations, Berry has served as a vice president of the American Historical Association and president of the Organization of American Historians, the first black woman to hold the latter position. Because of her critical analyses, prodigious research, and coverage of timely issues from a historical perspective, she continues to be a sought-after professor, graduate adviser, author, and lecturer.

Combining public service with political activism during the 1980s and early 1990s, Berry has been a member of the U.S. Commission on Civil Rights since her appointment in 1980, and she served from 1980 to 1982 as the commission's vice chairperson. Always emphasizing not only its political autonomy, but also its watchdog role, Berry has come into conflict with Presidents Reagan and George Bush because they have wanted the commission to support the conservative policies of their administrations, something Berry cannot do. In 1984, for example, she became known as "the woman the president could not fire" when she successfully sued President Reagan to retain her position on the commission. Although she has been a minority voice on the commission subsequent to appointments by Reagan and Bush, Berry continued to be outspoken in the cause of civil rights, stressing the critical nexus between economic and racial justice. President Bill Clinton appointed her chair of the commission.

Both in her capacity as a public servant and as a private citizen-political activist, Berry has emphasized the impropriety and immorality of racist policies at home and abroad. With Washington, D.C., delegate to Congress Walter Fauntroy, and Trans-Africa executive Randall Robinson, Berry was arrested on November 21, 1984, after holding a sit-in at the South African Embassy. Their sit-in was the catalyst for a series of grass-roots demonstrations, the arrest of thousands of U.S. citizens, and nationwide protests against Reagan's policy with regard to South Africa. It was through such activism that the national Free South Africa movement, of which Berry is a cofounder, had its genesis. Whether in the trenches with other activists such as Jesse Jackson, Roger Wilkins, and Sylvia Hill or doing advocacy history with scholars such as John Hope Franklin for *amicus curiae* briefs in defense of African Americans' civil rights, Berry has been uncompromising in the struggle for African-American liberation and for justice.

Mary Frances Berry has received numerous honors and awards. She was selected by *Ms.* magazine as one of its 1986 Women of the Year, and she has been awarded honorary doctorates by such institutions as Central Michigan University, Howard University, **Oberlin College, Bethune-Cookman College,** and the City College of the City University of New York. Numerous organizations have singled her out for special recognition; she is the recipient of the **Rosa Parks** Award of the Southern Christian Leadership Conference (SCLC), the President's Award of the Congressional Black Caucus Foundation, and not only the Roy Wilkins Civil Rights Award but also the Image Award of the **National Association for the Advancement of Colored People** (NAACP).

GENNA RAE McNEIL

Bethune, Mary McLeod
(1875–1955)

In October 1941, after black women had been excluded from membership in the national advisory council of the Women's Interest Section (a female public relations unit in the War Department), Mary McLeod Bethune, the president of the **National Council of Negro Women,** vigorously challenged the omission. The situation underscored the encompassing nature of racial segregation in the United States in the first half of the twentieth century. Though participation in a women's advisory group was an exceedingly small matter in the country's large defense picture, white decision-makers barred African-American representation. In responding, the superpatriotic Bethune demonstrated the essentials of her leadership. "We cannot accept any excuse that the exclusion of Negro representation was an oversight. . . . We are incensed!" she informed the public and most particularly the Secretary of War. Concurrently, she maneuvered behind closed doors with influential white supporters, chief among whom was First Lady Eleanor Roosevelt. Bethune's objective was characteristic: to attain a breakthrough opportunity for black leadership that would lend itself to promoting the general welfare and to assaulting racial discrimination. As usual, Bethune was effective. She established a connection to the War Department via the women's advisory council from which, most notably, she ensured the commissioning of black officers in the Women's Army Auxiliary Corps (as it was then called) when it materialized the following year.

In circumstances common to black Americans of her generation, the uncom-

Always interested in world affairs, Mary McLeod Bethune was an adviser to the U.S. delegation at the 1945 founding conference of the United Nations in San Francisco. She is pictured here at the conference with W. E. B. DuBois (left) and Walter White of the NAACP. (BETHUNE MUSEUM AND ARCHIVES)

mon Mary McLeod Bethune was born on July 10, 1875, near Mayesville, South Carolina, about fifty miles northeast of Columbia. She was the fifteenth of seventeen children. Her parents were Sam and Patsy (McIntosh) McLeod, ex-slaves liberated by the Civil War. Initially it appeared that, despite natural leadership qualities augmented by emulating her iron-willed Christian mother, Mary would become just another poor, rural, uneducated black girl. At age ten, however, she enrolled in the Trinity Presbyterian Mission School when

it opened a few miles from her family's farm. Three years later, through the initiative of her loving teacher and dynamic mentor, Emma Jane Wilson, Mary attended Scotia Seminary, a missionary outpost of Northern Presbyterians in Concord, North Carolina. She stayed at this female boarding school from October 1888 to her graduation in May 1894. Scotia's head-heart-hand educational strategy prepared the overwhelming majority of its students to earn a living at teaching other black Americans—whose slave heritage left them desperate for schooling. Before McLeod began to teach, however, she spent a year at evangelist Dwight Moody's Institute for Home and Foreign Missions in Chicago, an experience that gave her contact with a significant microcosm of the world's people. She had enrolled at the institute to receive training for the African mission field, but the Presbyterian church rejected her application because it declined to support African-American missionaries in Africa. McLeod returned home, therefore, grievously disappointed. Nevertheless, she possessed the experiences, talent, and character for a bright future. She saw herself as God's very own precious child—an equal to any other in the human family. Regardless of the limitations society imposed because she exhibited the physical appearance of her African forebears, regardless of her sex, her rural Southern background, and her lingering poverty, this woman believed in God and in herself. More specifically, along with her teaching ability, McLeod possessed a missionary spirit that demanded release. It bubbled over while she taught at Haines Institute in Augusta, Georgia, in 1896–97, and during that same year she organized the Mission Sabbath School for 275 of the city's poorest children. Then McLeod established a mission enterprise in 1902 in Palatka, Florida, a city located about seventy-five miles southwest of Jacksonville. She not only taught children unable to pay tuition but also routinely imparted material goods, encouragement, and the gospel of Jesus Christ to sawmill workers, prisoners, and others in need.

While at the Presbyterians' Kendall Institute in Sumter, South Carolina, McLeod met a store clerk, Albertus Bethune, five years her senior. They married in May 1898, but no long-term conjugal bliss resulted. Bethune pursued a career in Florida—first in Palatka for five years and then in Daytona, about fifty miles to the southeast. Her husband followed her from one location to another, until, although never divorced, the Bethunes separated late in 1907. He returned to his home in Sumter County, South Carolina, where he died in 1918. This experience may have been responsible for her view that marriage and family were only secondary institutions in race advancement.

The Bethunes did have one son. During their first married year in Savannah, Georgia, Albert McLeod Bethune was born on February 3, 1899. Mary was the primary caregiver but Albertus always maintained consistent interest. Their son dropped out of college and failed at several jobs. His greatest blessing to his mother was presenting her in 1920 with Albert McLeod Bethune, Jr., her only grandchild. Grandmother Bethune took this first grandchild as her very own, legally adopting him. As an adult with a master's degree in library science, the younger Albert settled into a rewarding career as a librarian in Daytona Beach at the institution his grandmother had established. (The elder Albert died on October 31, 1989.)

When Bethune moved to Daytona in 1904, it was to start a school. Having previously established an independent mission, she knew the essentials for success. Moreover, she knew she wanted an incarnation of her alma mater, Scotia Seminary. She planned to offer basic academics, a pious religious atmosphere, and training in homemaking and teaching. Around the turn of the century, home training was publicly conceded as the special province of black female boarding schools. No goal was considered worthier, given the notion that a people could advance only to the extent that women "purified" the home. Accordingly, Bethune planned her school with the idea of educating girls as the keepers of the home. This translated into offering them sewing and cooking, activities subsumed under the rubric "industry." Despite the theoretical foundations of black girls' schools, in reality most students used whatever skills or knowledge they acquired to earn a living as maids, cooks, seamstresses, and especially teachers.

Though Scotia was the model, Bethune did not intend to imitate it precisely. Like Emma Wilson's independent Mayesville Educational and Industrial Institute, established in 1892, she planned to have a large farm to feed students and teachers and to generate a cash income. Furthermore, like Haines Institute's Lucy Laney, the era's preeminent black female founder-educator, she planned to have a kindergarten, a nurse training program, and community outreach.

Few would have predicted the success of these plans when Bethune, on October 3, 1904, launched the Daytona Educational and Industrial Institute from a rented house. According to tradition, she began with "five little girls, a dollar and a half and faith in God." Since the material necessities of education were nonexistent, Bethune made do with dry goods boxes for benches, the charred splinters of burned logs for pens, and elderberry juice for ink. In three years, she had achieved enough support to relocate the school to a permanent campus, where the first building was a four-story white frame named Faith Hall.

In 1910, Bethune bought a farm across the street. Typically she toiled in the fields with her teachers and with students in blue uniforms and white aprons to bring to the kitchen sugarcane syrup, melons, pumpkins, tomatoes, peas, and other food. Yet Bethune's concerns reached beyond her students. She developed several groups and forums to address community issues. None was more important to her than temperance. On September 27, 1905, she and her students mobilized to assure an overwhelming vote to keep Volusia County "dry." In short order, Bethune had become a leader in Daytona's black community.

In 1912, with a budget of $5,000 for sixty boarding students plus a number of day students, Bethune enjoyed a rush of good fortune that included receiving for an overnight stay the famed Tuskegee educator Booker T. Washington. More important still, she caught the attention of the national black press. Media exposure was particularly helpful because it presented Bethune with a wider field of potential donors. She needed as many as possible to underwrite a trades cottage for rug weaving, broom making, and other industries as well as a hospital that would train nurses and care for the sick. Both of these facilities became a reality in 1912. Moreover, in that same year Bethune recruited Frances Reynolds Keyser, the superintendent of New York City's **White Rose Mission** and an executive committee member of the **National Association for the Advancement of Colored People** (NAACP). Keyser was, in effect, her school's dean and well suited to share the challenges of the Daytona Institute.

Of course, the number one challenge was money. To get it Bethune utilized the well-worn techniques of black activists: selling chicken dinners, singing for donations, and out-and-out begging. Like other heads of private black schools, she traveled north to meet America's wealthy philanthropists, but Bethune enjoyed an advantage over most of her fund-raising colleagues: she could find donors in her own front yard as well. The Daytona area enjoyed an ever-expanding economy thanks primarily to its tourist attractions: a near-perfect climate, white sand beaches, and auto racing. Moreover, a core of the white population assisted liberal causes. Bethune routinely solicited from tourists whose names appeared in the local papers. Having trained her students to render Negro spirituals and plantation melodies with great feeling, she marched them into Daytona's prominent hotels to perform. Afterward, in a magnetic fashion, she pleaded her cause. By 1912, both millionaire winter residents James N. Gamble and Thomas H. White backed her, as did the leading town fathers and mothers. With such benefactors the Daytona Institute became Florida's center of interracial goodwill. Bethune demanded the respect of all, and all gave it. Yet Daytona was still a Southern town, and as the decades unfolded this became clearer than ever.

Nonetheless, having laid solid foundations in the first decade, Bethune's school activities appeared to be headed toward continued success. She attracted large numbers of students and faculty, erected more buildings, and pushed the budget ever upward, so that in 1918 she operated a four-year high school under the banner of the Daytona Normal and Industrial Institute. By April 1920, forty-seven girls had completed the full high-school course, and ten

taught in Florida's public schools. In conjunction with her educational work, Bethune took on wide-ranging social service responsibilities, particularly with the Red Cross. She became known throughout the East, and her contacts eventually extended to Washington, D.C. On March 7, 1918, U.S. Vice President Thomas R. Marshall spoke to hundreds of eager listeners in the Daytona Institute's new auditorium.

Bethune's tremendous success with her girls' school led to its transformation. In 1923, with more than 300 students and a debt-free physical plant valued at $250,000, it became coeducational; the next year, while promoting its high school, it inaugurated a junior college curriculum. These events occurred under the auspices of the Board of Education for Negroes of the mostly Northern Methodist Episcopal Church, which had assumed responsibility for the school. The board wanted to merge Bethune's school with the coeducational Cookman Institute in Jacksonville. The combined institution became Bethune-Cookman College (BCC), named in honor of Mary McLeod Bethune and in recognition of Cookman Institute, founded in 1872 and named for Alfred Cookman, a white New Jersey Methodist minister who had passionately preached social justice and support for black Americans. The new name epitomized the continuing interracial commitment of Bethune's institution, which was probably the only college of its day to be named specifically to highlight such a commitment.

The merger had practical results as well. Bethune achieved institutional support and college status for her virtually unendowed school just in time. From the mid-1920s onward, the downturn in the economy, the demise of the tradition of individual do-nors, and the increasing selectivity of phil-anthropic agencies translated into the closing of many independent black institu-tions. Even some colleges affiliated with religious denominations went under, and most of those that survived did so only barely. This was the case with BCC, which had to close its hospital in 1927. Indeed, the Great Depression started to hit when the Florida land boom collapsed in 1925, and it intensified with two severe hurri-canes in subsequent years. Then the bottom fell out with the stock market crash in 1929.

Although she was sometimes given to dramatic hyperbole, when Bethune ob-served in a February 1935 letter that in the Great Depression "we are passing through the most severe test of our lives," she pro-claimed an unadulterated truth. Her hardships as a college president defied ex-aggeration; but she refused to relinquish the hard-won ground on which she had staked her life. BCC was the only black college in Florida south of St. Augustine, and had it ceased to exist, many would have lost the chance for college. If white Americans could maintain institutions of higher learning, the indomitable Bethune believed she could do likewise regardless of the handicaps of race, gender, and relative poverty. For this determination, Bethune paid a high price. In 1933 she canceled all athletic and social affairs, periodically cut the heat off in dormitories, and slashed teachers' salaries. Bethune, a champion of vocationalism, even dropped her business course. A facilitator of thousands of schol-arships, she withdrew in the middle of the semester the work scholarships essential

to many. Consequently, by fives and tens, students "quietly packed up their effects and slipped away."

Despite the ordeal of running a college for more than a decade with a gaping insuf-ficiency of funds, throughout this period Bethune presented to the public a positive and inspiring presence. She understood that in fund-raising one had to project opti-mism, enthusiasm, confidence, and thank-fulness. She succeeded in keeping the doors open. Moreover, in 1935, with two new brick buildings, a dining hall, and a science hall, she augmented plant facilities by $80,000. Most important, she steadily raised the caliber of the academic program to comply with accrediting agencies' re-quirements. In 1934, of the sixty-four stu-dents who completed the junior college curriculum, fifty-six concurrently earned state teaching certificates. The next year, in recognition of her standard junior col-lege, the NAACP bestowed on Bethune its annual Spingarn Award, its highest honor.

The year afterward, Bethune's relation-ship to her college changed. She became in effect a part-time president when she assumed a demanding government job in Washington, D.C., with the National Youth Administration. Under this arrange-ment of divided priorities, Bethune kept the college functioning by relying on Bertha Loving Mitchell, the secretary-treasurer for business matters, and on James Bond, the academic dean. Yet regardless of this assis-tance, Bethune had taken upon herself im-possible tasks: pursuing national interests while serving as her school's chief execu-tive. The latter meant nonstop solicitations to individual donors, foundations, and gov-ernment agencies. Bethune suffered grievously from her colossal burdens. Her health broke in 1940, and months of medical care and recuperation followed.

Despite Bethune's part-time presidency, BCC reflected, as it always had previously, Mary McLeod Bethune. It continued to cultivate better race relations and to emphasize Christian values and practices. Also, it still championed vocationalism—agriculture, secretarial work, cooking, and sewing—in tandem with academics. The addition of a Trades Building for National Defense in 1942, a building Bethune had financed through her government agency in Washington, symbolized her commitment to vocational skills. Young people trained there for occupations in auto mechanics, masonry, electricity, and tailoring. Academics also enjoyed renewal at BCC. In 1939–40, for example, the school graduated 118 junior college students. The next year it opened a new library and inaugurated the third-year program in teacher education; in 1942 it added the fourth year. Bethune had developed a senior college.

Though accurately reflecting Bethune's vision, the dualism of vocational and collegiate programs would prove unrealistic for the underfunded BCC. Bethune escaped having to choose between them by giving up the presidency on December 15, 1942, because of recurring ill health. At that time she exercised the same control over the school that she had in its beginning, but now the institution boasted total cash receipts of more than $155,000 and a $600,000 physical plant that included a thirty-four-acre campus with fourteen buildings plus a farm.

Although Bethune had become committed to the education of both men and women, her interest in elevating females was so compelling that she found channels beyond her school for achieving this. For many years she worked through the **National Association of Colored Women** **(NACW)**, America's premier black women's organization in the first quarter of the twentieth century. Fully controlling a girls' boarding school provided Bethune with an excellent institutional base for NACW's charitable and civic work. Moreover, she benefited from associating with leaders of Daytona's influential Palmetto Club, an affiliate of the General Federation of Women's Clubs, the white counterpart to NACW. She enjoyed the coaching of associate Frances Keyser, the highly respected first president of NACW's Empire State Federation. Given these factors plus her own missionary spirit and aggressiveness, Bethune's ascent in NACW was guaranteed.

Her essential grounding for national leadership occurred during her presidency of the Florida Federation of Colored Women's Clubs (1917–24). Bethune brought to the office the full resources of her school plus her businesslike efficiency manifested in fruitful conventions, a realistic constitution, published minutes, and a respectable periodical. Always she set an inspiring example for club sisters as they confronted great issues. Obviously, the first of these was responding to America's entry into World War I. This Bethune did by promoting canning and preserving food, making articles for soldiers and their families, buying Liberty bonds, and contributing to Red Cross chapters and emergency circles. The second great issue was female enfranchisement. When, in September 1920, the voter rolls opened to women in Daytona in accord with the Nineteenth Amendment to the Constitution, braving the intimidations of the Ku Klux Klan, Bethune registered along with her entire institute faculty and staff and other local black women attuned to her leadership. A third issue, made all the more urgent due to white supremacists, was forging links with egalitarian-minded white women for the common welfare. Bethune handled this primarily by organizing in 1920 the Southeastern Federation of Colored Women, to which she brought superb organizing and human relations skills and an inspiring presence. Though the scope of this Southern aggregation transcended race relations, one of its major triumphs was supplying leadership for the women's general committee of the regional Commission on Interracial Cooperation headquartered in Atlanta.

The most demanding issue Bethune faced stemmed from state conditions relative to a wholesome rehabilitative environment for delinquent black girls. The state provided accommodations only for adult lawbreakers at the state prison in Raiford. Therefore, the Florida Federation of Colored Women's Clubs established in Ocala an alternative facility for up to twelve residents. On Sunday, September 20, 1921, Bethune opened the new Industrial School with her arm around the first girl committed to the federation's care. From then on she shouldered the responsibility for its efficient operation, which included paying two matrons. A year and a half into operation, the school's needs were compelling enough for President Bethune to write to one matron, "as long as I have a penny I am willing to share it with you. Don't give up." Bethune shared deeply both from her own pocketbook and from renewed financial campaigns. She and the subsequent federation president managed to obtain relief in the late 1920s when the Florida legislature finally appropriated funds for this facility just as it had been doing since 1913 for the Industrial School in Ocala that nurtured white female juvenile delinquents.

In 1924, Bethune achieved the highest office to which a black woman could then aspire, the presidency of NACW. During her tenure, she turned the organization increasingly beyond itself to the broader society. The National Council of Women of the United States was NACW's primary institutional mechanism for expanded contacts. In 1925, this council of thirty-eight organizations—thirty-seven white and one black—was the avenue for NACW's participation in the International Council of Women at its quinquennial conference, which attracted representatives from thirty-five countries to Washington, D.C. Through unprecedented planning, Bethune had gotten her chief lieutenants from around the country to the meeting and had insisted upon desegregated seating at all events. When this policy was violated on the evening of May 5, 1925, NACW members and other black Americans walked out. Bethune vented their rage publicly by explaining that it was humiliating to the United States to be segregated in the presence of women from all over the world. The International Council then in earnest ensured open seating. Consequently, Bethune and her members returned to tracking the sixty-four resolutions of the meeting dealing with issues as diverse as approval for the League of Nations and the rights of children. This international meeting whetted Bethune's appetite for foreign travel, and she subsequently visited nine European countries in 1927 as the recognized emissary of African-American women. She observed that other large minorities suffered oppression similar to that of black Americans. In Marseilles, France, she saw a rose garden with a big black velvet rose growing as luxuriantly as the white rose, the red rose, and all of the others; from that point on, the imagery of humanity as a rose garden became Bethune's unique symbol of universality.

So strong was Bethune's sense of this universality that she espoused a limitless vision for her organization. It could be the equal of any other women's voluntary association. It could be great particularly in relating to people of color around the world and in assuming a position on salient national and international questions. Even before assuming office, Bethune began to nurture the organizational unity and machinery necessary to realize her aspirations. The centerpiece of her program was a national headquarters in Washington, D.C., operated by a full-time paid executive secretary. For this cause she recruited Rebecca Stiles Taylor of Savannah, the talented president of the Georgia Federation of Colored Women, to join her college staff in order to serve as her chief NACW aide.

Obstacles loomed forbiddingly. One was the crunching 1925–28 economy that preceded the Great Depression. The NACW possessed relatively little discretionary income, so economic pressures bombarded it from all sides. Another hurdle was the great schism existing in NACW over the advisability of establishing an independent headquarters. For about a decade, some NACW leaders had supported the Washington, D.C., home of Frederick Douglass, the

nineteenth-century civil rights giant, as a suitable NACW headquarters, and as an incentive for clubwomen to pay for its upkeep. Bethune's position was that NACW members should persist in the noble cause of maintaining the Douglass home but should establish headquarters elsewhere because NACW did not and could not legally own the Douglass property. Bethune's sense of business and awareness of the real possibility of power struggles between the Douglass home trustees and NACW elected officials (even though at times these were the same people) never permitted her to waver in acquiring a building to which NACW held the title. Bethune's view prevailed but always against a powerful undertow of resistance that necessitated superstrenuous efforts such as her fundraising mission to twenty-five states in one thirteen-month period. Finally, on July 31, 1928, with more than half the $25,000 mortgage paid, Bethune and NACW proudly opened, with appropriate ceremony, an imposing detached red brick building as the organization's first home. Furthermore, they installed in it a paid secretary. This was the first time that a national black organization was designed to function in Washington, D.C., in the same way as scores of other national groups.

Had NACW's constitution failed to limit a president to four years in office, Bethune may have stayed on indefinitely. She loved the presidency, though she may have found a prolonged tenure unsuitable. Although the NACW had always taken a stand on some public questions directly affecting its membership, it had been basically a decentralized organization responding to local and state self-help projects and, later, national self-help projects—such as maintaining the Douglass home and establishing a $50,000 scholarship fund. Bethune had attempted to mold it into a unitary body that could forcefully and consistently project itself into a myriad of public issues as the authoritative voice of black women. Although suited perfectly to the spirit of the equalizing decade for women and the renaissance decade for black Americans, the imposition of an orientation alien to many members faced rugged opposition in the long run. When the Great Depression dealt a blow to visionary projections, all but the stoutest hearts tended to retreat. The new NACW powers did so with a vengeance, paring the organization's twenty-two departments covering a broad range of interests down to only two that focused almost exclusively on the black family.

Bethune, however, could not flinch from her passion for black women's participation in the mainstream of the body politic and found reinforcement for it in the Depression. When more than 25 percent of black families were on relief and multitudes more were applying, Bethune longed for black women to become a channel through which public funds could reach some of them. She wanted black women to play a substantive role—as did white men and women and black men—in the governmental process undergirding individual and family survival. Bethune believed that she and her sisters could best assume such activities through an umbrella organization that encompassed all existing national women's organizations. To some degree modeled after the National Council of Women, this would be a national council of black women. It would "cement a spirit of cooperation and unified effort" among women's groups so that they could "speak as one voice and one mind for the highest good of the race." Bethune was the perfect creator for this new organization, for she possessed not only its central idea but also the organizational expertise to accomplish it. Moreover, she enjoyed preeminent leadership stature among black women, as symbolized in the Spingarn Award and through her strong identification with a federal agency. Consequently, on December 5, 1935, in New York's Harlem, thirty representative women of voluntary associations voted the National Council of Negro Women (NCNW) into being. They also made Bethune the president, a position she occupied for almost fourteen years until relinquishing it in November 1949.

Predictably, President Bethune worked wonders with the NCNW machinery. By the end of her tenure the council included twenty-two national women's organizations, including professional and occupational groups, both broadly based and subject-restricted academic sororities, Christian denominational societies, fraternal associations, auxiliaries, and various other aggregations. In addition, NCNW boasted eighty-two local councils and numerous individual life memberships. Bethune left in place noteworthy mechanisms for effective operations such as a debt-free headquarters building in Washington, D.C., a paid executive secretary, and a proud periodical.

Before these assets materialized, however, NCNW proceeded to give black women, for the first time ever, sustained visibility in the nation's capital. Bethune propelled NCNW to the forefront of women's race organizations in the national life of the country through its "Conference on Governmental Cooperation in the Approach to the Problems of Negro Women and Children," held on April 4, 1938, at the Department of the Interior and the White House. Sixty-five of America's most civic-minded women of African descent met with government personnel to discuss greater black female integration into social welfare bureaucracies. The conference was a harbinger of what became almost annual visits of NCNW members to the White House—powerful public relations parades projecting a new imagery of black women as citizens in American democracy.

The 1938 conference also revealed Bethune's basic strategy for advancement, which was to win policy-making and management positions in government for competent black women. This emphasis upon upper-level employment for the "talented tenth" was to benefit the black masses. At its first White House conference, NCNW found that black women and children failed to participate in welfare programs in proportion to their need because of the virtual exclusion of black women from designing and administering those programs. Bethune chose to chip away at the era's strong apartheid practices and gender prejudice through conferences, petitions, civil service reform, and other means that would provide greater opportunities for African-American female leadership.

Even though Bethune readily won recognition of her council from First Lady Eleanor Roosevelt, it was only after an episode in 1941 in which the War Department initially barred and then accepted NCNW as a member of its women's advisory council that organized black women could partici-pate in government programs at a level somewhat approaching that of other women's associations. Like nothing else had, this validated Bethune's concept of gaining power for her constituency through a unified council. With the War Department's acknowledging NCNW as the representative of black women, the private sector followed suit, as symbolized in the National Council of Women's decision to accept NCNW into membership. As a result, NCNW enjoyed a wider platform from which to promote its fundamental concerns about issues of federal employment, effective enfranchisement, antilynching, and internationalism.

Bethune's determination to involve herself and her organization in international affairs resulted in her participation as an adviser to the U.S. delegation in the 1945 founding conference of the United Nations in San Francisco. By that time the crisis of World War II had so elevated the value of national unity that NCNW had interacted with various government and private agencies to promote the general welfare, as in its sponsorship of the S.S. *Harriet Tubman*, the first Liberty ship to honor a black woman. In addition, it had devised its own wartime projects. Its greatest pride stemmed from black women's participation in the military. This had been a priority goal of NCNW and other black organizations, but one that leading white women's organizations viewed indifferently. The goal was not achieved in all service branches until 1949, when the women's Marine Corps finally admitted a black applicant. In that year, NCNW pledged to work for more public housing, army desegregation, and President Harry S. Truman's civil rights program.

As the NCNW program in 1949 suggested, Bethune concerned herself with improving the status of all black Americans regardless of socioeconomic position or gender. In this emphasis, she was most effective in assuming the role of the preeminent race leader at large from 1936 to 1945. From slavery until the recent present, a race leader in white-controlled America could at best win concessions to ameliorate some hardships. More specifically, in New Deal Washington, D.C., a race leader was needed to keep track of black involvement in proliferating federal programs, to develop recommendations to enhance black welfare through them, and then to effect contacts to facilitate consideration of the recommendations. Bethune brought sterling qualities and a new political edge to this self-appointed role. She was tied to the leadership of the frontline organizations including the NAACP, the National Urban League, and the Association for the Study of Negro Life and History, and she was held in the highest esteem in black academia. Moreover, Bethune tackled the problems of African Americans both intelligently and ardently. She dealt effectively with all types of people, using the language and nuances of diplomacy. She knew how to articulate and dramatize her causes; and she was in her sixties, an age that gave her more distinction than she would have had otherwise in a world of men unaccustomed to women in corridors of political power.

Ever the world citizen, Mary McLeod Bethune is pictured here with Madame Pandit, India's representative to the United Nations, Ralph Bunche of the United Nations, and President Harry Truman. The occasion is the NCNW's 1949 annual convention, which honored Bethune on her resignation as president. (BETHUNE MUSEUM AND ARCHIVES)

Because Bethune needed a highly trained staff wholeheartedly committed to black advancement, she organized what became the Federal Council on Negro Affairs, a highly informal network popularly called the Black Cabinet. Composed primarily of New Deal race specialists in September 1939, it consisted of twenty-seven men and three women working mostly in short-term emergency agencies such as the Works Progress Administration (WPA). With generous assistance from Housing Administrator Robert Weaver, Bethune maintained the Black Cabinet with an iron fist inside a velvet glove, a remarkable achievement especially considering that others before her had permitted such an association to falter. The cabinet was newly possible because the government recruited more than a hundred black managers and administrators for government positions during the Great Depression. These black Americans collectively constituted the twentieth-century emergence of a black political presence in Washington, D.C.

The only other prerequisite for at-large leadership was entree into the capital's inner sanctums of power. Even though African Americans lacked the political and economic clout that would have ensured them hearings on request, arranging such hearings proved easy for Bethune. She used a personal relationship with Eleanor Roosevelt. Having brought Bethune into government in 1936, Mrs. Roosevelt then extended her carte blanche assistance as long as the Roosevelts lived in the White House. This enabled Bethune to extend her at-large activity a year after leaving government. Mrs. Roosevelt interceded with a wide range of federal officials, including her husband, on Bethune's behalf, and Bethune developed an easygoing friendship with President Franklin Roosevelt. She gave the impression that their relationship was very close—an impression that generally enhanced her status and permitted her to talk with virtually anyone in government. The price Bethune gladly paid for this was loyalty to the Roosevelts, particularly at election time.

With all the factors for at-large leadership in view, Bethune sought to heighten the racial consciousness of the nation but most specifically that of the federal bureaucracy, since it was the institution possessing the greatest power to address black inequality. In this continuing effort, her most sensational feat was the federally sponsored National Conference on the Problems of the Negro and Negro Youth, held January 6–8, 1937, at the Department of Labor with guest speakers including Eleanor Roosevelt and the Secretaries of Commerce and Agriculture. Bringing together for the first time the Black Cabinet and the most important leaders in African-American life from the NAACP to Bethune's NCNW nucleus, the conference defined the most pressing difficulties of black Americans in a segregated society and outlined the needed government responses. It advanced pragmatic solutions for immediate implementation, advocating a fair share of federal resources to black citizens within the legally segregated South rather than insisting upon integration.

Framing its deliberations into four categories, the conference developed many recommendations. Some of the most prominent were as follows. Under the category "Security of Life and Equal Protection under the Law," it called for a federal anti-lynching law, equal access to the ballot in federal elections, and the elimination of segregation and discrimination on interstate transportation. Under "Improved Health and Housing Conditions," it emphasized federal aid to reduce tuberculosis and syphilis among black Americans, the building of health centers in black neighborhoods with black staff, a guarantee to black veterans that they would have access to veterans' hospitals, insurance of black involvement as tenants and managers in all federal housing projects, and an end to the total exclusion of black Americans in the new suburban communities developed through the Resettlement Administration. Under the category "Adequate Educational and Recreational Opportunity," it asked for an equitable share of federal education dollars and recreational and educational centers as integral parts of all public housing projects. The recognition of economics as the preeminent black issue in the Great Depression evoked a barrage of resolutions, including the provision that black workers receive the same apprenticeship training as did white workers; the abolition of the practice of requiring a photograph with a civil service application; the denial of benefits from federal legislation to any union excluding black Americans; decent wages and standardized norms for domestic workers; the extension of Social Security benefits to domestic and agricultural workers (the areas employing the overwhelming number of black Americans); and the end of discriminatory employment practices in the army and navy and all branches of the federal government and in all projects receiving federal funds, such as the Tennessee Valley Authority.

No other general black meeting on civil rights during the Roosevelt administration generated the interest and publicity of this 1937 conference. It signified not only that Bethune had "gathered everything and everybody under her very ample wing," as one journalist phrased it, but also that she was in the middle of a broad black consensus and could speak truly as black America's race representative at large in making the wide-ranging conference report her agenda for leadership. The most prominent formalized channels in which she pursued support for specific conference recommendations included her women's council and youth agency, the President's Special Committee on Farm Tenancy, and the Southern Conference for Human Welfare. Requiring more time and effort still were the numerous private meetings held to advance conference resolutions. Federal acceptance of them was necessary if black workers were to attain high-echelon government jobs. In this area, with the exception of Black Cabinet members (who were confined chiefly to advising and assisting), black Americans were virtually unrepresented. For example, in January 1940, only one black federal judge held court in the United States, and he presided in the Virgin Islands. Race-based discrimination barred more than 13 million Americans from the higher responsibilities of democracy. As Bethune pressed the employment issue, typically with either Franklin or Eleanor Roosevelt, she had in hand lists of positions and names of black Americans qualified to fill them. Nevertheless, the results she sought had to await the black revolution of the 1960s.

As a leader at large, Bethune identified with high visibility programs promising black advancement outside of government. She even walked the New Negro Alliance's picket line in 1939 to support the hiring of black clerks in a Washington, D.C., drug-store chain. She joined A. Philip Randolph's march on Washington movement in 1941, and nationwide support for the threatened demonstration led to Roosevelt's most important civil rights action. His Executive Order No. 8802 called for hiring in government and in defense industries without regard to race, and it established the Fair Employment Practices Commission.

Since Bethune was an administration insider and thus required to demonstrate loyalty to the administration, it was fortunate that she firmly believed in both the president and his programs. As the 1937 conference recommendations suggested, she was fully conversant with the glaring shortcomings of the administration's civil rights record and she flatly stated time and again that black citizens could not be satisfied or complacent. Yet at the same time, she implied that the Republicans offered less than the Democrats and she exhorted her constituency to uphold the administration's efforts for relief, recovery, and reform. As wartime considerations emerged, her commitment to the administration became even greater. She believed that black Americans must oppose Nazi Germany's Adolf Hitler and that they must support the president's foreign policy. Her concern was consuming enough for her to put aside her other commitments in order to secure, behind closed doors, an all-white training center in Daytona Beach, Florida, for the Women's Army Corps. Aside from the economic vitality it promised her hometown, Bethune must have reasoned that the facility would not be injurious to black women because they could receive identical training at Fort Des Moines, Iowa. For a black leader, this action, though unpublicized and controversial, required courage and constituted one measure of Bethune's devotion to country.

For her untiring patriotism and promotion of democratic ideals, Mary McLeod Bethune reaped the wrath of the congressional House Un-American Activities Committee. In the early 1940s, it branded her a Communist, and she suffered grievously from this stigma. Because of it, as late as 1952, she was denied a public school platform in Englewood, New Jersey. A groundswell of public support, however, eventually made her appearance there possible.

Though investing time and energy in at-large activities, Bethune's focus in Washington, D.C., from 1936 to 1943 had to be upon her job in the National Youth Administration (NYA), where she became director of the Negro division. The directorship (which became official in 1939) represented the highest federal appointment held by a black woman and facilitated her functioning in the agency's hierarchy. Behind both the appointment and the agency stood Franklin and Eleanor Roosevelt. They greatly enhanced Bethune's work, as did Aubrey Willis Williams, NYA's sole head administrator, who came to the agency via his deputy directorship in the government's massive Works Progress Administration.

Along with the Civilian Conservation Corps, the NYA was Washington's prescription for enabling youth to weather the Great Depression. During its 1935–44 lifespan, the agency offered young people ages sixteen to twenty-four job placement services and work relief through programs for those both in and out of school. When national defense became the country's preoccupation, NYA concentrated on training youth for war production jobs. During its final year, it transported trained youth when necessary to areas of labor shortages and then housed them temporarily in regional induction centers while they learned the ways of a new community. Through these arrangements black Americans, and women in particular, found employment in manufacturing as opposed to the agricultural and service sectors. Before budget-cutting imperatives conspired with the agency's powerful opposition—the educational establishment anxious to protect vocational territory and a resurgent Republican bloc determined to stifle New Deal relief—the NYA spent over $685 million on several million youth. Moreover, it firmly established the concept of direct federal assistance to deserving youth both in and out of school—a concept notably revived in the Great Society of the 1960s.

As a dazzling and magnetic personality, Bethune elevated support for the entire NYA program among black and white citizens. Yet, like most of her Black Cabinet associates, her specific function was to promote equal treatment for black employees within her agency. Though these young people needed NYA benefits more than any other category of youth, in the racial order of that era they were the least likely to get them. There was no way that proportionate benefits for black youth could be realized. Nonetheless, with a staff consisting of four successive excellent assistant directors and an extremely competent secretary, Arabella Denniston—who had graduated from the Daytona Institute—Bethune pursued this goal. Her office enabled the NYA to come closer to approximating equity between black and white benefits than perhaps any other federal entity. Generally, African-

American leaders lauded the NYA and worked zealously but unsuccessfully to establish it as a permanent federal institution. In the middle of the Depression, they valued most the work-study grants to students in school; during World War II, NYA shop training and work experience typically were the best available to black youth.

In the late 1930s, of necessity Bethune crisscrossed the country to realize the full potential of her NYA job, because at that time her agency maintained a decentralized structure permitting state directors considerable autonomy. These white directors typically oversaw projects for black participants that were of lesser complexity and quality than those for whites. Although the white directors and black participants sometimes divided along racial lines over an issue, Bethune managed to bring the sides together or, regardless of her position, at least to emerge politically unscathed.

Though the virtues of travel were indisputable, Bethune's most concrete contributions to the NYA derived from wielding influence in Washington, D.C. As the agency assumed new programs, she saw to it that black participants were included in initial phases, as in the Civilian Pilot Training Program (1939–41), through which six black colleges offered flight instruction. Their programs were foundational to black pilots in the military. In the agency's established programs, Bethune lobbied for equitable benefits. She pushed for outstanding black projects, especially ones centered in skilled training for modern manufacturing processes and proportionate job placement services. Wherever possible, Bethune sought to make expenditures equitable. She successfully moved the agency to adopt a policy in 1939 assuring a proportionate distribution of secondary school-aid funds between black and white students. Moreover, she persuaded the NYA to create a specific resource tailored to the special difficulties black students faced in higher education: her Special Negro Higher Education Fund advanced funding equality by disbursing $609,930 to 4,119 students over seven years.

Bethune believed that black involvement in the initial stages of new programs and equity in established programs, both in quality and funding, could all be advanced through placing black personnel in key positions. She saw black leadership in every phase of the NYA as translating into greater services to black youth. She argued that where racism produced dual programs, at least black Americans should have opportunities for leadership in one of them. In 1941, Bethune's most impressive achievement was to facilitate employment for twenty-seven black administrative assistants with state NYA directors. Though the effectiveness of these positions varied greatly, they did result in benefits for their constituencies.

Through her NYA employment, Bethune reached the zenith of her career. In the years immediately afterward, she focused on her national women's council. Increasingly, she spent less time in the Capitol in favor of greater involvement in the Daytona community and heightened support for an internationalism that projected the inherent unity of humankind. Moreover, to promote her social and educational ideals, she turned her home into the Mary McLeod Bethune Foundation. Another highlight of her active retirement was travel. In January 1952, she fulfilled a cherished girlhood dream by visiting Africa.

This was occasioned by her official representation of the United States at the inauguration of William Tubman as president of Liberia.

Bethune died of a heart attack in her home of more than fifty years on May 18, 1955.

By any measure, through more than three decades Mary McLeod Bethune was an extraordinary public figure, particularly considering the daunting obstacles to opportunity she faced as a poor, black, Southern female born between America's first and second Reconstructions. In promoting opportunities for young people to obtain an education and employment, and in asserting both personal and organizational equality, she lifted service to others to an exalted high.

Bethune fine-tuned her leadership to the racial climate in which she lived, a climate never characterized by a national commitment to change the subordinate status of African Americans but one affected greatly by the exigencies of the Great Depression and two world wars. This meant that though black Americans lacked equal opportunity, they experienced increasing opportunity. Bethune maneuvered at any given time within superimposed restraints that loosened only slightly from the 1910s to the 1950s. In her early years she emphasized the hallmarks of accommodation—vocationalism, self-help, and skillful appeals to influential whites; later she could agitate for higher educational opportunities, government assistance, and full citizenship rights. Though using the program and methods of Booker T. Washington in developing a private school in the South, she found it more difficult than he, even though she had vision, determination, an intuitive understanding of people, and persuasive powers. Because she was a black woman, she had to work harder to get less. Compared to the financial resources of Washington's Tuskegee Institute, Bethune's school wallowed in poverty. Still, Bethune exercised a level of leadership unavailable to any black male leader of the era. She led a female constituency into symbolic participation in national affairs. In the 1930s and 1940s, Bethune elevated her women's council to a level approaching that of other national women's organizations in Washington, D.C. She created the image and reality of black women going to the White House on affairs of state.

In assuming leadership during the New Deal, Bethune's gender posed no handicap. Supported by the Black Cabinet, she confronted influential federal officials and the nation with all issues relative to the status of black Americans. Always she pursued an array of benefits for all black Americans. Her forte was facilitating the flow of NYA funds to black youth for high school and college work-study, vocational training, and job placement. Her most identifiable beneficiaries came from the "talented tenth." At one level, they received essential assistance in paying their higher-education bills from her Special Negro Fund, which was the only financial resource any black New Dealer controlled. At another level, they secured responsible jobs in the federal establishment, setting precedents for the future that might have been unavailable otherwise. The most notable of these were in the officer cadre of the Women's Army Corps and in the NYA state offices. In the latter, the black administrative assistants to state directors gave Bethune what

amounted to a field staff across the country—another first for a black New Dealer. So tremendous was her impact that in July 1974 a seventeen-foot bronze statue of her was placed in a District of Columbia public park, a short distance from the Capitol. It was the first statue in the city to portray either a woman or a black American.

Though long deemed the most influential black American woman, more recently, a scholarly consensus has emerged ranking Bethune as one of the most important black Americans in history, along with Frederick Douglass, W. E. B. DuBois, and Martin Luther King, Jr. Unflinchingly, she championed the democratic values that define the nation. She took personally the well-being of the body politic, particularly in the crisis of two world wars. No less a personage than President Franklin D. Roosevelt viewed Bethune as a great patriot devoted to advancing all Americans. In fact, Bethune's accomplishments were so impressive in relationship to resources, and her interest in people regardless of nationality and locality was so genuine, that any freedom-loving country could feel proud to claim her as its own.

ELAINE M. SMITH

Black Women Mayors' Caucus

The Black Women Mayors' Caucus (BWMC) originated at the National Conference of Black Mayors (NCBM) in 1988. The thirteen female mayors in attendance at the first Leadership Institute for Mayors formed the organization in an effort to highlight and enhance the role of black women mayors, to focus national attention on the needs of black women elected officials, to expose young women to the challenges of elected office, and to examine issues of particular concern to women. Other issues addressed by the BWMC are child care, the needs of teenaged mothers, and the welfare of black youth.

As of 1992, sixty-seven black women mayors nationwide constituted the membership of the BWMC. They represented municipalities in twenty states and the District of Columbia. Mayor **Unita Blackwell** of Mayersville, Mississippi, chaired the association in 1991, and Mayor Calley Mobley of Alorton, Illinois, in 1992. Active members include Mayor Emma Gresham of Keysville, Georgia, who captured international attention for her leadership in reestablishing municipal government in this predominantly black town. The staff of the NCBM, along with other organizations, assisted Mayor Gresham and the Concerned Citizens of Keysville in their effort.

The BWMC has annual workshops in conjunction with the meetings of the NCBM. These seminars are designed to improve the leadership and management skills of black women mayors and to focus on topics affecting women. The first workshop in 1989, "Women Mayors Balancing Family, Career, and Elected Office," focused on enhancing awareness of the issues inherent in the multiple roles of women mayors. The role-model speaker was **Yvonne Brathwaite Burke**, an attorney and former U.S. representative and California assemblywoman as well as a wife and mother.

The second annual (1990) workshop, "Combatting Sexism in the Work Place through Changes in Language and Attitudes," was led by Dr. Gloria Mixon of Clark Atlanta University. Marion Delaney-Harris, national trainer, led the third annual (1991) workshop, "Breaking Down the Barriers to Non-Traditional Employment." She focused on the obstacles facing women in employment; identified training opportunities for women in nontraditional jobs; provided information on nontraditional occupations for women; examined discrepancies in hiring, wages, and promotions; and provided women mayors with technical assistance for local action.

In addition to these annual workshops, members participate in national forums that focus on women's issues, and the caucus is part of the Women's Agenda. The staff of the NCBM provides technical assistance to the BWMC.

GRETCHEN E. MACLACHLAN/EDIE C. PEARSON

Bolin, Jane Mathilda   (1908–   )

Judge Jane Bolin's view of her job upon her appointment to the Domestic Relations Court of the City of New York in 1939 was that she was a judge for the whole city and for all children who were in trouble. She was the first black woman judge in the United States. Her other notable firsts as a black woman include: the first to graduate from Yale Law School, the first to be admitted to the Bar Association of the City of New York, and the first in the New York City Corporation Council's office.

Jane Mathilda Bolin was born in Poughkeepsie, New York, on April 11, 1908, to Gaius C. and Mathilda Bolin. She received her elementary and secondary education in the public school system and attended Wellesley College. She graduated from Wellesley in 1928 and was named a Welles-

When he appointed her to the Domestic Relations Court of New York City in 1939, Mayor Fiorello La Guardia made Jane Bolin the first black woman judge in the United States, praising her for her broad sympathy for human suffering.   (LIBRARY OF CONGRESS)

ley Scholar, an honor reserved for the twenty women with the highest scholastic standing in their class. She went on to graduate from Yale University Law School in 1931.

Upon her admission to the New York Bar in 1932, Bolin began her career as an attorney in her father and brother's law firm in Poughkeepsie, New York. She married attorney Ralph E. Mizelle in 1933 and worked as his law partner until 1937. It was during this time that she ran for public office. In the 1936 election, she was the unsuccessful Republican candidate for the

state assembly seat from New York's seventeenth district.

On April 7, 1937, Bolin was assigned as assistant corporate counsel in New York City's law department. She felt that in her new office and position her biggest job was to educate private employers to give African Americans jobs without discrimination, according to their qualifications.

Perhaps the most important day in Bolin's career came on July 22, 1939. On that date, Bolin was appointed as justice of the Domestic Relations Court of New York by Mayor Fiorello La Guardia. She was responsible for bringing citywide attention to the ways in which private schools and child care institutions in New York City discriminated against children because of race or color. Bolin remained a justice when the court was reorganized to become the New York Family Court in 1962.

During her first ten years on the bench, Judge Bolin was never reversed by the higher courts. When asked why he had originally selected Bolin, Mayor La Guardia explained that she had common sense, patience, courtesy, and a broad sympathy for human suffering. Judge Bolin remained on the bench for over forty years, retiring on December 31, 1978. In recognition of her work on the bench, Bolin received honorary LL.D. degrees from Williams College, Morgan State College, Tuskegee Institute, Hampton Institute and Western College for Women.

Throughout her career, Judge Bolin remained active in the New York community. She served on the board of the New York Urban League, the New York branch of the **National Association for the Advancement of Colored People,** the Harlem Tuberculosis Committee, the legislative committee of the United Neighborhood Houses, and the Harlem Lawyers' Association, and she was a member of the New York County Lawyers Association. A woman ahead of her time, Judge Bolin retained her maiden name and is reported to have said it sounded strange to be addressed by her married name. She was cited for distinguished achievement and the improvement of race relations in 1939 in a nationwide poll conducted by the Schomburg Center for Research in Black Culture of the New York Public Library.

Bolin's first husband, Ralph E. Mizelle, died in September 1944. Bolin's only child, Yorke Bolin Mizelle, was born on July 22, 1941. Bolin married Reverend Walter P. Offutt, Jr., in November 1951, and was widowed a second time when Offutt died on October 7, 1974.

Since her retirement, Bolin has practiced family law as a consultant and has done volunteer tutoring in math and reading for public school children. Friends describe her as a "fighter," and a "courageous, no-nonsense, hard worker who never shirked an assignment." Judge Bolin describes herself as determined to wage a fight for racial justice.

WENDY BROWN

Brown, Corrine (1946–)

Congresswoman for the third congressional district of Florida, Corrine Brown was elected to represent the minorities of north central Florida. The third congressional district was part of a historic redistricting mandated by the 1982 Voting Rights Act, which permitted voting districts to be drawn by race. Brown was elected from the newly drawn district and became

part of the bloc of black women that confronted the 103rd Congress in 1992. Washington will never be the same.

Born in Jacksonville, Florida, on November 11, 1946, Brown grew up in the same area that she would later represent in Congress. She received a bachelor of science degree from Florida Agricultural and Mechanical University in 1969, and an education specialist degree from the University of Florida in 1974. She became a member of the faculty at Florida Community College of Jacksonville in 1977 and also taught at the University of Florida and

Born in Jacksonville, Florida, Corrine Brown grew up in the same area she would later represent in Congress. Brown has unapologetically used her position to win federal money for her constituents. When accused of "pork barrel" politics, Brown retorted, "We've been on a liquid diet for years. We need pork." (OFFICE OF CONGRESSWOMAN BROWN)

Edward Waters College. She was awarded an honorary Doctor of Law degree from Edward Waters College.

In 1982, Brown was elected to the Florida House of Representatives. Once in the statehouse, she was re-elected four times for a total of ten years of service. She served as Chairperson of the Prison Construction and Operations Subcommittee, and Vice Chairperson of the Regulatory Reform Subcommittee. She also served on the Appropriations and Finance & Taxation Committees.

Brown represented a relatively poor minority district and used her influence to get state monies appropriated for her area. She also represented a large population of elderly people who had moved to Florida to retire. In recognition of her work in the interests of the elderly, she was named Legislator of the Year by the Florida Association on Housing for the Elderly.

Having honed her skills in the state legislature, Brown was ready when the Voting Rights Act mandated a congressional district to represent minorities. The resulting district sprawls across parts of fourteen counties and includes 39 cities and townships. While the district map was controversial for its peculiar shape, it served the purpose of creating a district where minority voters could elect a representative to voice their interests. Brown won election in 1992, which made her one of the few black representatives from Florida since Reconstruction.

In Congress, Brown won assignments to the Committee on Transportation and Infrastructure, and the Committee on Veterans' Affairs. Brown is also a member of the Congressional Black Caucus, the Caucus on Women's Issues, the Older Americans Caucus, the Congressional Sunbelt Caucus, and the Congressional Space Caucus. All of these committees represent the special concerns of the people who elected her.

Brown has been unabashed about using her position to gain federal cash for her constituents. Defending her use of "pork barrel" politics, she once stated, "We've been on a liquid diet for years. We need pork." Brown has also been quick to challenge the established white male power structure that she found in Washington. Soon after election she played a powerful part in a confrontation over the controversial Hyde Amendment, which banned federal funds for abortions. More than willing to shout down the conservatives that opposed her, she stood with the black and women's caucuses in a spirited stand that made the newspapers. The new black congresswomen, including Corrine Brown, had made their presence felt.

ANDRA MEDEA

Burke, Yvonne Brathwaite
(1932–)

Yvonne Brathwaite Burke was the first black woman from California to serve in the U.S. House of Representatives. Before she was elected in 1972, she established an impressive record in state politics. Her national career was disappointing, however, cut short after only three terms.

Born in Los Angeles on October 5, 1932, Yvonne Watson received a J.D. degree from the University of Southern California in 1956. She worked for the Los Angeles Police Commission and in 1965 served on the commission that investigated the Watts riot. The next year she was elected as a

Her commitment to issues that concern blacks and women helped Yvonne Brathwaite Burke become the first black woman from California to serve in the U.S. House of Representatives. (MOORLAND-SPINGARN)

Democrat to the California State Assembly. During six years as a legislator, she helped pass tenants' rights legislation and child health care bills, and also was active in the League of Women Voters. In 1972, she reached a national audience as official co-chair of the Democratic Party convention in Miami. When she ran for the U.S. House of Representatives from Los Angeles, prominent black Americans and feminists across the country endorsed her campaign.

She won easily, taking 64 percent of the vote. During the campaign she married businessman William A. Burke, and in 1973, she had a daughter, Autumn Roxanne. Burke predicted that her daughter might one day become president, but she herself found service in the House of Representatives frustrating. She was named to the Appropriations Committee, and in 1976 she became chair of the Congressional Black Caucus, but she was unable to get any major legislation passed in the areas of child care, housing, or education.

Burke abruptly resigned her seat in 1978, citing the difficulty of having an impact on such a large assembly, but personal reasons also figured in her decision. She was exhausted from six years of commuting (her husband remained in Los Angeles). Furthermore, many politicians believed her husband's involvement in a bankrupt corporation under federal investigation was a serious liability. She ran instead for California attorney general but lost to Republican George Deukmejian; she then served as a Los Angeles County supervisor. Beginning in 1981 she practiced law in California and served on the boards of corporations, banks, and public institutions, including the University of California Board of Regents.

She resumed her political career in 1992, when she became the first African American to be elected to the Los Angeles County Board of Supervisors.

JOAN E. CASHIN

C

Carson, Julia (1938–)

When Julia Carson was elected to the House of Representatives from Indiana's tenth congressional district on November 5, 1996, she became only the second African-American congresswoman from the state. Her election was a natural step in the career of a dedicated and determined public servant.

Born in poverty to a teen-age mother, the young Julia Carson worked as a waitress, a newspaper "girl," and summer farm-laborer to help her family make ends meet. While she worked, she was educated in the Indianapolis Public School system and graduated from Crispus Attucks High School in 1955. Carson describes herself as "the natural mother of two children and surrogate mother of many." As a single working mother, she raised her own children and, later, two grandchildren.

Carson's political career began in 1965 when she was hired away from her job as a secretary for UAW Local #550 by the newly elected congressman Andrew Jacobs, Jr. She served Congressman Jacobs and the people of his district for eight years, first in Washington and then in his Indianapolis office. In 1972, Carson decided to enter electoral politics and successfully ran for the Indiana House of Representatives. In 1974, during her first term, she was awarded the first of two *Indianapolis Star* "Woman of the Year" citations. After two terms in the Indiana House, Carson was elected to the Indiana Senate in 1976. During her tenure, Carson drafted numerous pieces of legislation, including laws designed to encourage in-home health care and to ease the collection of child support.

Carson gained valuable business experience while a member of Indiana's citizen-legislature. For ten years, she worked as an executive for Cummins Engine. Later, Carson owned and operated her own small business in downtown Indianapolis.

While serving in the Indiana Senate, Ms. Carson became increasingly concerned about both the plight of the poor people in her district who were not receiving the local services they needed and the burden already being shouldered by the local taxpayers. The local township government, mandated to provide welfare to the needy of central Indianapolis, had fallen heavily into debt and was widely accused of mismanagement of taxpayer funds as well as mistreatment of applicants seeking assistance. In 1990, Carson successfully ran for the position of Center Township Trustee on the platform that she knew how to fix the agency she was forced to rely on in her youth for a ration of corn meal and lard for her family.

Carson had her job cut out for her. Indianapolis was over $20 million in debt and faced the imminent possibility that this debt would depress its bond rating and drastically curtail its ability to attract new

Born in poverty to a teenage mother, Julia Carson grew up to help reform the welfare system on which she depended as a child. When she was elected to Congress from Indiana's tenth congressional district, she became only the second congresswoman from the state. (MARY ANN CARTER/NYT PICTURES)

business. Through effective management, including the elimination of fraud and waste and the requirement of "workfare" for able-bodied relief recipients, Carson trimmed the deficit while still assisting those truly in need. Center Township became debt-free and property taxes were actually reduced as a result of Carson's efforts. As the admiring Marion County auditor, John Von Arx (a Republican), said to the *Indianapolis Star:* "Julia Carson wrestled that monster to the ground."

Julia Carson has a wealth of personal experience as a manager, legislator, businessperson, and as a woman who pulled herself and her family out of poverty. Her experience will clearly be an asset in the 105th Congress, as it strives to come to

grips with the momentous issues facing the United States as it legislates for the twenty-first century.

RALPH CARLSON

Carter, Eunice Hunton (1899–1970)

The appointment of Eunice Hunton Carter as the first black woman district attorney in the State of New York made her one of the "twenty against the underworld," as special prosecutor Thomas E. Dewey called his prosecution team. Carter's work on theories about organized crime triggered the biggest organized crime prosecution in the nation's history in New York City in the late 1930s.

Eunice Hunton was born in Atlanta, Georgia, on July 16, 1899, to William A. Hunton and Addie Waites. She attended Smith College in Northampton, Massachusetts, and graduated cum laude with both a bachelor's and a master's degree in 1921. She attended Fordham School of Law, graduated in 1931, and was admitted to practice law in New York in 1934. After a short time in private practice, she began work in the district attorney's office in 1935.

Carter was hired by New York County District Attorney William C. Dodge to handle primarily low-level criminal prosecutions, many of them prostitution cases. After handling several prostitution cases, she began to suspect the links of prostitution with the underworld. She began to note that defendants told nearly identical stories, that all of the women were represented by the same law firms, and that if they were fined, the same bondsmen would appear with the money. Based largely on her research, special prosecutor Dewey ordered a major raid of more than eighty

"Twenty against the underworld" was Thomas E. Dewey's name for his crack prosecution team, which included Eunice Hunton Carter, the first black woman district attorney in the State of New York. (NATIONAL ARCHIVES)

houses of prostitution. Information from the raid provided Carter with enough details on the prostitution racket to convict the top Mafia leader in New York. Dewey, who subsequently was appointed New York County District Attorney, chose Carter to head the Special Sessions Bureau where she supervised more than fourteen thousand criminal cases each year.

Carter remained with the district attorney's office until 1945 and then returned to private practice. Her other professional achievements include being a consultant to the United Nations and International Council of Women; vice president of the National Council of Women of the U.S. YWCA; member of the U.S. National Committee of Educational, Scientific and Cultural Organizations; trustee and chairman of the **National Council of Negro Women**; and a member of the American Association of University Women.

Hunter married Lisle C. Carter and had one son, Lisle Carter, Jr. She died on January 25, 1970.

WENDY BROWN

Carter, Pamela Fanning (1949–)

In the 1992 race for the office of Indiana attorney general, Pamela Carter's Republican opponent distributed a life-size cutout of her picture. Its presumed aim, to tell possibly racist voters that Carter was black, backfired. What may be more noteworthy than her becoming Indiana's and the nation's first black and first woman elected to such a post was that she won it in a state with a population less than 10 percent black. As attorney general, Carter has demonstrated her credo that crime victims are "to be treated with fairness and respect."

Carter has credited much of her success to the inspiration of her parents, businessman Roscoe Fanning and teacher Dorothy Elizabeth Hadley Fanning, and to Roscoe's father, who lived to be 101 years old and quoted law to the young Pamela. Born Pamela Lynn Fanning on August 20, 1949, in South Haven, Michigan, she was raised in Indianapolis, Indiana.

Carter went to St. Agnes Academy. When she was fifteen, she met Martin Luther King, Jr., who advised that she "be courageous in any pursuit." She went on to the University of Detroit, where she concentrated on social work and pre-law and received a B.A. with honors in 1971. That year she married Michael Anthony Carter, and they have a son and a daughter. In 1973, at the University of Michigan in Ann Arbor, she received her master's degree in social work. She resumed her education in 1984 with a J.D. from Indiana University's School of Law in Indianapolis.

In the 1970s, Carter held research and administrative positions with the University of Michigan and Detroit's Mental Health Center for Women and Children. Upon passing the Indiana bar in 1984, she became a consumer litigation attorney for both the United Auto Workers and General Motors in Indianapolis and later, focusing on white-collar crime, a securities and enforcement lawyer for Indiana's secretary of state.

Pamela Carter won the race for Indiana attorney general in 1992 despite the fact that less than a tenth of the state's population is black. The nation's first black and first woman elected to such a post, Carter is also a journalist and poet. (OFFICE OF ATTORNEY GENERAL CARTER)

Carter worked under Indiana governor Evan Bayh from 1988 to 1992, first as executive assistant for health and human services, then as deputy chief of staff. The following year she developed her campaign for attorney general while a member of the Indianapolis law firm of Baker & Daniels.

Indiana's first Democrat in twenty-four years to be attorney general, Carter acted quickly as head of the $10 million-budgeted office. The office's staff of 250 included no women or minorities, so she brought a dozen aboard. The Victims of Crime Constitutional Amendment that she proposed in 1993 was passed by two consecutive state legislature sessions and went on the ballot in 1996.

In 1994 her office recovered nearly $4 million in Medicaid overpayments. She altered her office's Consumer Services Division, which now quarterly issues a Buyer Beware List, and upgraded the Lemon Law protecting auto buyers, as well as the Deceptive Consumer Sales Act that greatly aids senior consumers. When the boxer and convicted rapist Mike Tyson's case came up for appeal, she showed that she was immune to his celebrity. When she opposed the appeal, she dispelled, wrote an observer, "the myth that women cannot be strong law enforcement officials."

Honored by the Society of Professional Journalists, the Southern Christian Leadership Conference (SCLC), *Ebony* magazine and others, she belongs to several civic organizations and is a published poet.

GARY HOUSTON

Chisholm, Shirley (1924–)

Shirley Chisholm, the first black woman to be elected to the U.S. House of Representatives, was born Shirley Anita Saint Hill in 1924 in the Bedford-Stuyvesant section of Brooklyn, New York. Her parents, both natives of Barbados, had left the island during the famines of the 1920s for a better life in the United States. When Chisholm was four years old, she and her sisters were taken to live on her grandmother's farm in Barbados. During the six years that Chisholm lived in Barbados, her grandmother became one of the major influences in her life and her first black female role model.

When Chisholm returned to Brooklyn, she excelled in her academic work at a public high school and was offered scholarships to both Vassar and Oberlin Colleges. Because of financial constraints, she chose instead to remain close to home and attend Brooklyn College. She decided upon a career in teaching, which was one of the

In 1968 Shirley Chisholm was the first black woman ever to be elected to the United States House of Representatives. (MOORLAND-SPINGARN)

few occupations open to educated black women in the 1940s. After her graduation in 1946, she took evening classes at Columbia University toward a master's degree in early childhood education while she also worked during the day as a teacher's aide. During this period she married Conrad Chisholm, also a native of the West Indies.

It was during this time that Chisholm first became seriously involved in politics through her local political organization, the Seventeenth Assembly District Democratic Club. As Chisholm described it in her first autobiography, *Unbought and Unbossed* (1970), it was through her involvement with this club that she began to perceive the lack of power of both black people and women in regular Democratic Party politics in Bedford-Stuyvesant. Black residents were by far the majority group in the district, but there were no prominent black elected officials, and black concerns often were ignored by the people in power. Also, although women were the main organizers of the fund-raising committee, their opinions on concrete political matters were not solicited and, when offered, often were ignored.

Chisholm eventually joined the Bedford-Stuyvesant Political League, an alternative to the regular all-white Democratic machine, led by Mac Holder, a local politico concerned with electing black leaders in the community. In 1960, however, after a period of inactivity in politics as a result of a falling-out with Holder, Chisholm and several others formed another alternative organization, the Unity Democratic Club, with the explicit purpose of challenging the regular political machine by running black candidates for all elected positions. It was through this organization that Chisholm

herself ran as a candidate for New York State Assembly in 1964—and won. For four years she was the only woman and one of only eight black representatives in the assembly.

In 1968, using the slogan "Unbought and Unbossed," Chisholm ran against James Farmer, former leader of the Congress of Racial Equality (CORE), for the seat in the newly formed twelfth congressional district of Brooklyn, which included Bedford-Stuyvesant. The race would have made history no matter what the outcome, for either way Brooklyn would have had its first black member of Congress. However, Chisholm's overwhelming victory made her the first black woman ever to be elected to the House of Representatives. She remained in the House for fourteen years, during which time she was a staunch advocate for many diverse progressive issues, most prominently civil rights and women's liberation issues. Chisholm was an early member of the National Organization for Women (NOW), a founder of the National Women's Political Caucus, and a spokesperson for the National Abortion Rights Action League (NARAL).

In 1972, Chisholm attempted to coalesce her various potential constituencies into a potent force for change when she became the first African American to make a bid for the presidential nomination of the Democratic Party. In spite of a lack of money, organization, and serious consideration from either the press or her male opponents, Chisholm remained in the race until the convention, where she captured more than 150 votes on the first ballot. The experience was a watershed event in her political life. In her second autobiography, *The Good Fight* (1973), which concen-

Before Eva Clayton became the first woman from North Carolina to be sent to the U.S. Congress in 1992, she was already widely respected as a public servant. As a chair of Warren County's Board of Commissioners, Clayton was responsible for attracting more than 900 jobs and $55 million in investments to the state. (OFFICE OF CONGRESSWOMAN CLAYTON)

trated solely on her run for the presidency, she described her disappointment and hurt at the coolness her candidacy received from both black male-led and white female-led organizations.

Shirley Chisholm retired from the House in 1983 and has not run for political office since. In 1984 she founded the **National Political Congress of Black Women** (NPCBW), which encourages black women to enter and participate in the political process. She made a show of support for Jesse Jackson in both his 1984 and 1988 presidential campaigns. She has lectured widely around the country, especially on college campuses, and has taught at Mount Holyoke and Spelman colleges. She and her second husband live in upstate New York.

LISA WOZNICA

Clayton, Eva (1934–)

Eva M. Clayton, a Democrat, is the first woman from North Carolina to be sent to the U.S. Congress. In the 103rd Congress, she became the first woman president of the Democratic Freshman Class, the largest such incoming group since 1948. Her state and national record in affairs of rural health and economic development, in housing, and in jobs training and creation has been effective and exemplary.

Born on September 16, 1934, in Savannah, Georgia, Clayton went to North Carolina to attain her B.S. from Johnson C. Smith University in Charlotte and her M.S. from North Carolina Central University in Durham. She studied law at the latter, as well as at the University of North Carolina in Chapel Hill.

Executive director of the Soul City Foundation, a project of the federal government's New Town program, she was also director of the North Carolina Health Manpower Development Program. As assistant secretary for community development with North Carolina's Department of Natural Resources, Clayton oversaw program management and policy development and administered special programs for the

Office of Community Development. In addition, she was supervisor of the Division of Community Assistance and Employment Training.

In 1981 she founded Technical Resources International Ltd., a management and consulting firm specializing in local and state economic growth. The many projects she managed at TRI ranged from affirmative action to market development.

Between 1982 and 1990 Clayton chaired Warren County's Board of Commissioners, which under her leadership attracted more than 900 jobs, drew $55 million in investment, built a rural health care facility, and gained bond funding for school renovation and construction. At the close of her board service, fellow commissioners named her Outstanding North Carolina County Commissioner.

Brown moved toward her present position when she was appointed to fill a seat in the state's First Congressional District upon the death of Rep. Walter B. Jones, Sr. She then won the seat in her own right in the November, 1992, election.

In the House of Representatives Brown was named the 103rd Congress' most influential newcomer by congressional staffers. She distinguished herself in agricultural and small business-related committee work and cowrote legislation that salvaged the Section 515 Housing Program meant to make housing affordable for thousands of North Carolinians. Winning her next term, she continued her previous committee assignments while vice-chairing the Democratic Policy Committee on Research and serving the Executive Committee of the House Rural Caucus.

Clayton's many recognitions include awards from the Housing Assistance Council and the Food Research Action Committee. Active in the Presbyterian Church, she traveled to Berne, Switzerland, in 1991 as a participant in the Ecumenical Consultation on the Environment.

Married for 39 years to Warrenton, North Carolina, attorney Theaoseus T. Clayton, Sr., she is mother of four grown children and has two grandchildren.

GARY HOUSTON

Collins, Barbara-Rose (1939–)

Barbara-Rose Collins' political career began in a very personal way, out of concern for her daughter's education, and led to the United States Congress.

Born on April 13, 1939, in Detroit, Collins is the daughter of Lamar and Verna Jones Collins. She attended the public schools and then majored in anthropology and political science at Wayne State University.

At 31, her interest in improving the schools her daughter would be attending prompted her to run for a seat on the Detroit Region I Public School Board. After she was elected, she proposed mandatory homework for children and spearheaded a drive for a multicultural and Afrocentric curriculum.

Collins left the board in 1973 and won a 1974 race for the Michigan House of Representatives. She remained there for seven years. During that time she sponsored or strongly supported legislation to create urban enterprise zones, to safeguard proper foodstuffs dating, to offer sex education courses, to combat sexual harass-

Barbara-Rose Collins got involved in politics out of concern for her daughter's education. She joined her local school board in 1970, went on to the Michigan House of Representatives, and in 1991, was elected to the U.S. House of Representatives. (OFFICE OF CONGRESSWOMAN COLLINS)

ment and to equalize pension benefits. She founded and chaired the Michigan Legislative Black Caucus.

In 1981, she joined the Detroit City Council and initiated ordinances on toxic waste cleanup and single-room occupancy for the homeless. She also proposed that the city of Detroit sell any investments they had made in South African companies. She chaired task forces on litter and teenage violence and served on New Detroit's Mi-

nority Business Committee. Her work on the Council lasted until 1990.

In 1991, she was elected as a Democrat to represent Michigan's thirteenth congressional district in the U.S. House of Representatives. State redistricting shifted her to Michigan's fifteenth congressional district in November 1992, yet she won 87 percent of the vote in the next election and so launched her second term in the House.

For the 103rd U.S. Congress she was appointed majority whip-at-large. She has served on many committees and subcommittees and has also lent her insight and talents to the Congressional Black Caucus, the Steel Caucus, the Hispanic Caucus and others.

Despite a busy life, Collins has raised a family, learned to play both piano and harp, become a portrait-painter in her leisure hours, and been an active member of the Shrine of the Black Madonna, a Pan-African Orthodox Christian church.

GARY HOUSTON

Collins, Cardiss (1931–)

Cardiss Robertson was born on September 24, 1931, in St. Louis, Missouri, the only child of Finley and Rosia Mae Cardiss Robertson. Her father was a laborer, and her mother was a nurse. When she was ten years old, the family moved to Detroit, Michigan, where she attended Bishop and Lincoln elementary schools. Upon graduation from Detroit's High School of Commerce, she moved to Chicago to find a job.

After hand-tying mattress springs and working as a stenographer for a carnival equipment company, Robertson found a job as a secretary with the Illinois Department of Revenue and enrolled in night school. Her studies in accounting at Northwestern University led to her promotion to accountant and then to auditor. At about this time, she met George Washington Collins. They were married in 1958, when she was twenty-seven. They had one son. When her husband ran for political office, Cardiss Collins became involved in his career. She worked in his campaigns and later became politically active herself, representing the Democratic Party as a committeewoman.

After serving as alderman, George Collins ran for and won the office of U.S. Representative from Illinois' sixth district. He remained in close contact with his constituency and his family, flying back from Washington, D.C., to Chicago nearly every weekend. On one of those flights, his airplane crashed into a residential area near the Chicago airport, and he was killed. Mayor Richard Daley immediately offered to support Cardiss Collins in a bid for her husband's vacant seat in Congress. With the encouragement of her son, she decided to make the attempt to carry on her husband's work.

Collins won the election by a comfortable margin and began her new career on June 5, 1973. Two years after she first took office, she became the first black American and the first woman to be appointed Democratic whip-at-large. Not long after that, she repeated both "firsts" as chair of the House Government Operations Subcommittee on Manpower and Housing.

In 1979, Collins became chair of the Congressional Black Caucus. She was determined to unify the seventeen members of the caucus, giving them more power in Congress. Her skills in dealing with people helped her achieve that goal, and she was highly praised as both forceful and tactful.

Standing together became a greater and greater necessity as legislation was proposed that would move the country further from the goals that had been set during President Lyndon Johnson's War on Poverty. As Collins said to her fellow caucus members, "We're going to have to be in there fighting for butter, because they're going to give everything to guns." She also warned that attempts would be made to roll back gains in civil rights, and they were. Still, under her leadership the caucus helped defeat an antibusing amendment to

The longest-serving black congresswoman, Cardiss Collins of Illinois was the first African American and the first woman to be appointed Democratic whip-at-large. (OFFICE OF CONGRESSWOMAN COLLINS)

Pictured here are four of the eleven black women members of the 104th Congress. They are Senator Carol Moseley-Braun (second from right) and House of Representatives members (from left to right) Barbara-Rose Collins, Eddie Bernice Johnson, and Carrie P. Meek. (TOM HORAN)

the Constitution, monitored the 1980 census to protect minorities, and pushed for economic sanctions against apartheid governments in Africa.

While serving on a number of important congressional committees, Collins was a strong defender of civil rights. She was a critic of administration policies during the Reagan era and battled discriminatory hiring practices in the private sector. She had the full support of her constituency. Every time she ran for reelection, she won decisively. In 1988, she ran unopposed. Her district, 55 percent black, 22 percent foreign-born, and 17 percent Hispanic, knew that she would represent them with integrity and defend them with courage.

She retired in 1996.

KATHLEEN THOMPSON

Congresswomen

Senate
Moseley-Braun, Carol (D-IL)
1993–

House
Chisholm, Shirley (D-NY)
1969–1982

Burke, Yvonne B. (D-CA)
1973–1978

Collins, Cardiss (D-IL)
1973–1996

Jordan, Barbara C. (D-TX)
1973–1978

Hall, Katie (D-IN)
1982–1984

Collins, Barbara-Rose (D-MI)
1991–1996

Norton, Eleanor Holmes (D-DC)
1991–

Waters, Maxine (D-CA)
1991–

Clayton, Eva (D-NC)
1992–

Brown, Corrine (D-FL)
1993–

Johnson, Eddie Bernice (D-TX)
1993–

McKinney, Cynthia (D-GA)
1993–

Meek, Carrie (D-FL)
1993–

Lee, Sheila Jackson (D-TX)
1995–

Carson, Julia (D-IN)
1997–

D

Delco, Wilhelmina R. (1929–)

A determined state legislator with the courage to fight for education, Wilhelmina Delco has become well known throughout Texas for her support of state schools and black students. As Delco stated, "I wanted my own kids to be successful, and I figured what was good for my kids would be good for all kids."

Born in Chicago on July 16, 1929, Delco was the daughter of Juanita Fitzgerald Watson and William P. Watson. Both of her parents worked in the court system. Her father was a court deputy, and her mother was a probation officer. Her parents helped instill in her a sense of personal responsibility and a respect for public service.

Delco attended the Chicago public schools, graduating from Wendell Phillips High School. She was salutatorian and president of her senior class. In 1946, she went to Fisk University, graduating in 1950 with a B.A. in sociology, with minors in economics and business administration.

At Fisk, Delco met her future husband, Exalton A. Delco, Jr. Upon graduation, she moved with him to his home state of Texas, where they settled and raised four children. As a concerned parent, Delco became president of the local PTA and was elected to the Travis County school board in 1968. The county board served the city of Austin. Delco was the first African American ever elected to the board.

Delco was on the school board for six years, from 1968 to 1974. From 1972 to 1973, she was also on the founding board of the Austin Community College, an accomplishment of which she is particularly proud. But soon Delco found she could not make the changes she wanted at the school board level and she decided to run for the Texas House of Representatives. She won the election on her first try, taking office in January, 1975.

Delco was the first black representative from District Fifty, Travis County, and she found her work was cut out for her. State schools were still recovering from segregation practices that dated back to the Civil War. Schools that were primarily black had been mandated by the state, but were underfunded in comparison to primarily white schools. Delco set about getting more equitable funding for black students and opening doors for black and female faculty.

Since Texas was not offering minority students the kind of opportunities available in other states, promising students went elsewhere. And Texas was the poorer for it. "Other states come into Texas and raid talented black students," Delco pointed out. She was determined to gain more balanced funding. One of Delco's major accomplishments was an amendment to the Texas constitution that gave a predominantly black school, Prairie View A&M University, a share of funds previously enjoyed only by Texas A&M and the University of Texas.

Delco has also criticized the tenure system, which had been used to protect the jobs of established white males against younger blacks and women seeking opportunity. As Delco puts it, "I think tenure has evolved into a kind of a security blanket which happens to give security to some people who happen to be part of the good-old-boys' network and denies security to young people who might really have a lot to offer the institution."

At times Delco has clashed with Hispanics over school funding. There were instances when the Texas legislature would make funds available to either predominantly black schools or to south Texas districts with large Hispanic populations. Delco often won the funds for African Americans.

Delco served repeatedly as Chairman of the Texas House Higher Education Committee. She was cited as Distinguished Professional Woman for 1987 by the Committee on the Status of Women at the University of Texas Health Science Center at Houston and inducted into the Texas Women's Hall of Fame in 1986.

After twenty years of service in the House of Representatives, Delco decided to retire from the statehouse. Her term expired in January of 1995 and she declined to seek reelection. Since retiring, Delco has been nearly as active as ever in education policy, although as she says, "I now have the ability to say 'No,' which is difficult when in office." Delco is chair of a national advisory committee on Institutional Quality and Integrity for the Department of Education, and Chair of the National Advisory Committee for the Compact for Faculty Diversity. She also advises on educational funding.

Wilhelmina Delco continues to be a public speaker in great demand for her forceful and incisive views on education. While no longer in elected office, she has the ability to remain a voice in statewide and national education policy.

ANDRA MEDEA

E

Elliott, Daisy (1919–)

For almost twenty years, Daisy Elliott served as an elected official in the State of Michigan, first as a delegate to the Michigan Constitutional Convention, and then as a member of the Michigan State Legislature. In these capacities she successfully engineered constitutional and legislative provisions that significantly expanded the civil rights laws of the state.

Daisy Elizabeth Lenoir Elliott was born on November 26, 1919, in Filbert, West Virginia, the sixth of eight children of Robert Lenoir and Daisy (Dorum) Lenoir. Coal mining provided Robert with regular employment that allowed reliable but modest support for his family's needs. Daisy (Dorum) Lenoir was a homemaker who created a positive environment for her children's development. When Daisy was quite young, the family moved to Beckley, West Virginia, where Daisy attended school, graduating from Stratton High School in 1936. A few months after her graduation at seventeen, Daisy married Robert Elliott, a carpenter. They had one child, Doris Mae Elliott, in 1938. In the early 1940s, Daisy and Robert Elliott moved to Detroit hoping to find wartime factory work, and Daisy did work as a riveter and inspector in California before returning to Detroit. In 1947, Daisy and Robert divorced; in 1964, Daisy married Charles Bowers, who worked in the Detroit Department of Transportation. Daisy added to her education by attending college classes both in Detroit and in California but without completing a formal degree. She did complete a course of study and graduate from the Detroit Institute of Commerce in 1950. In the 1950s, she sold real estate and worked in a Michigan Secretary of State branch office, rising to the position of assistant manager.

For many years, Daisy Elliott had longed for greater social and economic opportunities for black men and women. Her World War II experiences convinced her that pressure from private civic groups and labor unions, combined with federal government orders against job discrimination, could bring needed changes. She resolved to enter politics to serve as a catalyst for these changes. In addition to her activities with several civic organizations, Elliott became active in the Michigan Democratic Party and also sought election to the Michigan State Legislature. From 1957 to 1959, she was president of the Michigan Federal Democratic Clubs and in 1961, she won election to the Michigan Constitutional Convention, in which she played a key role on civil rights issues. Elliott was instrumental in establishing the Michigan Civil Rights Commission as part of the new Michigan Constitution, the first time a state had included such an agency in its constitution. The commission's authority allows it to investigate charges of discrimination based on race, religion, color, or national origin and to enforce antidiscrimination laws. Elected to the Michigan State Legislature in 1962, she served through 1978 and was reelected again in 1980 and served through 1982. Elliott played a significant role in the legislature, serving for several terms as chair of such important committees as Constitutional Revisions and Labor and sponsoring valuable reform legislation. More than eighty laws which she sponsored or cosponsored were enacted by the legislature, including the Elliott-Larsen Civil Rights Act of 1977, often cited as the most comprehensive state civil rights law in the United States. It added prohibitions against discrimination based on sex, weight, height, age, or marital status and increased the amount of damages the Civil Rights Commission could award.

In 1982, Elliott's electoral district was combined with the district of another black female representative, requiring two incumbents to oppose each other. Four months before the August primary election, Elliott was charged with knowingly driving a stolen car. News stories led to her defeat in the primary. Elliott maintained her innocence, claiming she bought the car legally at a car dealership, but she was convicted. Claiming that she was "set up" because powerful people wanted her out of the state legislature, Elliott appealed the conviction, but was not able to overturn it.

DE WITT S. DYKES, JR.

F

Fauset, Crystal Bird (1894–1965)

Crystal Bird Fauset was the first African-American woman to be elected to a state house of representatives. She was born in 1894 to Benjamin O. and Portia E. (Lovett) Bird in Princess Anne, Maryland, but was raised in Boston by her maternal aunt, Lucy Groves. There she attended public schools and was considered an outstanding student. Later in life Fauset maintained that her social and political conscience was shaped by her experiences as a child in Boston. She went on to Teachers College, Columbia University, where she earned a B.S. in 1931.

Upon graduation Crystal Bird worked as a social worker and administrator of Negro affairs for the **Young Women's Christian Association** in New York City and Philadelphia. In 1933, she was named executive secretary for the Institute of Race Relations at Swarthmore College. While serving in that position, she became convinced of the necessity of political action for economic change. In 1935, after marrying author and educator Arthur Huff Fauset, she became director of Negro women's activities for the Democratic National Committee. Through that position she established numerous political contacts and was appointed in 1936 as an assistant personnel director in the Philadelphia office of the Works Progress Administration (WPA).

In 1938, the leadership of Philadelphia's local Democratic Party organization asked Fauset to run for a seat in the Pennsylvania House of Representatives from the eighteenth district in Philadelphia, and she accepted. Upon election in November 1938, she became the first African-American woman ever to achieve such a position. She remained in the legislature only one year, however, before accepting an appointment in November 1939 to the Pennsylvania WPA as assistant director in charge of education and recreational programs. She remained in that position until 1941, when, with the assistance of Eleanor Roosevelt, a close friend, she was appointed as the special consultant on Negro affairs in the Office of Civilian Affairs in Washington, D.C.

By 1944, however, Fauset had become disappointed with the Democratic Party because of its handling of black Americans in the war effort, and she announced her support of Governor Thomas E. Dewey's bid for the Republican presidential nomination. After meeting with Dewey and other Republican leaders, she became an advisor to the Republican National Committee's division on Negro affairs.

Fauset held a number of other important posts during her distinguished career. For a time she was chair of the Philadelphia Negro Women's Democratic League and served on the board of trustees of Cheyney State Teachers College. In 1963, Philadelphia Mayor James Tate appointed her to the board of directors of the Small Business Opportunities Corporation.

Crystal Bird Fauset, who believed in going to the heart of the economic situation through political action, was the first black woman to be elected to a state legislature. (NATIONAL ARCHIVES)

Fauset suffered a heart attack and died in Philadelphia on Sunday, March 27, 1965. She believed that wide economic gaps between human beings interfered with human relationships and she spent most of her life attempting to close those economic gaps to improve the quality of human life.

V. P. FRANKLIN

Federal Judges, by Appointing President, 1966–1995

Lyndon B. Johnson (1963–1969)
1966
  Motley, Constance B. (b. 1921–)
    Southern District of New York

James Earl Carter (1977–1981)
1978
  Lowe, Mary Johnson (b. 1924–)
    Southern District of New York

1979
  Kearse, Amalya L. (b. 1937–)
    2nd Circuit Appeals Court, New York
  McDonald, Gabrielle Kirk (b. 1942–)
    Southern District of Texas
  Taylor, Anna Diggs (b. 1932–)
    Eastern District of Michigan
  Thompson, Anne E. (b. 1934–)
    New Jersey District
1980
  Johnson, Norma H. (b. 1932–)
    District of Columbia
  Marshall, Consuela B. (b. 1936–)
    Central District of California

Ronald Reagan (1981–1989)
1985
  Williams, Ann C. (b. 1949–)
    Northern District of Illinois

George Bush (1989–1993)
1991
  Armstrong, Saundra Brown (b. 1947–)
    Northern District of California
1992
  Jackson, Carol E. (b. 1952–)
    Eastern District of Missouri

William Clinton (1993–)
1994
  Batts, Deborah (b. 1947–)
    Southern District of New York
  Collins, Audrey (b. 1945–)
    Central District of California
  Gilmore, Vanessa (b. 1956–)
    Southern District of Texas
  Hood, Denise (b. 1952–)
    Eastern District of Michigan

Fisher, Ada Lois Sipuel (1924–1995)

Ada Lois Sipuel was an honors graduate of all-black Oklahoma State College for Negroes (now Langston University) and the

Refused admission to the University of Oklahoma Law School in 1946 because of her race, Ada Sipuel Fisher was named to the university's Board of Regents in 1992. (UNIVERSITY OF OKLAHOMA NEWS SERVICES)

first African-American woman to attend an all-white law school in the South.

The daughter of a minister, Ada Lois Sipuel was born on February 8, 1924, in Chickasha, Oklahoma. Her brother had planned to challenge the segregationist policies of the University of Oklahoma but instead went to Howard University Law School, in part because he did not want to delay his career further by protracted litigation, having already been delayed by serving in World War II. Ada, who was younger and who had been in college during the war, was willing to delay her legal career in order to challenge segregation.

In 1946, Sipuel applied for admission to the University of Oklahoma law school. She was denied admission because of her race, and a lengthy court battle ensued. The Supreme Court ruled in 1948 that the state of Oklahoma must provide instruction for blacks equal to that given whites. Unfortunately, since this decision did not invalidate segregated education, the regents created the Langston University School of Law located at the state capital. Further legal action was necessary to prove that this law school was inferior to the University of Oklahoma law school. Finally in the summer of 1949, Sipuel was admitted to the University of Oklahoma law school.

By the time the law school allowed her to register, the semester had already begun. She had married Warren W. Fisher, and was pregnant with the first of her two children. The law school gave her a special chair marked "colored" and roped it off from the rest of the class. Her classmates and teachers welcomed her, however, sharing their notes, studying with her, and helping her catch up on the material she had missed. Although she was forced to eat in a separate chained-off and guarded area of the law school cafeteria, she recalled many years later that white students crawled under the chain and ate with her when guards were not around. Adding to these circumstances, and the usual difficulties of law school, was the added pressure of the lawsuit. "I knew the eyes of Oklahoma and the nation were on me," she said in an interview years later. Her lawsuit and tuition were supported by hundreds of small donations, and she believed she "owed it to those people to make it."

After graduating from the law school in 1951, Fisher earned a master's degree, also from the previously all-white university. In 1952, she began practicing law in her hometown of Chickasha, and as early as 1954 she represented a client before the Oklahoma Supreme Court. In 1957, she joined the faculty at Langston University, where she served as chair of the social sciences department and later as assistant vice president for academic affairs. In 1988, she became counsel to Automations Research Systems, Ltd., in Alexandria, Virginia. That same year, the Oklahoma Legislative Black Caucus honored her on the fortieth anniversary of the U.S. Supreme Court's decision in *Sipuel* v. *Board of Regents of the University of Oklahoma*. In 1974 and 1975, she served on the Advisory Committee on Civil Rights for the Oklahoma Regents for Higher Education. Throughout her career she was active in civil rights organizations, serving the Urban League, the **National Association for the Advancement of Colored People** (NAACP), and the American Civil Liberties Union (ACLU).

In 1992, Oklahoma governor David Walters appointed her to the Board of Regents of the University of Oklahoma, which, she noted in an interview, "completes a forty-five-year cycle." Of her appointment, she said it brings "a new dimension to university policies. Having suffered severely from bigotry and racial discrimination as a student, I am sensitive to that kind of thing."

Ada Lois Sipuel Fisher died of cancer at her home in Oklahoma City on October 18, 1995. She was 71 and had served for three years on the University of Oklahoma's Board of Regents, the same body that had denied her admission to the university.

PAUL FINKELMAN

G

Guinier, Lani (1953?–)

Until April of 1993, she was simply a good lawyer, and an outstanding legal scholar who was trying to explore ways to make the democratic process more democratic. On April 29th, however, she became President Bill Clinton's nominee for head of the Justice Department's Civil Rights Division. On April 30th, she became "the Quota Queen."

Lani Guinier grew up in a working-class neighborhood in Queens in New York City. She was the daughter of a black father and a Jewish mother and grew accustomed early to answering the question "What are you?" Her father was a frequently unemployed academic who finally gained the status he deserved when he became chair of the Afro-American studies department at Harvard University.

Guinier went to New York City public schools and then to Radcliffe College, where she received her bachelor's degree in 1971. She went on to Yale Law School, graduating with her J.D. in 1974. It was at Yale that she met Bill Clinton, who, she wrote later, "stood out as a white student who was obviously comfortable eating at a table in the company of more than one black person."

After Yale, Guinier was law clerk for Damon J. Keith, then Chief Judge of the United States District Court in the Eastern District of Michigan. She then became a juvenile court referee in Detroit, Michigan.

In 1977, she went to work for the Civil Rights Division of the U.S. Department of Justice, where she remained for a little over three years. From 1981 to 1988, Guinier worked as assistant counsel for the

Before Lani Guinier drew public attention when President Bill Clinton withdrew her nomination for head of the Civil Rights Division of the Justice Department, she was a highly respected attorney, law professor, and scholar. Though Clinton never gave Guinier the opportunity to defend her position publicly, she did so in her 1994 book, The Tyranny of the Majority. *(THE FREE PRESS)*

NAACP Legal Defense and Educational Fund, Inc.

During all this time, Guinier was considered a practical, effective, highly competent attorney. It was only after she left the public arena to become a scholar that she became controversial. In June of 1988, Guinier became an associate professor at the University of Pennsylvania Law School. She began to write about ways that minorities might have more say in a democracy. As she describes it, "Inspired by the work of James Madison, I explored ways to insure that even a self-interested majority could work with, rather than 'tyrannize,' a minority. I imagined a more consensual, deliberative, and participatory democracy for *all* voters, despite religious, political, racial, or sex differences."

These writings, which were respected and debated in an academic setting, became the primary weapon used against Guinier in the attack against her after her nomination for the Justice Department post. Innovative approaches became "breathtakingly radical." Guinier was accused of being "race-obsessed" and "divisive."

In one of the least shining moments of his presidency, Clinton failed to support his nominee. Guinier was not even allowed to defend her positions publicly, and Clinton withdrew her nomination.

Lani Guinier went back to her work as teacher, scholar, and public speaker. But she did find a way to tell her side of the story. Her book, *The Tyranny of the Majority,* was published in 1994.

KATHLEEN THOMPSON

H

Hall, Katie (1938–)

"Men and women of good will on both sides of the aisle showed this was a human concern, not a political or racial issue," commented Katie Hall, representative from Indiana, when the U.S. House of Representatives passed the bill she had introduced designating the birthday of Martin Luther King, Jr., a federal holiday. Signed into law by President Ronald Reagan on November 2, 1983, this legislation embodied the wishes of many Americans to honor the slain civil rights leader, following a legislative process mired in controversy since it was first introduced, shortly after King's assassination on April 4, 1968.

Katie Beatrice Green was born in Mound Bayou, Mississippi, on April 3, 1938, attended local schools, and graduated from Mississippi Valley State University in 1960. She married John W. Hall in August 1957. She received an M.S. from Indiana University in 1968. She spent her first years out of college as a teacher in the Gary, Indiana, public schools; later she taught social studies at the Edison School from 1964–75. A member of the Gary Council of Social Studies and vice chair of the Gary Housing Board of Commissioners, Hall became involved in politics while participating in the mayoral campaigns of Richard Hatcher. Eventually Hall entered electoral politics, serving as Indiana state representative (1974–76) from her northwestern Indiana district, state senator (1976–82), and chair of the Lake County Democratic Committee (1978–80).

Well connected in local Democratic politics, Hall was nominated to run for the U.S. House of Representatives seat left vacant by the death of Representative Adam Benjamin, Jr. In November 1982, she defeated the Republican candidate, Thomas Krieger, and immediately took the first district seat to complete the term in the Ninety-seventh Congress and serve in the succeeding term in the Ninety-eighth Congress.

While best remembered for her tireless efforts as floor manager in support of the King holiday, Hall also served on the House Committee on Post Office and Civil Service (as chair of the census and population subcommittee and as a member of the civil service subcommittee) and the Committee on Public Works and Transportation (aviation, economic development, and public buildings and grounds subcommittees). She focused her efforts on legislation that would remedy her district's significant unemployment rate and its associated social problems. Hall supported the Fair Trade in Steel Act, designed to infuse new energy into the lagging steel industry, and she supported the Humphrey-Hawkins bill for prevention of family violence and child abuse. She also supported the Equal Rights Amendment to the U.S. Constitution.

Running for reelection in 1984, Hall was defeated in the Democratic primary by Pe-

Representative Katie Hall, to the left of Coretta Scott King, at the official signing of the bill to create a national Martin Luther King holiday, November 2, 1983. Hall, who was responsible for introducing the bill, was a representative from Indiana from 1982 to 1984. (CALUMET RE-GIONAL ARCHIVES)

ter Visclosky. She became the city clerk of Gary, Indiana in 1985.

LYNDA ALLANACH

Hamilton, Grace Towns (1907–1992)

There are many trailblazers and among them is Grace Towns Hamilton—Georgia's first black female legislator. She brought power to minority voters and served as a catalyst for racial cooperation. She helped

rewrite the Atlanta charter to give black citizens self-government. "At a time when there was very little interracial cooperation and very little of any kind of discussion, she was a real pathfinder. . . . She set a standard for civic involvement that was difficult for any of her peers to meet and will be difficult for any who come after her to meet," said former Georgia state representative Julian Bond.

Grace Towns was born February 10, 1907, in Atlanta, the eldest of four children of George A. Towns and Nellis McNair Towns. Young Grace Towns graduated from Atlanta University in 1927, then enrolled in graduate school at Ohio State, paying her way by working as a **Young Women's Christian Association** (YWCA) secretary. She earned a master's degree in psychology in 1929.

In 1930, she married Henry Cooke Hamilton, dean and professor of education at LeMoyne College, now LeMoyne-Owen College, in Memphis, Tennessee.

Grace Towns Hamilton taught psychology at the Memphis college from 1930 to 1934, had a job making a Works Progress Administration survey of black workers in Memphis in 1935–36, and was a YWCA employee helping to develop interracial programs on college campuses from 1936 to 1941. In 1941, she and her husband returned to Atlanta to live when Henry became principal of The Atlanta University Laboratory School. He joined the faculty of Morehouse College in 1943.

Hamilton, the first black woman to serve in the Georgia legislature, represented the Vine City area from 1966 to 1984. Hamilton was elected to the House after court-ordered reapportionment in 1965 that created eight new Fulton County seats and increased political opportunities for black people. As executive director of the Atlanta Urban League and later as a legislator, she was a champion for fair housing, more job opportunities for black workers, and the integration of Atlanta's Grady Memorial Hospital.

Hamilton was the major architect of the current Atlanta city charter, which became law in 1973. It reduced at-large representation and paved the way for black self-government through district voting. She brought "one person, one vote" to local government. It was first actualized in a 1962 Georgia case before the Supreme Court and later swept Southern states and local governments.

Five years after she was elected to the Georgia House, Hamilton authored a bill creating an Atlanta Charter Commission. She served as vice-chairman of the twenty-seven-member commission during its deliberations in 1971–73. Hamilton and fellow Commissioner Everett Millican developed the current political map of Atlanta, with its twelve voting districts (the legislature later added six at-large seats). Before then, whites had used at-large voting to maintain control. Council members were not required to live in the districts they represented. Consequently Atlanta had no black council member until 1966. Seven years later in October 1973, Maynard H. Jackson was elected the first black mayor of a major Southern city.

Hamilton was one of Atlanta's greatest activists as executive director of the Atlanta Urban League for eighteen years, from 1943 to 1961. As a fierce advocate of greater opportunities for black school children, she waged a successful campaign in 1944–46 for the black community to get a share of a $9.9 million school-bond issue. At the same time, she and others led a 1946 drive to register black citizens to vote, as the federal courts were weighing a suit to outlaw the state's notorious white primary. Only whites could vote in the Democratic primary, which in a one-party state was tantamount to election.

During the pivotal 1954–55 period, when the Supreme Court was deliberating the *Brown* decision to eliminate segregated schools, Hamilton was on a leave of absence from the Urban League and was serving as associate director of the Atlanta-based Southern Regional Council, which worked to end discrimination.

She also was a seminar leader and member of the Executive Council of the Highlander Folk School in Monteagle, Tennessee. Liberals, black and white, attended seminars at the school on voter registration and peaceful school integration. Hamilton's Highlander ties provoked racists. In 1957, segregationist Georgia governor Marvin Griffin sent a state employee to the school to photograph black attendants. The governor then published a four-page hate sheet charging that Highlander was a hotbed of Communism. Its principal news was that Dr. Martin Luther King, Jr., had visited the school, and Grace Hamilton was a member of the school's executive council.

Grace Towns Hamilton also was a champion of fair housing, more job opportunities for black Americans, and the integration of Grady Memorial Hospital. She engaged in a struggle with the Fulton-Dekalb Hospital Authority over conditions at Grady Memorial Hospital many times. The Hughes Spalding Pavilion exists because Grace Hamilton convinced the authority that there had to be a place where black patients who could afford to pay could receive medical treatment. At that time Grady Hospital was restricted to those too poor to pay. She was also primarily responsible for the hiring of Grady's first black doctor in 1958.

Spurred by her triumph in recasting city government, she tried in 1975 to do the same with county government. She authored a bill to shorten the terms of county commissioners from four to two years. Not only did the commissioners get the bill defeated, they removed her from the Ful-

ton-Dekalb Hospital Authority, a post she had held since 1971.

Political opposition began to mount in 1982 after she allied with Georgia House speaker Tom Murphy to oppose a congressional reapportionment committee. Hamilton's critical miscalculation, however, was her support of Walter Mondale and not Jesse Jackson for the Democratic nomination for president in 1984. That year, she sought a tenth term in the legislature from the 31st District. Mable Thomas, her opponent, charged that Hamilton was "out of touch with her district." Thomas led in a primary, 1,401 votes to 1,170, and won in a runoff, 2,483 to 983.

Her husband, Henry, died in 1987 at the age of eighty-seven. They had a daughter, Eleanor Hamilton Payne, four grandchildren, and seven great-grandchildren.

In 1989, Emory University in Atlanta, Georgia, honored Hamilton by inaugurating the Grace Towns Hamilton Lectureship, the first lecture series at a major university named for a black woman. In 1990, she was honored again when Emory endowed a distinguished chair in her name. Both occurred through the initiative of the African American and African Studies program at Emory.

Grace Towns Hamilton died at the age of eighty-five on July 17, 1992. Described as "the quiet warrior," she fought for better health facilities, improved education, help for the indigent, and rights for the disenfranchised.

DELORES P. ALDRIDGE

Harris, Patricia Roberts (1924–1985)

An acute intelligence and tremendous confidence in herself led Patricia Roberts Harris to a brilliant political and academic

Patricia Roberts Harris was the first black woman to serve as U.S. ambassador and to hold a cabinet position. (MOORLAND-SPINGARN)

career filled with "firsts"—the first black woman to head a United States embassy, to serve in a president's cabinet, and to head a law school. She was born in 1924 in Mattoon, Illinois, to Bert and Chiquita Roberts. She and her brother were brought up by their mother after their father abandoned the family. The Roberts family was one of the few black families in Mattoon, and Patricia was aware of racism by the age of six, though she was determined to do whatever she was able to do.

After graduating from a Chicago high school, Roberts went to **Howard University.** Four years later, she received her A.B. summa cum laude. While at Howard, Roberts participated in one of the first student sit-ins in an attempt to integrate the Little Palace cafeteria.

Back in Chicago, Roberts went to work for the Chicago **Young Women's Christian Association** and then became executive director of **Delta Sigma Theta.** She also met and married William Beasley Harris, a lawyer. Her husband encouraged her to go to law school and, in 1957, she enrolled in the George Washington University School of Law. Upon graduation, she went to work for the criminal division of the United States Department of Justice for about a year before joining the faculty of the Howard University Law School. In 1965, Harris was appointed ambassador to Luxembourg by President Lyndon Johnson. She served in that capacity until September 1967, when she returned to Howard. At this time she was also an alternate delegate to the United Nations.

For a brief time in 1969, Harris was dean of the School of Law at Howard, making her the first black woman to head a law school. However, she resigned within a month after she was appointed, following student and faculty conflicts. She joined a prestigious Washington, D.C., law firm and practiced corporate law until she was appointed U.S. Secretary of Housing and Urban Development by President Jimmy Carter in 1977, a position she held until 1979, when she became U.S. Secretary of Health, Education and Welfare until the Reagan administration in 1981.

In 1982, Harris ran for mayor of the District of Columbia but was defeated by

Marion S. Barry. The following year she joined the faculty of George Washington University. She taught there for less than two years before dying of cancer on March 23, 1985.

KATHLEEN THOMPSON

Harvard, Beverly (1950–)

When Beverly J. Harvard bet her husband and a family friend one hundred dollars that a woman could be an effective police officer, little did she know what the future would bring. "It was 1973, and my husband, Jimmy, and a friend of his were talking about how the women who might be suited to be police officers had to be six foot three inches tall, weigh two hundred pounds, and have deep voices," says Harvard. "I really thought my husband would say, 'My wife, she could be anything,' and go on with the conversation. But he said, 'Yeah, you're right, she could never be a police officer.'" Harvard took the doubtful comments as a challenge, made the bet, and embarked on a career path that would eventually take her to the rank of Police Chief for the City of Atlanta. She would be the first African-American woman to run a major American police department.

Born in Macon, Georgia, on December 22, 1950, Harvard was the youngest of seven children. She studied sociology at Morris Brown College in Atlanta, earning her bachelor's degree in 1972. Determined to win the hundred-dollar bet, she took an assignment handling 911 calls in the Atlanta police department's communications department. But her growing interest in law enforcement and its potential to help people drew her into the police academy. By 1974, she was an officer walking a beat.

Harvard's husband was not comfortable with the idea of his wife's first assignment—foot patrol in a high-crime neighborhood. He worried about her safety and insisted on following her around in his car to make sure she was okay. But in time he came to realize that his wife was a trained professional who could take care of herself. He relaxed and let her pursue her life's work.

After two years on street patrol, Harvard moved on to other kinds of police work. She served as affirmative action specialist

When Beverly Harvard first joined the Atlanta Police Department in 1974, her husband was so worried about her safety that he followed her around in his car when she was on foot patrol. Little did he know that in 1994 she would become Atlanta's first African-American female chief of police. (OFFICE OF BEVERLY HARVARD)

and public affairs director. She then won a place in the Atlanta police department's Executive Protection Unit (the first woman to do so). She moved up through the ranks to deputy chief (the first African-American woman to do so). In that capacity, she supervised various units, acquiring a reputation as a capable manager and a skillful administrator. Along the way, she earned a master's degree in urban government and public administration from Georgia State University, graduated from the FBI National Academy, and received an honorary Doctorate of Laws degree from Morris Brown College.

In 1988, Harvard took time off from police work to have a baby, daughter Christa, but she was soon back on the job. In 1994, she was named acting police chief by Atlanta mayor Bill Campbell. Six months later, having proved herself, Harvard was named chief.

As the first African-American female police chief in a major American city, Harvard was proud of her achievement and yet frustrated by the attitudes of some skeptical male law enforcement colleagues who seemed to regard her as an oddity. "It was lonely at the top, not having a female counterpart to empathize and sympathize and help to assess whether [my] perceptions were right," she says. But she held on and focused her energies on the job, working to reduce major crimes, youth violence, and the use of handguns, among other priorities. And at last Beverly J. Harvard is no longer alone at the top: Betsy Watson is police chief in Houston, Texas; Penny Harrington is police chief in Portland, Oregon; and **Jacqueline Barrett** is sheriff of Fulton County, Georgia, the county in which Atlanta is located.

CHRISTINE SUMPTION

Hedgeman, Anna Arnold
(1899–1990)

"I had been forced to spend my whole lifetime discussing the implications of color. . . . This was to me a waste of time and of whatever talent I had. . . . The opportunities I really wanted were closed to me." Anna Arnold wanted to teach, but, because of her color, she could not find a teaching position in the North. She found a job with the **Young Women's Christian Association** (YWCA) in a branch located in a black neighborhood, and from then on her varied career as educator, public servant, and civil rights advocate was determined by her race.

Anna Arnold was born in Marshalltown, Iowa, on July 5, 1899, the daughter of Marie Ellen Parker and William James Arnold II. Her father, born the son of slaves in South Carolina, had attended high school and then Clark College in Atlanta, Georgia, and was a strict disciplinarian. Anna grew up in an Irish neighborhood in Anoka, Minnesota, a small town without any signs of real poverty and without a black community. Raised in a religious household, she was taught to read at home by her mother and did not attend school until the age of seven. Anna had reached high school when she first realized that hers was the only black family in town. Because her father would not allow his daughters to date before college, the issue of a white boy dating a black girl never emerged.

After she graduated from high school in June 1918, her father sent her to Hamline University, a Methodist college in St. Paul, Minnesota. Because she lived with white friends of her father's, Arnold never knew whether, as Hamline's first black student, she would have been accepted in the dormitory. Her best friend at college was white, and her sense of her race was only incidental in her life. The fact that she was female, however, did limit her choice of a career, because teaching was the only occupation open to women at the time. Anna Arnold did her practice teaching at Hamline, learning only later that she would not have been allowed to do so at St. Paul High School because of her race.

Deciding she wanted to teach in the South, Arnold found a teaching job at Rust College, a black school in Holly Springs, Mississippi. Her first experience with segregation came on the train trip south, in September 1922, when she was forced to change to the "colored" coach at Cairo, Illinois. Not only was racial segregation a constant affront in the South; Rust College was sex segregated as well. Anna Arnold lived with the women students, serving as their chaperone when they needed to go into town. Like many other Southern towns, Holly Springs' black grade school was inferior and, because town leaders assumed that black children neither needed nor were capable of high school training, there was no black high school. Consequently, in addition to its college offerings, Rust maintained a grade school and high school for black students. Many came from sharecropping families, so they could not begin classes until after harvest, and they left early in the school year for spring planting. Parents paid tuition out of their often meager earnings.

Disillusioned by Southern segregation, Arnold decided to return to the Midwest to teach in 1924. After learning that racism prohibited her from getting a teaching job in the North, Arnold accepted a position with a YWCA in Springfield, Ohio, beginning in the fall of 1924. The Springfield

The only woman on the organizing committee of the 1963 March on Washington, Anna Hedgeman had a long career in community service which began with black chapters of the YWCA and progressed through government service in New York City and on a national level. Although she protested the sexual discrimination to the committee, no woman made a major address at the march. (MOORLAND-SPINGARN)

YWCA was segregated by neighborhood and lacked a gym, swimming pool, cafeteria, and adequate staff. Anna Arnold found it difficult to give black children confidence in the face of such discrimination and even more difficult to give lectures on race relations because there were no relations. Yet, the national YWCA was ahead of its time for even hiring black executives, and her relationship with the YWCA, where she helped develop a variety of international programs in education, continued on and off for twelve years.

Having spent time in the summer of 1926 in the freer atmosphere of New York, Arnold was eager to return. Requesting a transfer from the national YWCA, she became the executive director of a black branch in Jersey City. There black Americans were represented on all committees, and there were even a few black teachers in the public schools. Her days off were spent in Harlem, where she became acquainted with the culture of the Harlem Renaissance at A'Lelia Walker's soirées. In 1927, Anna Arnold became membership secretary of the Harlem YWCA. Endowed by the Rockefellers, the Harlem YWCA had a well-equipped physical plant, a business school, a beautician training program, an employment agency, and meeting rooms. Because African Americans were barred from white branches of the YWCA just as they were from other public accommodations, this branch was particularly important to the community. For two years Arnold had a good job and was surrounded by black colleagues and friends. The Great Depression, however, brought more difficult times. The branch's membership shrank dramatically as people could no longer afford to pay for its services. Yet the community was now faced with the reality of starvation and a burgeoning Harlem population that had increased more than 600 percent in twenty-five years.

In fall 1933, Arnold became the executive director of the black branch of the Philadelphia YWCA. She made the black branch a vital part of the life of the community but only stayed one year. She returned to New York City in November 1933 to marry Merritt A. Hedgeman, a concert artist, an interpreter of black folk music and opera, and a former member of the **Fisk Jubilee Singers.** By this time, her parents and siblings had also settled in New York. By fall 1934, the city's Emergency Relief Bureau had begun to hire a few black supervisors, and Anna Hedgeman began working for the agency as the city's first consultant on racial problems. Hedgeman served Jews and Italians as well as black Americans. In fall 1937, the Emergency Relief Bureau became the Department of Welfare, whereupon Hedgeman resigned and accepted the directorship of the black branch of the Brooklyn YWCA. She used this position to organize a citizens' coordinating committee to seek provisional appointments for black Americans to the Department of Welfare. They secured the first 150 provisional appointments the city had ever given to the black community. With the aid of white women on the race relations committee of the Federation of Protestant Churches, she also succeeded in expanding employment opportunities for black clerks in Brooklyn department stores. Hedgeman resigned from the Brooklyn YWCA, however, after her activities became a point of contention with the central board. Her organizing tactics—including picket lines and challenges to the old guard leadership—proved too militant.

Anna Hedgeman continued to lobby for change. She defended the picketing of a local defense plant that refused to hire black workers on the grounds that government contracts should be denied to contractors who discriminate against black workers. She joined the civilian defense program as a race relations assistant. Then she joined A. Philip Randolph's March on Washington Committee, designed to fight segregation and discrimination against African Americans in defense industries and the military. In 1944, Randolph offered Hedgeman the job of executive director of the National Council for a Permanent Fair Employment Practices Committee (FEPC). Because she had come to believe that permanent legislation was needed to outlaw discrimination in employment, Hedgeman took the job and moved to Washington, D.C., and began lobbying on behalf of FEPC. The National Council was unable to obtain a permanent FEPC, and after a major legislative drive in 1946 failed, she resigned and then became dean of women at **Howard University.**

In summer 1948, Congressman William L. Dawson, vice chair of the Democratic National Committee, asked Hedgeman to join the presidential campaign of Harry Truman by becoming executive director of the national citizens' committee to raise funds among African Americans. Pollsters predicted that Truman would lose, and Hedgeman was reluctant to align with racist Southern Democrats, but Dawson had supported FEPC, and she accepted the offer. After the election, Hedgeman received a patronage appointment as assistant to Oscar R. Ewing, administrator of the Federal Security Agency (later the Department of Health, Education and Welfare). She was sworn in on February 12, 1949, the first black American to hold a position in the Federal Security Agency administration. At the request of Ambassador Chester Bowles, Hedgeman spent three months in India in 1952 as an exchange leader for the State Department. She resigned upon her return to the United States, following the Republican victory in the presidential election.

Hedgeman returned to New York City after a ten-year absence and was met by a Harlem delegation that urged her to delve into city politics. So, on January 1, 1954, when Robert F. Wagner invited her to be a mayoral assistant, she accepted. She was responsible for eight city departments, acting as their liaison with the mayor, and she remained in the post until 1958. As the first black woman at the cabinet level, Hedgeman gave speeches, represented the mayor at conferences and conventions, hosted United Nations' visitors to the city, and participated in weekly cabinet meetings. In 1955, when Mayor Wagner was on a European tour, Hedgeman was designated as his representative at the tenth-anniversary meeting of the United Nations in San Francisco. In 1956, she was invited on a study tour of Israel and the Middle East through the American Christian Committee on Palestine. Because she was a board member of the United Seamen's Service, she continued on to Munich, Germany, where she chaired a panel at the International Conference of Social Work as a representative of the Seamen's Service. In the same capacity, she attended the International Conference of Social Work in Japan in 1958. Hedgeman served as secretary to the board of the United Seamen's Service from 1955 to 1960.

By fall 1958, frustrated by City Hall's lack of response to black concerns and the black community, Hedgeman accepted the offer of S. B. Fuller to join his cosmetics firm as a public relations consultant and an associate editor and columnist for the *New York Age,* one of the oldest black newspapers in the United States.

In 1960, a group of black and Puerto Rican reformers asked Hedgeman to run for Congress as an insurgent from the East Bronx. She ran, but she lost.

That same year, Hedgeman was invited to be the keynote speaker at the First Conference of African Women and Women of African Descent held in Accra, Ghana, in July. She also became a consultant for the division of higher education of the American Missionary Association to help six black colleges prepare for their centennial anniversaries in 1966, and she had her own radio program, "One Woman's Opinion," on a local New York City station.

In February 1963, Hedgeman played a key role in conceptualizing the 1963 March on Washington as a joint effort. A. Philip Randolph had called for a march on Washington for job opportunities to be held in October 1963. When Hedgeman learned that Martin Luther King, Jr., was planning a march for that July to pressure public opinion on behalf of a strong civil rights bill, she suggested that they combine efforts into a March on Washington for Jobs and Freedom to be held in August. Hedgeman was the only woman on the organizing committee of the march; indeed the heads of all the sponsoring organizations and all of the proposed speakers were male, even though women had played major roles in fund-raising. While plans for the march were taking shape, Hedgeman was appointed to the newly formed commission on religion and race of the National Council of Churches as coordinator of special events. The intent of the commission was to mobilize the resources of Protestant and Orthodox churches to work against racial injustice in American life. Her first assignment was to relate the march on Washington to this renewed commitment of Protestant churches to justice for all. In this capacity she was asked to help mobilize

30,000 white Protestant church leaders to march. About a third of the 250,000 marchers were white; some credit for that figure certainly belongs to Hedgeman.

In 1965, granted a leave from the commission on religion and race, Hedgeman campaigned unsuccessfully for president of the City Council of New York on the Reform Democratic ticket. She was the first woman and the first black woman to run for the office. In 1968, she unsuccessfully ran in the Democratic Party primary for an assembly seat.

On December 31, 1967, Hedgeman retired from her work with the National Council of Churches. She and her husband established Hedgeman Consultant Services in 1968. Their clients included educational institutions and civic, business, and community organizations.

The recipient of many honors and awards for her work in race relations, Hedgeman garnered, among others, the Frederick Douglass Award from the New York Urban League, the National Human Relations Award from the State Fair Board of Texas, and awards from the Schomburg Collection of Negro Literature and the American Federation of Labor-Congress of Industrial Organizations (AFL-CIO). She received citations from the **National Association for the Advancement of Colored People** (NAACP), the Southern Christian Leadership Conference (SCLC), the **National Council of Negro Women,** and United Church Women. In 1948, she was awarded an honorary doctorate of humane letters by Hamline University, the first woman graduate of Hamline to be so honored. In 1983, she received a "pioneer woman" award from the New York State

Conference on Midlife and Older Women. Hedgeman was also a board member of the National Council of Christians and Jews. In 1964, she published her auto-biography and study of black leadership, *The Trumpet Sounds,* following it with an assessment of the civil rights movement from 1953 to 1974, *The Gift of Chaos* (1977).

In later years, Hedgeman used a restaurant at 22 West 135th Street as her unofficial office and meeting place for friends during the breakfast and dinner hours. From there she continued her efforts to improve conditions for the people of Harlem. After fifty-four years of marriage, Merritt Hedgeman died in 1988; Anna Hedgeman died on January 17, 1990, at the age of ninety.

Despite her indisputable accomplishments, Hedgeman never received the recognition due her. Partly from her own desire to better her situation and partly forced by circumstances, she constantly changed jobs, never remaining in one long enough to achieve prominence as a leader. Still, her long career as a civil rights advocate deserves further attention.

PAULA F. PFEFFER

Herman, Alexis M. (1947–)

When President Bill Clinton's 1994 Crime Bill needed a push to pass it through Congress, it was Alexis M. Herman to whom he turned for help. As assistant to the president and director of the White House office of public liaison, Herman quickly arranged a series of appearances in order to mobilize support. The bill eventually passed—one of the most resounding achievements of Clinton's first year in office—and Herman was dubbed "Clinton's Ms. Fix-it" by *The New York Times.*

Alexis M. Herman was born in Mobile, Alabama, on July 16, 1947. She was introduced to the realities of politics early on, when her father sued the Democratic Party for denying African Americans the vote. The effort eventually bore fruit in his being elected Alabama's first black wardsman.

After graduating from Xavier University in 1969, Herman plunged into community activism. She was a social worker for Catholic Social Services from 1969 to 1972 and followed that with stints with the Black Women's Employment Program (1972–1974) and the Minority Women's Employment Program (1974–1977). There she came into conflict with the sexism that she has since battled at every turn. "I was not prepared for, not just the overt forms, but the institutional barriers, the real stereotypes about what you can do as a woman, what you can do as a black woman," she says. Herman's life and achievements are a resounding reproof to that kind of stereotyped thinking.

Herman came to Washington in 1977 as director of the Women's Bureau of the Department of Labor for the Carter Administration. She also served as the White House's representative to the Organization of Economic Cooperation and Development on the role of women in the economy in Paris, France.

In 1981, she took a hiatus from government work to found her own marketing and management firm, A.M. Herman and Associates. She also ran a New York–based manufacturing company. However, she came back into Democratic politics in

Alexis Herman at her desk in the White House. Herman is assistant to the president and director of the White House office of public liaison.   (DAVID SCULL/NYT PICTURES)

1988, as deputy chairwoman and chief of staff of the Democratic National Committee. In 1991, she took over as chief executive officer of the 1992 Democratic National Committee, with the responsibility of overseeing the management and production of the presidential nominating convention. She has been characterized by Ernest Green, Managing Director of Lehman Brothers, as "talented, smart, aggressive, and she doesn't get herself associated with losers." Having worked with a winner in the 1992 election, she earned an appoint-

ment as assistant to the president and director of the White House office of public liaison after Bill Clinton took office in January 1993.

As director, she supervises communications between the president and a number of volatile constituencies, ranging from the Congressional Black Caucus to the Republican-dominated business community. Her background as a committed social activist, a savvy and successful businesswoman, and a canny political manager has given her the ability to walk the precipitous tightropes of modern American politics with a maturity, sense of balance, and thoroughness that have distinguished her as one of the Clinton administration's most effective appointees.

Alexis M. Herman has been the recipient of honorary doctorates from Xavier University, Central State University, and Lesley College. Her outstanding leadership skills and experience in management and public policy earned her recognition as one of *Ladies' Home Journal*'s "Women of the Future." In December 1996, she was nominated for the post of secretary of labor by President Clinton.

RICHARD E. T. WHITE

Hill, Anita (1956–)

"She is scrupulous, conscientious and ethical beyond reproach," said the associate dean of the University of Oklahoma law school. But there have been those who portrayed her as a vindictive, scheming liar. In 1991, this quiet, well-spoken law professor jolted the nation by testifying that a Supreme Court nominee had sexually harassed her. By detailing her accusations in public, and by facing the disbelief of men in power, she opened a firestorm of national debate. The country has not been the same since.

Anita Hill was born on her parents' farm outside the small town of Morris, Oklahoma, on July 30, 1956. Her parents, Albert and Irma Hill, were hardworking and extremely religious. The youngest of thirteen children, Hill attended public schools in Oklahoma. Both parents stressed education, and four of their children, including Anita, were valedictorians of their high school class. Their youngest daughter was popular in school, with both black and white friends, at a time when integration in Oklahoma was still unusual.

Hill went on to Oklahoma State University, where she majored in psychology. She graduated with honors in 1977. While still in Oklahoma, she served an internship with a local judge, which convinced her to study law. She went on to Yale Law School,

There are certain events in American history after which subsequent history is never seen in the same light. One such event was Anita Hill's testimony before the Senate Judiciary Committee, which was considering the nomination of Clarence Thomas to the Supreme Court. (REUTERS BETTMANN)

which she attended on a NAACP scholarship and graduated in 1980.

Having served a summer internship at the Washington law firm of Ward, Harkrader, and Ross, she returned to work there as a lawyer after graduation. In 1981, she accepted a job as personal assistant to Clarence Thomas, who headed the Office of Civil Rights at the Education Department in Washington. When Thomas was promoted to chairman of the Equal Employment Opportunity Commission, she was offered a promotion to follow him.

However, by 1983, she was hospitalized with stress-related stomach problems. At that time she decided to leave Washington. Hill became civil rights professor at Oral Roberts University School of Law, where she served from 1983 to 1986. When the school was reorganized and moved to Virginia, Hill became a professor at the University of Oklahoma School of Law at Norman. There she became a tenured professor after only four years. She served on the faculty senate and was named faculty administrative fellow in the Office of the Provost.

Hill became famous suddenly and unexpectedly. Clarence Thomas, her past boss, had been nominated to the Supreme Court to take the seat of famed black judge Thurgood Marshall. Thomas' nomination did not go smoothly. Considered by many to be a Republican political appointee rather than a jurist, Thomas had only one year's experience as a judge. Then Hill entered the proceedings.

Hill had been approached by the investigating committee, who had heard rumors of her being sexually harassed by Thomas. Eventually, and rather reluctantly, Hill testified before the Senate judiciary committee. Before television cameras she detailed a pattern of sexual harassment that included crude suggestions, descriptions of pornographic movies and pressures to date Thomas. Thomas passionately denied everything.

Hill's description of sexual harassment was like dropping a match into a neglected pool of gasoline. People were riveted to their televisions. The nation divided in angry debate. Many women said, "I've been treated like that. I didn't speak out because I didn't think anyone would believe me, either." Many men said, "She's lying. She's just jealous or vindictive." Blacks were shocked at a black accusing another black.

Either Hill or Thomas had to be lying. As one writer put it, "To accept Anita's story, you had only to believe that Clarence Thomas would lie to salvage his honor in front of the country and his family. To accept Thomas's denial, you had to believe that Hill was a psychopath."

Not only was Hill's character dragged through the mud, information was suppressed. Another woman who experienced similar treatment under Thomas offered to testify but was not called as a witness. Attempting to bring sanity back to the hearings, Hill underwent a lie detector test to confirm her statements. She passed the lie detector test, but this didn't end the controversy. Opponents attacked the ex-FBI agent who administered the test. Meanwhile, Thomas refused to undergo a similar lie detector test. In the end, Thomas was confirmed as Supreme Court justice.

However, the fight did not stop there. Many people, especially women, were outraged that Hill was treated so badly by the Senate judiciary committee. The next year, several senators who were involved in the hearings were up for reelection. Angry women organized against them. Senator Alan Dixon of Illinois, who assumed an easy reelection, was defeated in the primary by Carol Moseley-Braun, the first black woman to become a senator. Two other female senators were elected as part of the same reaction, creating a female voting bloc in the Senate for the first time in American history.

Hill was remarkable for her strength, dignity and poise during the hearings and after. She clearly did not anticipate that the senators would defend Thomas by attacking her. As she said later, "I was so caught up with the idea that this was a fact-finding hearing and that I was going to be giving testimony that I was not even thinking about what other people seemed to be trying to accomplish, and it only dawned on me over a period of time. . . . I didn't expect that they would go to the length that they did."

A year and a half later, a reporter wrote a book, *The Real Anita Hill,* which purported to cast doubts on parts of Hill's testimony. Several reviewers doubted the reliability of this book. After this, two reporters from the *Washington Post* made a more thorough investigation from a wide range of witnesses who were reluctant to come forward at the time of the hearings. Their book was called *Capital Games,* and their conclusion was that Hill was telling the truth.

In 1991, Anita Hill was given the **Ida B. Wells** Award from the **National Coalition of 100 Black Women,** and was named one of *Glamour* magazine's ten Women of the Year. In 1996 Oxford University Press published *Race, Gender, and Power in America: The Legacy of the Hill-Thomas Hearings,* co-edited by Hill and Emma Coleman Jordan.

ANDRA MEDEA

I

Ingram, Edith J. (1942–)

" 'The law' in the South has been viewed for many years by blacks as the action arm of the oppressor," notes Edith J. Ingram. "The three standard qualifications for becoming a law enforcement officer were (1) to be white, (2) to be strong enough to carry a revolver, and (3) to be mean enough to utter 'Nigger! Nigger! Nigger!' " However, in 1969, all that began to change when Ingram was appointed the first African-American judge in the state of Georgia.

Edith J. Ingram was born near the town of Sparta in Hancock County, Georgia, on January 16, 1942, the daughter of Robert T. and Katherine Hunt Ingram. Following her 1963 graduation from Fort Valley State College with a bachelor's degree in education, she worked for four years as a schoolteacher at Moore Elementary School in Griffin, Georgia. She then went on to a one-year teaching stint at Hancock Central Elementary School in her hometown of Sparta.

But Ingram was to make her mark on a larger scale. In 1969, she was appointed Judge of the Court Ordinary of Hancock County. Her appointment was an historic occasion. "In the past," says Ingram, "when a black individual found himself in a confrontation with whites, there was never an opportunity to call 'the law' for help because a call for help meant a call for hell." But with Ingram as Georgia's first African-American judge, there was an opportunity for change at last.

Ingram was awarded the Outstanding Courage in Southern Political Arena Plaque by the NAACP in 1969 and, in 1971, she received the Community Leaders American Award as well as a Certificate of Merit from the Booker T. Washington Business College of Birmingham, Alabama. She was named "Woman of the Year" by the *Mirror* newspaper of Augusta, Georgia in 1972.

The year 1973 saw Ingram's ascent to Judge of the Probate Court of Hancock County, where her duties include hearing cases involving everything from traffic to probate as well as performing marriages, taking care of vital records, and supervising county, state, and federal elections. In the meantime, Ingram has remained an active voice in her community, holding board memberships on the East Central Committee for Opportunity, the Hancock Concerned Citizens Club, the Georgia State Democratic Executive Committee, and the Georgia Council of Human Relations. She is active in the National and International Association of Probate Judges, the Macedonia Baptist Church, and the NAACP, among other organizations.

CHRISTINE SUMPTION

J

Johnson, Eddie Bernice (1935–)

The representative for the thirtieth congressional district of Texas, Eddie Bernice Johnson knows how to be effective as an outsider. As a black woman in a predominately white male congress, and as a nurse in a sea of lawyers, Johnson has made a career of providing an alternate point of view. She has delivered for her constituents and created controversy doing so.

Born on December 3, 1935 in Waco, Texas, Johnson was the child of Lee Edward and Lillie Mae White Edward. At the time she decided to go to college to become a nurse, no school in Texas would train black nurses. Johnson had to go to St. Mary's College at Notre Dame in South Bend, Indiana, to get her degree. She received her nursing diploma in 1956.

Johnson returned to Texas that same year and married Lacy Kirk Johnson. She became a psychiatric nurse at the Dallas Veterans Administration Hospital, where she worked for sixteen years. In 1967, she received her B.S. in nursing from Texas Christian University. She received her master's degree in Public Administration in 1976 from Southern Methodist University.

In 1972 Johnson decided to stand for election to the Texas House of Representatives. Running as an underdog, she won by a landslide and became the first black woman elected from Dallas.

Johnson served five years in the Texas House, until 1977. At that time President Carter appointed her regional director for the Department of Health, Education, and Welfare. This enabled her to combine her talents in medicine, politics and public administration.

Johnson left her position in 1980, when Ronald Reagan was elected president. She opened Eddie Bernice Johnson and Associates, Inc., a consulting agency that advised companies wishing to expand or relocate in the Dallas area.

In 1986, Johnson won a seat in the Texas state senate. She actively lobbied for economic development, job expansion, health care, education, racial equity, and public housing. Her legislation included bills to prohibit discrimination and improve medical access for AIDS patients, and a bill to put teeth into housing discrimination laws. In 1988 her consulting company expanded to manage concessions at the Dallas-Ft. Worth airport.

One of Johnson's most controversial assignments came after the 1990 census awarded Texas three additional districts for the U.S. Congress. Voting rights legislation in 1965 and 1982 allowed the re-drawing of voting districts to create minority blocs. Johnson chaired the reapportionment committee for Texas, and drew the boundaries for what was to become her own thirtieth district. This proved so controversial that *Texas Monthly* magazine named Johnson one of the state's ten worst legislators.

Eddie Bernice Johnson had a successful six-teen-year career as a psychiatric nurse before she ran for public office. She has served in the Texas House of Representatives, the Texas Senate, and in 1992, she won a seat in the U.S. Congress. (OFFICE OF CONGRESS-WOMAN JOHNSON)

After the thirtieth Texas district was created, Johnson ran in it in 1992 and won a seat to Congress—the only registered nurse in the House or the Senate. She became the Congressional Black Caucus whip and won appointments to the Public Works and Transportation Committee and the Science, Space and Technology Committee. In the close vote over NAFTA, which was controversial for its likelihood of costing American jobs, Johnson came under fire once again. She was accused of trading a vote for NAFTA for promises of two expensive

projects being built in her district. Johnson denied the charges.

Committed to creating a positive economic and civic climate in her district, Johnson has been willing to fight for what she believes in.

ANDRA MEDEA

Johnson, Norma Holloway
(1932–)

President Jimmy Carter appointed Louisiana native Norma Holloway Johnson to the U.S. District Court for the District of Columbia in March 1980. When the Senate confirmed her appointment that July, she became the first black woman to be appointed to the federal bench in the District of Columbia. In addition to presiding over trials, Holloway has served on two judicial conferences and assisted committees concerned with judicial management.

After graduating from Miner Teachers College in 1955, and inspired by the 1954 U.S. Supreme Court decision in *Brown v. Board of Education*, Johnson decided against a career in dentistry and chose instead to enter the Georgetown University Law Center. Motivated by a passion to pursue legal equality for African Americans, her initial goal was to become an attorney for the legal defense fund of the **National Association for the Advancement of Colored People** (NAACP).

After becoming the first black woman to graduate from Georgetown's law school in 1962, Johnson became a trial attorney in the civil division of the U.S. Department of Justice, where she served until 1967. She then went to the Office of the Corporation Counsel for the District of Columbia, where she eventually became chief of the juvenile division. In 1970, President Richard Nixon asked her to accept a judgeship on what would become the Superior Court for the District of Columbia. She served in that court until her appointment to the federal bench.

Norma Johnson has played numerous roles other than that of federal judge. She is a founding member of the National Association of Black Women Attorneys and the National Association of Women Judges, and she is active in many professional and public interest organizations. Juvenile justice continues to be a major concern, and she spends much of her spare time attempting to reform the juvenile justice system.

PHILIP A. PRESBY

Jones, Elaine R.   (1944–)

In 1993, attorney Elaine R. Jones became the first woman to hold the position of Director-Counsel of the NAACP Legal Defense and Educational Fund, Inc. This is the job and the organization made famous by Thurgood Marshall and his team (including **Constance Baker Motley**) when they argued such cases as *Brown* v. *Board of Education* before the Supreme Court.

Jones was born on March 2, 1944, in Norfolk, Virginia. Her father was a Pullman porter, her mother a teacher. In 1970, she became the first black woman to graduate from the University of Virginia School of Law. After graduation, Jones joined the NAACP Legal Defense and Educational Fund, Inc., where she argued death penalty cases throughout the South. She won a landmark Supreme Court case abolishing the death penalty in thirty-seven states. In 1973, Jones became managing attorney in

the New York office. From 1975 to 1977, she took a brief leave to work as a special assistant to the U.S. Secretary of Transportation. There she worked to open the Coast Guard to women.

In 1977, she rejoined the fund as head of its new office in Washington, D.C., and in 1988 she became director-counsel. In that capacity, she supervised the many lawyers who donate their services to the LDF, and monitored federal judicial appointments and civil rights initiatives of the House and Senate Judiciary Committees.

The first African American ever elected to the board of the American Bar Association (1989), Jones is a member of numer-

Elaine R. Jones is the first woman to be director-counsel of the NAACP Legal Defense and Educational Fund, Inc. (OFFICE OF ELAINE JONES)

ous professional associations, including the National Bar Association and the International Federation of Women Lawyers. Jones has been honored by the National Association of Black Women Attorneys, as well as the Black American Law Students Association. She is a member of the **Delta Sigma Sorority.**

In her position as director-counsel of the LDF, Jones manages a staff of approximately thirty lawyers, a $9 million budget and a docket of close to 300 cases. When she talks about how she sees her "job" in relation to the black community, Jones speaks with passionate conviction: "We are a wonderful, competent, vibrant people. All we need is opportunity. I want my life to help create that opportunity. I'm not the social worker. I'm not the parole officer. What I do is understand the operation of the law and how it helps to limit legitimate, lawful opportunities for black people. My job is to break down those barriers."

KATHLEEN THOMPSON

Jones, Star (1962–)

First a winning prosecuting attorney and now a television legal correspondent with a program of her own, Star Jones has made her own career on her own terms. Her sharp intelligence, quick rapport, and sense of humor have served her well in the courtroom and on the airwaves.

Starlet Marie Jones was born in 1962 and raised by her grandparents for her first six years, in Bodin, North Carolina. Her mother, Shirley Byard, was in New Jersey, earning her college degree. Jones got the idea of becoming a lawyer from her grandmother's soap operas. Her grandmother always would say about a particular char-

acter, "That child needs a lawyer." Jones decided to become one. While other little girls were pretending to sing rock and roll, Jones was pretending to sum up before the jury.

Once Jones' mother completed school and settled in a housing project, she sent for her two daughters, Starlet and Sheila. Jones' mother eventually became a human services administrator for the City of Trenton. Later she married Jones' stepfather, James Byard.

Jones and her sister attended parochial schools in New Jersey. In 1979, Jones enrolled at American University, paying her tuition by working clerical jobs and taking out student loans. She received her law degree in 1986 from the University of Houston Law Center. She promptly joined the Kings County District Attorney's office in Brooklyn. She wanted to be a prosecutor in New York because it had one of the highest crime rates in the country. Jones was assigned to the demanding General Trial and Homicides Bureaus. In 1991, she was promoted to senior assistant district attorney.

While a prosecutor in Brooklyn, Jones racked up an outstanding record. In her last two years as prosecutor, she tried forty homicide cases and received thirty-eight convictions. Some of these cases were high-profile, politically sensitive cases. One such was the 1991 "Crown Heights" case, in which a Hasidic Jew was accused of driving a car that killed one black child and injured another, touching off a serious racial incident. In another case, Jones got a long prison term for a sex offender who had escaped conviction four times previously.

While she was prosecuting in Brooklyn, a colleague turned down a chance to do legal commentary for *Court TV,* a cable series. Instead, the colleague recommended Jones. Jones' insightful commentary caught the attention of NBC's *Today* show. When she first received the call from NBC, Jones hung up. She thought it was a prank call. They called back and persuaded her to become NBC's legal correspondent.

In 1994, Jones began her own half-hour TV show, *Jones & Jury.* She and the audience question actual people from the California small-claims courts. The audience votes on the cases, but Jones makes the final decision, which the plaintiff and defendant have legally agreed to abide by. As part owner of the show, Jones is not just talent, but one of the day-to-day decision makers.

Jones has maintained her sense of humor in the face of fame and fortune. Back in Brooklyn, a judge asked her if she would know him after she became famous. Jones replied, "Well, Your Honor, I already think that I'm a grand diva, so what in the world could this do to me?"

ANDRA MEDEA

Jordan, Barbara Charline
(1936–1996)

I felt somehow for many years that George Washington and Alexander Hamilton just left me out by mistake . . . But through the process of amendment, interpretation and court decision, I have finally been included in 'We, the people.' . . . My faith in the Constitution is whole, it is complete, it is total, and I am not going to sit here and be an idle spectator to the diminution, the subversion, the destruction of the Constitution.

Congresswoman Barbara Jordan,
July 25, 1974

Congresswoman Barbara Jordan is pictured here in 1972 on learning that she had won her first election to the U.S. House of Representatives. She was the first black and the first woman ever elected to Congress from Texas. (SCHOMBURG CENTER)

Barbara Jordan's speech at the Watergate hearings in her now legendary rich and impassioned voice mesmerized the nation. And, her faith in the Constitution was complete. Her students recall that she was never without a copy of it in her purse. Representative Charles B. Rangel, the Manhattan Democrat who served with Jordan during the impeachment hearings said: "You know, Barbara wasn't really concerned about the guilt or innocence of Nixon. She was most concerned that the Constitution not be distorted for political reasons."

The youngest of three sisters, Barbara Charline Jordan was born on February 21, 1936, in Houston, Texas, to a black Baptist minister, Benjamin Jordan, and a domestic worker, Arlyne Jordan. Barbara attended Roberson Elementary and Phyllis Wheatley High School. While at Wheatley, she was a member of the Honor Society and excelled in debating, and she graduated in 1952 in the top five percent of her class. In 1956, she graduated magna cum laude from Texas Southern University with a double major in political science and history. As leader of the debating team, Jordan later proudly recalled maneuvering the Harvard team to a draw. "When an all-black team ties Harvard, it wins," she declared.

She earned her J.D. from Boston University in 1959 and returned to Houston to set up a private law practice.

Barbara Jordan's interest in politics was solidified in 1965 when she received her first public appointment as administrative assistant to the county judge of Harris County. Following this appointment she was elected to the Texas State Senate in 1966, the first black Texan to serve in that august body since 1883.

Her record in the Texas State Senate was remarkable. On March 21, 1967, she became the first black elected official to preside over that body; she also was the first black state senator to chair a major committee, Labor and Management Relations, and the first freshman senator ever named to the Texas Legislative Council. When the Texas Legislature convened in special session in March 1972, Senator Jordan was unanimously elected president pro tempore. In June of that year, she was honored by being named Governor for a Day.

Shortly thereafter, she decided to run for Congress and was elected, in November 1972, from Houston's eighteenth congressional district. She was the first black and the first woman elected to Congress from Texas.

Both as a state senator and as a congresswoman, Jordan sponsored bills that championed the cause of poor, black, and disadvantaged people. One of her most important bills as a senator was the Workman's Compensation Act, which increased the maximum benefits paid to injured workers. As a congresswoman she sponsored legislation to broaden the Voting Rights Act of 1965 to cover Mexican Americans in Texas and other southwestern states and to extend its authority to those states where minorities had been denied the right to vote or had had their rights restricted by unfair registration practices, such as literacy tests.

In 1976 she was the first black woman to deliver a keynote address at the Democratic National Convention, riveting both the delegates and the national television audience as she spoke magisterially from the stage at New York's Madison Square Garden:

One hundred and forty-four years ago, members of the Democratic Party first met in convention to select a Presidential candidate. Since that time, Democrats have continued to convene once every four years and draft a party platform and nominate a Presidential candidate. And our meeting this week is a continuation of that tradition.

But there is something different about tonight. There is something special about tonight. What is different? What is special? I, Barbara Jordan, am a keynote speaker.

A lot of years have passed since 1832, and during that time it would have been most unusual for any national political party to ask that Barbara Jordan deliver a keynote address, but tonight here I am. And I feel notwithstanding the past that my presence here is one additional bit of evidence that the American Dream need not forever be deferred.

Along with, and because of, her political accomplishments, Jordan received numerous honorary doctorate degrees. She was named the Democratic Woman of the Year by the Women's National Democratic Club. *Ladies' Home Journal* picked her as 1975 Woman of the Year in Politics. *Time* magazine recognized her that same year as one of its ten women of the year, and a poll conducted by *Redbook* (1979) magazine selected Jordan as one of the top women who could be president.

Barbara Jordan retired from public office in 1978 and gave her congressional papers and memorabilia to her alma mater, Texas Southern University. She taught political ethics at the University of Texas' Lyndon B. Johnson School of Public Affairs. She died on January 17, 1996. Afflicted with multiple sclerosis, Jordan died from viral pneumonia as a complication of leukemia.

In her acceptance speech in 1992 to the NAACP Convention when she received their seventy-seventh Spingarn Medal she summed up her dedication and that of the organization. "For more than 77 years we have been trying to get this country right, and it is still not right. But we are not going to stop!"

MERLINE PITRE

K

Kearse, Amalya Lyle (1937–)

The first woman judge of the federal appeals court in Manhattan, Amalya Lyle Kearse is known for her astute legal mind capable of unraveling complex judicial and financial issues. From her post in Manhattan Kearse not only writes opinions on issues pertaining to the rights of individuals, she also writes opinions on corporations that make a difference in millions—if not billions—of dollars.

Born on June 11, 1937, in Vauxhall, New Jersey, Kearse is the daughter of Myra Lyle Smith Kearse and Robert Freeman Kearse. Her mother was in medicine, and later worked for the government in the war against poverty. Her father was a postmaster, who had always wanted to practice law.

Kearse went to Wellesley, where she graduated in 1959 with a B.A. in philosophy. She went on to study law at the University of Michigan. While there, she was editor of the school *Law Review,* and was research assistant to legal scholars such as Alan N. Polasky and John W. Reed. She was awarded the Jason L. Honigman prize for her work on the editorial board, and graduated cum laude in 1962.

Kearse returned to the East Coast and went into private practice with the Wall Street law firm of Hughes, Hubbard, and Reed. She was a trial lawyer with the firm from 1962 to 1979. There she became the first black woman to become a partner in a major Wall Street law firm, advancing because of her shrewd analysis of legal matters and extraordinary taste for hard work. Within this same period, from 1968 to 1969, Kearse also taught law classes at the New York University Law School.

In 1979 Kearse was appointed by President Carter to serve on the U.S. Court of Appeals in New York City. This was an excellent use of Kearse's talents. Appellate judges are usually asked to write legal opinions on cases that are on appeal from lower courts. An important judgment on an appeal can have consequences across the country. Considering cases on appeal requires a judge with outstanding analytic skills and clear, precise writing. These were not only skills Kearse possessed, these were talents she enjoyed using.

Kearse was involved in a number of far-reaching cases. She was on the appeals court that decided to allow television stations to broadcast the Abscam tapes. Using her corporate background, she gave the decision on a tax dispute with RCA Corporation that resulted in their paying an additional five million dollars in taxes, and affected similar corporations across America. In all, Kearse has written hundreds of decisions on a wide range of issues, maintaining her workload by regularly putting in 100-hour workweeks. In 1994 her name was fielded by President Clinton as a possible candidate for the Supreme Court.

Kearse also found time for organizations apart from her work in court. From 1970 to 1979 she was on the executive committee of the Lawyers Committee for Civil Rights under Law. From 1977 to 1979 she was on the board of directors of NAACP's Legal Defense and Educational Fund, Inc., and from 1978 to 1979 she was on the board of the National Urban League.

Aside from Kearse's legal ability, she is also known as an expert bridge player. She has written several books on bridge, including *Bridge Conventions Complete* and *Bridge at Your Fingertips,* and edited the *Official Encyclopedia of Bridge.* She won two major national championships in the early 1970s, and in 1986 was part of the team that won the Women's Pair Championships, a world-class bridge event. Clearly her talent for analysis has made its mark in her hobby as well as her profession.

ANDRA MEDEA

Kelly, Sharon Pratt Dixon (1944–)

The first black woman mayor of Washington, D.C., Sharon Pratt Kelly admires Franklin Delano Roosevelt and Martin Luther King, Jr., for their power to shape public policy. A resolute and optimistic newcomer to political office, Kelly is charged by her firm belief in the possibility of creating a more caring and responsible society.

She was born in Washington, D.C., on January 30, 1944, the oldest child of Carlisle and Mildred Pratt. Following her mother's death when Sharon was four, she and her younger sister, Benaree, moved in with their paternal grandmother and aunt. Her father, a former Washington, D.C.,

The first Washington, D.C., native as well as the first woman to be elected mayor of the nation's capital, Sharon Pratt Kelly promised voters that, if elected, she would "clean house with a shovel, not a broom." (MOORLAND-SPINGARN)

superior court judge, proved to be an important influence in her childhood: when she was still a girl he gave her a copy of *Black's Law Dictionary* as a birthday present. Sharon Pratt attended Gage and Rudolph elementary schools, MacFarland Junior High School, and Roosevelt High School. In 1965, she graduated from **Howard University** with a B.A. in political science and went on to the Howard University School of Law, receiving a J.D. in 1968. While in law school, she married Arrington Dixon, with whom she had two daughters,

Aimee Arrington Dixon, who was born in 1968, and Drew Arrington Dixon, who was born in 1970. The couple divorced in 1982. Sharon Pratt Kelly married James Kelly III, in late 1991.

Kelly began her legal career in 1970 as house counsel for the Joint Center for Political Studies in Washington, D.C. In 1971, she became an associate with the Pratt and Queen legal firm and a year later joined the faculty of Antioch School of Law. She held both positions until 1976, when she became employed by the general counsel's office at Potomac Electric Power Company (PEPCO). In 1979, PEPCO appointed Kelly director of consumer affairs and then, in 1983, vice president of consumer affairs. She was both the first black person and the first woman to be named to that position. In 1986, Kelly became vice president of public policy for the company, and in that capacity she worked to develop programs to assist low-income and senior citizens.

Sharon Pratt Kelly has a long record of involvement in many different organizations. Between 1985 and 1989, she was the first woman to serve as national treasurer of the Democratic Party. She served as Democratic national committeewoman from the District of Columbia from 1977 to 1980 and was vice chairperson of the District of Columbia Law Revision Committee from 1970 to 1971. She has been a member of the National Women's Political Caucus and the American Bar Association. Her other affiliations include the Legal Aid Society, the American Civil Liberties Union (ACLU), and the United Negro College Fund. Kelly also is a member of Holy Comforter Church. She is a recipient of the Falk Fellowship, Howard University, 1962–65;

the Federation of Women's Club's Distinguished Service Award, 1986; and the Presidential Award from the NAACP, 1983.

In 1990, she stepped down from her vice presidency with PEPCO in order to make a long-shot bid for the office of mayor of Washington, D.C. An outsider in the field of politics, Dixon ran for office promising "I'll clean house with a shovel, not a broom," a statement that reflected both her concern about the city's cumbersome and ineffectual administration and the enormous social and economic problems affecting its citizens. Kelly's election on November 6, 1990, was not only a triumphant win for a contender with less money and a smaller staff than any of her four rivals, it also resulted in two historic firsts: she became the first Washington, D.C., native as well as the first woman to be elected mayor of the nation's capital.

FENELLA MACFARLANE

Kidd, Mae Street (19??–)

Even though Mae Street Kidd was very active in Louisville and civic affairs, she had no real interest in elective politics until she was drafted by the Democratic Party to run for the Kentucky legislature in 1967. Once seated in the Kentucky House of Representatives, she candidly affirmed that she was there to get all she could for her constituents. Serving on the banking and insurance and the cities and rules committees, and as vice chair of the elections and constitutional amendments committee, Kidd sponsored or co-sponsored bills on women's rights, collective bargaining for public employees, education, welfare, age discrimination, civil rights, law and order, and housing. Two housing bills bear her name; one provided for open housing, the other for low-cost housing.

Born in Bourbon County, Kentucky, and educated at Lincoln Institute of Kentucky at Lincoln Ridge, Kidd served as assistant club director for the American Red Cross in Europe during World War II. After the war she became a public relations consultant and businesswoman. She is married to J. Meredith Kidd III. She is a vibrant activist in the Plymouth Congregational Church; a member of Iota Phi Lambda Sorority, the Urban League, and the **Young Women's Christian Association** (YWCA); and a recipient of the Louisville Kennedy-King Award (1968). She retired in 1984 and devotes her time to local civic matters.

JEWEL LIMAR PRESTAGE

L

Lafontant-Mankarious, Jewel Stradford (1922–)

"Well, I don't know about this tokenism. People say to your face, 'They selected you because you are a twofer.' It means two for one—a black and a woman—and I laugh about it. But they are serious. I can't look into the person's mind, why they selected me. All I can say is, 'thank you.' It is up to me to turn tokenism into something real." Jewel Lafontant-Mankarious has not only turned her opportunities into something real, she has opened the doors for others to follow behind. Lafontant-Mankarious' career in law, business, and government has been marked by firsts. She has not only broken through barriers of race and sex, she has worked within the system to attempt positive change for minorities and women.

Jewel Stradford Lafontant-Mankarious was born on April 28, 1922 in Chicago, Illinois, to Cornelius Francis and Aida Carter Stradford. Jewel was born into a family of successful lawyers and businessmen. Her grandfather and father were both **Oberlin College** graduates, attorneys, and active in Republican politics. She continued the family tradition when she received a B.A. from Oberlin College in 1943 and a J.D. from the University of Chicago in 1946. While in law school, Jewel Stradford was one of the founding members of the Congress of Racial Equality (CORE). She also participated in sit-ins during the early 1940s.

Jewel Stradford began her career after admission to the Illinois state bar in 1947 as the first black trial attorney for the Legal Aid Bureau of the United Charities of Chicago (1947–53), where she worked on a volunteer basis. She also worked in the law firm of Rogers, Rogers, and Strayhorn, the firm of her husband John Rogers, from 1952 to 1954, and served as precinct captain for the sixth ward of Chicago. President Dwight D. Eisenhower appointed her Assistant U.S. Attorney for the North District of Illinois, where she served from 1955 to 1958. She left her appointment after the birth of her son, John Rogers, Jr., and practiced with her father's firm. Married to Ernest Lafontant in 1961, they opened a law office and she practiced there until 1983. Ernest Lafontant died in 1976. Jewel Lafontant was a senior partner in the law firm of Vedder, Price, Kaufman, Kammholz, and Day from 1983 to 1989, where she practiced corporate and labor law.

In addition to her legal career, Lafontant-Mankarious, a lifelong Republican, seconded the nomination of Richard M. Nixon for president in 1960 as an alternate delegate to the Republican National Convention. She served as U.S. representative to the United Nations from September 1972 to December 1972. President Nixon also appointed her to the position of Deputy Solicitor General of the United States in 1973, the first female and the first black to hold this position. As Deputy Solicitor

120

General, she was chairperson of federal women's programs for the Department of Justice. She served as Deputy Solicitor General from February 1973 to June 1975.

In 1968, Lafontant-Mankarious was elected to the board of directors of Jewel Foods. Prior to her appointment as an ambassador, she served as a corporate director of seventeen major corporations. She used her influence on these boards not only to provide leadership to the corporations but also to increase minority hiring, among other concerns.

Lafontant-Mankarious served as commissioner of the Martin Luther King, Jr., Federal Holiday Commission and chair of the Illinois Advisory Committee to the U.S. Civil Rights Commission. In recognition of her professional achievements and civic service, she has received numerous awards including awards from OICs of America (Opportunities Industrialization Centers), the National Coalition of Black Women, and PUSH (People United to Save Humanity). She is also the recipient of honorary degrees from fourteen universities including **Howard University,** Providence College, Loyola University, and the University of Chicago.

Lafontant-Mankarious served as Ambassador at Large and United States Coordinator for Refugee Affairs, beginning in 1989. She was responsible to the President for the development of overall U.S. refugee assistance, admission, and resettlement policy. She also negotiated on behalf of the United States with foreign governments and international organizations concerning refugee affairs.

Lafontant-Mankarious is married to Naguib S. Mankarious, an international business consultant. Her son, John W. Rogers, Jr., is president and chief executive officer of Ariel Capital Management. She is currently a partner in the Chicago-based law firm of Holleb & Coff.

SONYA RAMSEY

Lawson, Marjorie McKenzie
(1912–)

Marjorie McKenzie Lawson was the nation's first black woman judge appointed by a president. For her it was a peak in a career that included civil rights activism, journalism, and a law firm partnership with husband Belford V. Lawson, Jr.

Lawson was born on March 2, 1912, in Pittsburgh, Pennsylvania. Her father, T. Wallace McKenzie, died when she was five. Reared by her mother, Gertrude Stiver McKenzie, she was the only black child in the Pittsburgh grammar and high school classes she attended. She graduated from the University of Michigan in Ann Arbor with a B.A. in sociology in 1933 and there earned, the next year, a social work certificate. She moved to Washington, D.C., took night classes at Terrell Law School and received a law degree, in 1939. In that same year she married Lawson and passed the District of Columbia bar exams. Career circumstances would cause her to seek a second law degree, which she earned in 1950 from New York's Columbia University School of Law.

From the Washington office of Lawson and Lawson she specialized in administrative law while her husband handled civil rights cases. Her service in the firm ended only with the Kennedy appointment. In addition, she worked in the Roosevelt and Truman administrations from 1943 to

1946 as assistant director, then director, of the Division of Review and Analysis of the President's Commission on Fair Employment Practices. In 1950, the Lawsons' victory in the Supreme Court case, *Henderson v. United States*, abolished segregation in train dining cars.

More and more concerned to improve black community conditions, Marjorie Lawson wrote for over fifteen years a *Pittsburgh Courier* column mainly covering federal policies toward African Americans. She was vice-president, and later general counsel, of the **National Council of Negro Women** from 1952 to 1954 and assisted the council's planning of Bethune House. With D.C. Congressman Walter Fauntroy she founded the Model Inner City Community Organization in 1966.

From 1956 on, Lawson and her husband advised Kennedy on civil rights and helped him enlist the support of influential blacks in his bid for the presidency. An active Kennedy campaigner, she became a key member of the inaugural committee. In 1962, Kennedy named her both juvenile court judge and a member of his Committee on Equal Employment Opportunity.

She left the judgeship in 1965, but President Lyndon B. Johnson immediately appointed her to represent the United States on the Social Commission of the United Nations Economic and Social Council. She served on several federal and city commissions and task forces relating to housing, crime, and urban renewal throughout and beyond the Johnson Administration. She later joined the boards of the National Bank of Washington and the Madison National Bank.

Lawson credits much of her career's success to the support of her husband, who died in 1985. They had one son, Belford Lawson III.

GARY HOUSTON

Lee, Sheila Jackson (1950–)

Elected representative to the United States Congress from Houston in 1994, Sheila Jackson Lee was then promptly elected president of the Democratic freshman class.

When Representative Sheila Jackson Lee was elected to the U.S. Congress from the eighteenth congressional district in Houston, Texas, she stepped into the shoes of several famous predecessors. The seat was first held by the great orator Barbara Jordan, then by Mickey Leland, who was killed in a plane crash while investigating famine in Ethiopia. (OFFICE OF CONGRESSWOMAN LEE)

A champion for minority rights at a time when affirmative action is under siege, Jackson Lee is not afraid to stand for something—even if that something does not happen to be fashionable that year.

A native of Queens, New York, Jackson Lee acquired a distinguished academic background before moving into politics. She majored in political science at Yale University, graduating from their honors program. She went on to receive her law degree from the University of Virginia School of Law in Charlottesville, Virginia.

Before she entered politics, Jackson Lee was an active member of the state bar of Texas, eventually serving as director of the state bar. She was also former director of the Texas Young Lawyer's Association, chairing its minority affairs committee.

In time, Jackson Lee became an associate municipal judge for the city of Houston, before becoming a member of the Houston city council. She was one of the first African-American woman at-large council members in the city of Houston. While a council member, Jackson Lee was primarily concerned with issues of human rights. She was particularly concerned with the problem of homelessness, and gun safety and responsibility. Since Houston is a major center of the aerospace industry, Jackson Lee was also involved with aviation and economic redevelopment.

Jackson Lee was elected to the United States Congress from the eighteenth congressional district in Houston, which was created by the 1965 Voting Rights Act. This has been historically a black district and has been the home of several distinguished black representatives.

The district was first represented by **Barbara Jordan,** the gifted orator who served on the committee that investigated President Nixon's involvement with the Watergate scandal, which led to his resignation. After Jordan came Mickey Leland, whose concern for world hunger cost him his life in a plane crash while he was investigating famine in Ethiopia. The seat then was won by Craig Washington, who was a powerful contender for the chairmanship of the Congressional Black Caucus. Jackson Lee unseated Washington in a fierce battle.

Jackson Lee's notable win against Washington caught the attention of the national press and media, as well as President Clinton and the head of the Republican opposition, Newt Gingrich. Marked as a promising newcomer, she was not only chosen to head the Democratic freshman class, but was the only freshman member named to the influential steering and policy committee. Jackson Lee also serves on the crime subcommittee of the committee on the judiciary and on the subcommittee on space and aeronautics, within the committee on science. She is also a member of the House Democratic Caucus task force on hunger and the Human Rights Caucus.

Jackson Lee is married to Dr. Elwyn C. Lee, who is vice president of student affairs and special assistant to the president of the University of Houston.

As a fresh Democratic representative, Jackson Lee is looking forward to pressing the agenda on affirmative action and welfare reform. She is not daunted by the conservative majority in Congress. As she says, "I'm more than happy to listen and to learn from those who have been there. But I'm also willing to stand for what I believe in."

ANDRA MEDEA

M

McKinney, Cynthia (1955–)

The young black woman with the gold sneakers, slacks, braided hair and Mickey Mouse watch stepped into the elevator in the Capitol.

"This elevator is for members only," the elevator operator said frostily.

"Yes, thank you," Cynthia McKinney replied, her glittering shoes planted firmly in place.

"This elevator is for members only," the women running the elevator repeated, even more coldly.

"Yes, thank you," Ms. McKinney said, even more insistently.

"This elevator is for members only," the operator tried once more, before finally spotting the blue pin with the Congressional seal, worn by members, hanging on a gold chain around Ms. McKinney's neck.

"The elevator lady was very apologetic, and I told her that it's wonderful now that members of Congress come in all shapes and hues," the freshman Representative from Georgia said, recalling the recent standoff.

The New York Times, March 5, 1993

She was one of the stars of the freshman Congressional legislators of 1993. The representative for the eleventh congressional district of Georgia, Cynthia McKinney got her seat from voter reform, and got her style from her father, an activist politician. Fiery, articulate, intelligent, and game, Mc-

Kinney is one of the bloc of black women who are challenging the power structure on Capitol Hill. She is also the first Congressperson ever seen to wear gold tennis shoes on the floor of the House.

Born on March 17, 1955, in Atlanta, McKinney is the daughter of Leola McKinney and J. E. "Billy" McKinney. Her mother was a nurse and homemaker. Her father was a man who knew how to take on the system. He came back as a G.I. from World War II and got thrown in jail for refusing to use segregated drinking fountains. In 1948, he became one of the first black police officers in Atlanta. In his spare time he picketed the force for its racist practices.

Young McKinney was sent to Catholic schools, where she challenged a nun over racist language in class. She got in trouble when the authorities didn't believe her, so she secretly tape-recorded the sister's words to prove her point.

As the civil rights movement gained force, Billy McKinney took his little daughter along to demonstrations. This worried her mother but it formed the basis for McKinney's political education.

McKinney attended the University of Southern California, majoring in international relations. Southern California culture did not suit her, but her mother made her stick it out until she got her degree in 1978. The next year she joined her father at a demonstration in Alabama, where she encountered armed Klansmen in full cos-

Probably the first person to wear gold tennis shoes on the floor of the U.S. House of Representatives, Cynthia McKinney has made a name for herself as a fiery and fearless congressperson. She was responsible for introducing the Motor Voter bill, which would register people to vote when they apply for their driver's licenses. (OFFICE OF CONGRESSWOMAN MCKINNEY)

tume. There was a violent confrontation, and the National Guard had to be called in. The experience changed McKinney. "That was probably my day of awakening. That day I experienced hatred for the first time. I learned that there really are people who hate me without even knowing me. . . . Prior to that day, everything was theory. On that day, I saw fact."

McKinney's father went on to be elected to the Georgia state legislature, where he became a pivotal figure in black politics.

Meanwhile, McKinney entered a doctoral program in international relations.

McKinney married a Jamaican and was living in Jamaica when her father entered her name as a candidate for state representative in 1986. Neither one of them expected her to get elected. Says Billy McKinney, "I got mad with one of my colleagues and told her, 'I'm going to put you out of office.' I registered Cynthia."

McKinney thought he was kidding. She didn't campaign and she still picked up 20 percent of the vote. That's when she learned how ripe the district was for an outspoken black leader. In 1988, she ran in earnest and won a seat in the Georgia state legislature. She served in the legislature from 1989 to 1992, when she was elected to Congress.

McKinney got her seat in Congress when the eleventh Georgian congressional district was redrawn according to the Voting Rights Act of 1982. This allowed for the creation of a black majority district, even though the boundaries stretch from the eastern suburbs of Atlanta, to Augusta across rural Georgia and down to coastal Savannah. McKinney won with a 75 percent landslide.

McKinney was a Congresswoman unlike any they had seen before in Washington. Her hair is parted down the middle and set in neat braids. She wears bright, flowing outfits, and the trademark gold tennis shoes. She insists she now has to wear the shoes, "otherwise people are so disappointed."

The shape of the district proved to be both a blessing and a curse. The extensive boundaries gave McKinney a district where she could run for Congress and win, showing just how well she could perform in

Congress. But the district was challenged on the grounds that the voters had little in common but race. The new district boundaries were eventually overturned by a Supreme Court ruling.

In fact, there were many issues about the curious district that made for difficulties, aside from the usual racial politics. Her largely urban following was matched by rural constituents, who did not especially want to be represented by someone from the city. Fellow Democrats resisted the redistricting because it took black voters away from other districts where they were critical swing voters. However, even with the boundaries redrawn once again, McKinney is still expected to succeed. A political analyst predicts, "You can cut big chunks out of her district and she wins again." However, the lengthy fight over boundaries required a great deal of attention during her freshman term.

McKinney also challenged some of the powers that reside in her congressional district. Her extensive district includes mines of kaolin, a white clay that is used in toothpaste and medicines. She is an environmentalist and member of the Sierra Club, and she has asked the Department of Justice to investigate possible antitrust violations in the industry. The kaolin industry was believed to be essential in helping to overturn her district.

McKinney has taken a number of spirited stands. When it appeared that the federal government might shut down due to political fighting over the budget, McKinney joined a handful of representatives who insisted that Congress do without their paychecks if other federal employees could not be paid. She introduced legislation that would call for a "Code of Conduct" that would restrict arms sales to dictators. She also introduced the Motor Voter bill, which would register people to vote when they applied for their driver's licenses.

As a member of the new generation of black politicians, she is even willing to battle with her father, as a member of the previous generation of black politicians. They vehemently disagree on gay issues (she is for them, he against), and she scolds him for making deals with conservatives. They both seem to delight in the arguments, but there is no mistaking that Billy McKinney is very proud of his daughter.

McKinney is proving to be part of the force that is making a conservative Congress re-think its ways. From an early confrontation with powerful Henry Hyde, the black women's bloc has made its presence felt.

"It's been said that they (white Congressmen) just don't know how to deal with black women, and that's probably true. Because they've never been dressed down the way we're prepared to dress them down. . . . Perhaps before the Hyde fight we were viewed with some novelty. But when they saw the black women so united, they saw the white women rally with us, they saw black men *daring* them to touch us, it was like, 'Wow, we have a new dynamic here that we have to contend with.' "

After the Supreme Court ruled in 1995 that race could not be used as a predominant factor in designing legislative districts, McKinney's district was redrawn, with the black voting age population going from 60 percent of the total to only 33 percent. McKinney won the July 1996 primary in this newly drawn district against three white challengers, receiving a remarkable 67 percent of the votes. In the general election of 1996 she defeated her Republican challenger.

ANDRA MEDEA

Meek, Carrie (1926–)

Granddaughter of a slave, Carrie P. Meek became the first African American to be elected to the U.S. Congress from her native state of Florida since Reconstruction, in 1992.

Herself the mother of three children, Meek was born in Tallahassee in 1926. She received her bachelor's degree in biology and physical education from Florida A&M University in 1946 and her master's in public health and physical education from the University of Michigan in 1948.

Meek coached women's basketball at **Bethune-Cookman College** in Daytona Beach, Florida, while teaching biology and gym. She also taught these classes at Florida A&M. Some time later, she was special assistant to the vice president of Miami-Dade Community College in Miami.

Before being sent to the U.S. House of Representatives from Florida's seventeenth congressional district, Meek had been a member of both the Florida house and, between 1982 and 1992, its senate. As senator from the state's thirty-sixth district, she was responsible for a great deal of the housing finance policy that is in place today in Florida. Two major legislative contributions made home ownership more possible for more people and provided for the construction of some 1,000 more affordable rental units.

During her final term she chaired the education subcommittee of the senate appropriations committee and oversaw a school budget of nearly $10 billion. Her

Judging by her career, Carrie Meek is nothing like what her name suggests. Granddaughter of a slave, in 1992 Meek became the first African American to be elected to the U.S. Congress from Florida since Reconstruction. Among her many accomplishments was the acquistion of more than $100 million in federal assistance to Florida's Dade County in the devastating wake of Hurricane Andrew. (OFFICE OF CONGRESSWOMAN MEEK)

decisions impacted statewide education from kindergarten to the graduate school level.

In the U.S. House she quickly attracted attention as the only Democrat in her incoming congressional class to be put on the House's powerful Appropriations Committee. She has since sat on its Budget and Government Reform and Oversight Committees and on the latter's subcommittees affecting regulatory affairs, economic growth and the postal service.

Within a short time, Meek has championed federal programs for job creation and retirement security for household workers. Through her initiatives, business parties from her district gained access to key government contracting and trade officials. But perhaps her most visible achievement for her state was the acquisition of more than $100 million of federal assistance to Dade County in the wake of Hurricane Andrew's devastation there. This included the rebuilding of such former facilities as the Homestead Air Reserve Base and the building of various new ones, such as a family and child care center.

Her drives in both state and nation to create jobs and affordable housing, assist senior citizens, erase gender and race discrimination, and enhance the quality of life of all citizens have given Carrie Meek a solid reputation as legislator and social activist.

GARY HOUSTON

Mitchell, Juanita Jackson
(1913–1992)

Juanita E. Jackson Mitchell was the first national youth director of the **National Association for the Advancement of Colored People** (NAACP) and, later, the first African-American woman to be admitted to practice law in Maryland. Although these distinctions significantly marked her transition from one career to another, Mitchell's prominence is primarily a conse-

quence of her civil rights advocacy for more than half a century.

Juanita E. Jackson was born in Hot Springs, Arkansas, on January 2, 1913, to Lillie M. Carroll Jackson, a schoolteacher, and Keiffer Albert Jackson, a traveling promoter and exhibitor of religious films. With the exception of occasions when the family traveled with Keiffer Jackson on business, Jackson was raised in Baltimore with her two sisters and her brother, Virginia, Marion, and Bowen Keiffer. Jackson graduated from the Frederick Douglass High School with honors in 1927. For two years she attended Morgan State College in Baltimore but then transferred to the University of Pennsylvania in Philadelphia; she graduated in 1931 with a B.S. in education. Racial consciousness nurtured by her parents and her sorority, **Alpha Kappa Alpha,** and her leadership in the interracial national Methodist youth movement motivated her to return home during the Great Depression to try to improve conditions for African Americans in Baltimore.

Jackson saw the crises of the economic depression—massive unemployment, racial segregation, other forms of racist discrimination, and continued lynching—as challenges. Implementing her idea to hold a forum to address such challenges, Jackson, along with Lincoln University (Pennsylvania) graduate and friend Clarence M. Mitchell, Jr., and approximately one dozen other African-American youth of high school and college ages, founded the City-Wide Young People's Forum of Baltimore. As its first president, Jackson collaboratively developed programs and projects with other officers, older advisers, and many of Baltimore's African-American citizens. The forum held well-attended weekly public meetings featuring black leaders and prominent educators. The forum also sponsored antilynching petition drives and various demonstrations and employment campaigns for African Americans in Baltimore. Jackson led the forum through 1934, even after she found employment in 1932 as a secondary schoolteacher in the Baltimore public schools. As Jackson had hoped, the forum proved to be a boon to the Baltimore African-American community from 1931 through 1940.

In 1935, having observed the success of Baltimore's forum in mobilizing youth as well as adults, and having been impressed by Jackson's skills, talent, and education (she had earned an M.A. in sociology), Walter White, the executive secretary of the NAACP, invited Jackson to assume the leadership of the NAACP's first nationwide youth program. From 1935 to 1938, headquartered in New York City but traveling throughout the nation, Jackson served as national youth director and special assistant to Walter White. She wrote a constitution, organized youth councils, revived junior NAACP branches, established a national network, and worked with youth primarily on four problems—education, jobs, civil rights, and lynching—doing for youth what **Ella Baker** had done for the NAACP's branches. Support from other women for this youth work came as a result of Jackson's participation with **Mary McLeod Bethune** in the founding conference of the **National Council of Negro Women** (NCNW) and its subsequent activities.

Juanita Jackson's August 1938 marriage to Clarence M. Mitchell, Jr. (then the Na-tional Youth Administration's Maryland director of the Division of Negro Affairs, but later the NAACP's chief lobbyist until 1978), interrupted her employment with the NAACP but did not end either her association with the NAACP or her political activism. As a new wife and mother in the early 1940s, Mitchell coordinated a civil rights march of 2,000 citizens on the state capital, participated in a White House conference on children, and directed the first NAACP citywide voter registration campaign in Baltimore. After giving birth to four sons, Clarence III, Keiffer, Michael, and George, and desiring to be better armed for the civil rights struggle, she decided to change vocations. She studied law at the University of Maryland, served on the *Law Review*'s staff, and earned her law degree by 1950.

When Mitchell became the first African-American woman admitted to practice before the courts of Maryland, she had one objective in mind: to litigate on behalf of African Americans seeking an end to racial discrimination. Her legal achievements were notable throughout the 1950s and 1960s. She was counsel in Maryland litigation initiated in 1950 to eliminate the racial segregation of state and municipal beaches and swimming pools, which she won in November 1955. A Baltimore secondary school desegregation case filed in 1953 and handled successfully by Mitchell resulted in Baltimore becoming the first Southern city to desegregate public schools after *Brown* v. *Board of Education*. During the 1960s she served as counsel for students who had engaged in sit-ins to desegregate Maryland restaurants, in *Robert Mack Bell* v. *Maryland*. On appeal in 1964, the students represented by Mitchell and the NAACP Legal Defense Fund prevailed in the U.S. Supreme Court. Viewing the Baltimore commissioner of police's authorization of mass searches of private homes without warrants, known as the Veney raid, as a particular affront to African-American residents and a gross violation of civil liberties affecting all citizens, Mitchell represented several home owners in proceedings to enjoin further such mass searches. As counsel for the home owners she won the Veney raid cases on appeal from the U.S. District Court for Maryland to the U.S. Court of Appeals, Fourth Circuit, in September 1966.

Although Mitchell devoted considerable time and energy to the firm of Mitchell, Mitchell and Mitchell (both her husband and her son Michael eventually earned law degrees) during the late 1950s through the 1980s, public advocacy of civil rights continued to be a priority. Recognition of Mitchell's particular talents and expertise resulted in her holding several important positions with the NAACP and other organizations. She directed, both in 1957–58 and in 1960, two major voter registration campaigns that placed more than 50,000 new voters on the books. She presided over the Baltimore NAACP branch, later served as the legal redress chairperson of the Maryland state conference, and, in the 1970s, succeeded her mother as president of the state conference of NAACP branches. A life member of NCNW, Jackson also chaired for a time that organization's legal committee.

Juanita Jackson Mitchell slowed her pace after her husband's death in 1984 and her subsequent illness, but she continued to maintain a lively interest in protecting the rights of African Americans, including opposition to official repression of activists and African-American elected officials during the 1980s. Her distinguished careers and activism of more than fifty years have resulted in her being the recipient of such honors as the NCNW's award for Special Distinction in Law, the Outstanding Service Award of the Youth/College Division of the NAACP and the Bicentennial Award of the University of Maryland's Black American Law Students Association. As was her mother, in recognition of achievements as a state citizen and woman, Juanita Jackson Mitchell was inducted into Maryland Women's Hall of Fame in 1985.

On July 7, 1992, at the age of seventy-nine, Juanita Jackson Mitchell, who had been in poor health for some time, succumbed to a heart attack and stroke. Benjamin Hooks, the executive director of the NAACP, praised her as "one of the greatest freedom fighters in the history of Maryland and the nation," and Maryland Governor William Donald Shaefer paid tribute to Mitchell as "an inspiration, a fighter . . . [who] never deviated from her principles." A memorial service attended by many admirers and friends was held at the Sharpe Street Memorial Methodist Episcopal Church, where she had so often met to further civil rights causes and to worship a God in whom she had great faith. Her principal legacy was a life of courageous and consistent struggle for civil rights.

GENNA RAE McNEIL

Morris, Carolyn (1939–)

The highest ranking black woman in the Federal Bureau of Investigation, Carolyn Gatling Morris is the assistant director

As assistant director of the Information Resources Division of the FBI, Carolyn Morris' job is to bring the FBI into the computer age. The highest ranking black woman in FBI history, Morris oversees 2,000 employees and manages a budget of over $200 million. (FEDERAL BUREAU OF INVESTIGATION)

of the Information Resources Division. As crime investigation becomes less hard boiled and more high tech, it is Morris' job to see that the FBI adapts to the twenty-first century.

Born in Jackson, North Carolina, on January 2, 1939, Morris is the daughter of Flora M. Gatling and Joseph Russell Gatling. She attended North Carolina Central University and, in 1960, graduated summa cum laude with a bachelor of science degree in mathematics. She received a full academic scholarship from the Na-

tional Science Foundation in order to attend graduate school at Harvard. She graduated from Harvard with a master of science degree in mathematics in 1963.

After Harvard, Morris went on to do post-graduate work in applied mathematics and later in computer science. She did post-graduate work in statistics at Virginia Tech, then operations research at the University of Michigan. She also worked in the field of artificial intelligence at George Washington University.

In 1980, Morris was hired by the FBI as chief of the Systems Development Section within what was once known as the Technological Services Division. In the old FBI, technological services consisted of basic technologies such as fingerprinting and chemical analysis. However, advances in computers have produced a quantum leap in criminal science and investigation. The FBI needed an information specialist who could design a world-class system.

In 1995, Morris was appointed assistant director in charge of the Information Resources Division. At this time, her division assumed responsibility for overseeing the next generation technology project, the National Crime Information Center otherwise known as NCIC 2000. This project will make law enforcement information readily accessible to police at state and local levels. Under this system, a local sheriff in Flagstaff, Arizona, can speedily and efficiently access information banks that cover the entire country. The project will place particular emphasis on identifying and tracking wanted persons and stolen property.

Morris' computer background in theory and applications make her particularly suited for this assignment. As FBI director

Louis Freeh stated, "Her expertise in telecommunications and computer science, programming, graphics, software languages, design and theory, is widely known and respected in law enforcement and throughout industry."

Morris was previously the acting assistant director of the same division. Her expertise was critical as leader of the FBI's Rapid Start investigative support team. The team was called in to help undertake the massive FBI investigation of the Oklahoma City bombing.

Morris oversees a division with nearly 2,000 employees and a budget of over $200 million. She will be in charge of all automation concerns, including four FBI technical centers in Georgia, New Jersey, Montana, and Idaho. She will also be in charge of the vast mainframe computers at Ft. Monmouth and FBI headquarters in Washington, D.C.

In many ways Morris represents the changes that have occurred in the FBI. Not only is Morris the highest ranking black woman in the FBI, she is also the first person to head the Information Resources Division who came to the post as a computer expert, rather than as a special agent.

ANDRA MEDEA

Moseley-Braun, Carol (1947–)

"I am—by definition—a different kind of senator," said Carol Moseley-Braun after her swearing-in to the United States Senate. "I am an African American, a woman, a product of the working class. I cannot escape the fact that I come to the Senate as a symbol of hope and change. . . . [But my] job is emphatically not to be a celebrity or a full-time symbol. Symbols will not create jobs and economic growth. They will not do the hard work of solving the health-care crisis. They will not save the children of our cities from drugs and guns and murder."

The first African-American woman in the Senate, Moseley-Braun has spent her first years there proving that her constituents elected a hard-working politician. And she has done so with great success.

Carol Moseley was born in Chicago, Illinois, on August 16, 1947, the daughter of a Chicago police officer, Joseph J. Moseley, and a medical technician, Edna W. Davie Moseley. During the early years of her childhood, the family lived in a middle-class neighborhood and lived a middle-class life. However, in 1963, her parents were divorced. Carol moved with her mother and brothers and sisters to live with her grandmother, in a neighborhood known as "Bucket of Blood."

What Moseley-Braun remembers of that time is the "crushing poverty" with which she was surrounded and the "people who are really trapped and don't have options." But she was not crushed by the environment she lived in. Brought up to believe that working for a better world was a primary human responsibility, she fought back. When she was still in high school, she staged a one-person sit-in at a restaurant that refused to serve her. At sixteen, she marched with Martin Luther King, Jr., in an open-housing demonstration in an all-white neighborhood. She also worked hard at school and went on to the University of Illinois.

During college, Moseley-Braun was a campaign worker for state representative Harold Washington, who later became the

first African-American mayor of Chicago. She graduated in 1969, with a bachelor's degree in political science and went on to the University of Chicago Law School. She received her law degree three years later.

For three years, she worked as a prosecutor in the U.S. Attorney's office. Her boss was James R. Thompson, later governor of Illinois. Her success in the job won her the U.S. Attorney General's Special Achievement Award. In 1978, she ran for, and was elected to, the Illinois House of Representatives.

Moseley-Braun quickly earned a reputation as a skilled legislator, one who could forge coalitions and get things done. From 1980 to 1987, she was the chief sponsor of every school funding bill that affected the city of Chicago. In 1985, she was chief sponsor of the Urban Schools Improvement Act, which created parents' councils in Chicago schools. She also sponsored a bill that allowed public aid recipients to go to college without losing their benefits.

After two terms, she became the first woman and the first African American to serve as assistant majority leader in the Illinois House. Mayor Harold Washington chose her over older and more experienced colleagues to be his floor leader. For each of her ten years in the legislature, she won the Best Legislator Award given by the Independent Voters of Illinois-Independent Precinct Organization (IVI-IPO).

In 1986, Moseley-Braun's name came up for lieutenant governor. However, the young legislator had shown herself to be

When the Senate was debating whether or not to end the system of welfare that had been in place since the New Deal, Senator Carol Moseley-Braun was clear where she stood. "This bill takes a Pontius Pilate approach to federal responsibility. We are washing our hands of our responsibility to poor children." (TOM HORAN)

independent of Harold Washington and, as a result, he blocked her nomination.

That same year, her marriage to Michael Braun ended. Her brother, Johnny, died of a drug and alcohol overdose. Her mother suffered a serious stroke. It was a terrible time for Moseley-Braun, but she had the strength to get through it and, in 1987, she left the House of Representatives to run for the office of Cook County Recorder of Deeds. She was elected, becoming the first woman and the first African American to hold executive office in Cook County government.

When she took office, Moseley-Braun called together a group of experts to help her make a plan to reform the recorder's office. It was a huge job. There were three hundred employees and a budget of $8 million, but what made the job so formidable was that the office was out of date, disorganized, and, according to many reports, filled with corruption. But Moseley-Braun followed the recommendations of her panel and turned things around. When she left the office in 1992, she had streamlined methods for recording deeds, established a code of ethics for employees, and eliminated the lowest level of the pay scale—$12,000 per year—which had been a great temptation to graft.

It is difficult to speculate on what Moseley-Braun's next career move might have been if Clarence Thomas had not been nominated for United States Supreme Court. She was already bored with her job as recorder of deeds. She was ready to take on something else. And then she, along with the rest of the nation, watched Thomas' confirmation hearings on television.

"To be honest," she told *Ebony* magazine, "I couldn't bring myself to watch the hearings full time. The whole thing was an embarrassment. I mean, it was an embarrassment from the very beginning and by the time [it began to concentrate on] the sexual harassment issue, it was beyond embarrassing, it was mortifying."

It was more than embarrassing, in the end. People all over the country were startlingly reminded that the most powerful legislative body in the country was made up almost entirely of white men over fifty. They saw these men treat a respectable and respected black woman with a lack of sensitivity that brought into question their touch with reality. And women, particularly, saw men who were busily closing ranks to protect their privileged status.

"The Senate had exposed itself and demystified itself," Moseley-Braun said in an *Essence* interview. "Most folks had thought of the U.S. Senate as this lofty body of great thinkers dealing with the issues of our time, and what they saw were some garden-variety politicians making bad speeches." She decided that the Senate "absolutely needed a healthy dose of democracy."

When Moseley-Braun announced her intention of running in the Democratic primary, it was a shock even to her friends and supporters. To the other candidates, it was like a fly buzzing on a battlefield—a nuisance, but not the main issue. She was going up against Al "The Pal" Dixon, who had been in politics for forty-three years and never lost an election. The third candidate was Al Hofeld a multimillionaire who was willing to spend whatever was necessary to defeat Dixon. The two Als proceeded to run high-powered, mud-slinging campaigns—against each other. A Hofeld consultant later remarked, "We were hammering [Dixon], and he was hammering us and nobody was hammering [Moseley-Braun]."

Moseley-Braun, of course, didn't have enough money to hammer anyone. She could afford only one television commercial. Feminist Gloria Steinem went to bat for her, trying to raise funds from women across the country. But it looked so unlikely that she could win, even political organizations specifically founded to help women run for office gave her little or nothing.

The morning after the primary, however, Moseley-Braun no longer had to buy time to get on television. First she did ABC's *Good Morning America*. Then she was on NBC's *Today* and *First Thing in the Morning*. At noon, she was interviewed on the Chicago midday news and later in the day she was on CNN. She had been nominated with 38 percent of the vote to Dixon's 35 percent and Hofeld's 27 percent.

Her election made history, too. In spite of some rough times when questions were raised about her mother's finances and the lack of discipline in her campaign, Moseley-Braun sailed into office with a ten-point victory. Now, she had to prove that she was more than the "Year of the Woman" flash in a pan.

If the Washington community expected the junior senator from Illinois to be eaten alive, they underestimated both her political savvy and her eloquence. The woman who confronted them was not an innocent idealist; she had survived and prevailed in Chicago politics.

Moseley-Braun was appointed to the Senate Judiciary Committee, the Senate Banking, Housing, and Urban Affairs Committee, and the Small-Business Committee. A few months after taking office,

she managed to keep the Judiciary Committee from extending a federal patent on the insignia of the United Daughters of the Confederacy, which includes the flag of the Confederacy. Two and a half months later Senators Strom Thurmond and Jesse Helms tried to extend the patent by attaching it as an amendment to a bill on national service. A test vote passed the Senate, 52 to 48. Then Senator Moseley-Braun took the floor.

"On this issue," she said, "there can be no consensus. It is an outrage. It is an insult." The senator continued to talk, refusing to yield the floor. She talked about the Civil War, "fought to preserve our nation, to keep the states from separating themselves over the issue of whether or not my ancestors could be held as property, as chattel, as objects of trade and commerce in this country."

To those who said she was blowing things out of proportion, that it was a small matter, just the proud insignia of a group of women, "most of them elderly, all of them gentle souls who meet together and work together as unpaid volunteers at veterans hospitals," Moseley-Braun had an answer. "This is no small matter," she said. "This is not a matter of little old ladies walking around doing good deeds. There is no reason why these little old ladies cannot do good deeds anyway. If they choose to wave the Confederate flag, that is their right." However, she continued, a flag that symbolized slavery must not be "underwritten, underscored, adopted, approved by this United States Senate."

It was, all in all, an astonishing performance for a freshman senator. What was more astonishing still is that it worked. Minds, and votes, on the floor of the Senate are seldom changed by speeches. But it happened here. A "daughter of slavery" spoke out, and the Senate voted down the amendment, 75 to 25.

Since then, Moseley-Braun has amended the major education bill of the 103rd Congress to include the Education Infrastructure Act, thus securing $100 million for repairing and rebuilding unsafe and hopelessly inadequate schools. "The question is," she said in support of her amendment, "are we providing the physical environment for education our children need as they go into the next century. The answer is a resounding no." She has also successfully introduced legislation requiring the Armed Services to establish procedures for handling cases of racial or sexual harassment.

The Senate and the country were stirred when Carol Moseley-Braun went up against Jesse Helms to keep the insignia of the Daughters of the Confederacy from receiving Senate approval. But, powerful as it was, that was the action of a bold, naive, angry freshman. In September of 1995, a plan was afoot in the Senate to significantly weaken fair-housing enforcement in a housing appropriation bill. Moseley-Braun grabbed Senate Majority Leader Bob Dole and said, "You're not going to let this happen, are you? We'll be riding on the back of the bus again."

When they had finished talking and bargaining, Bob Dole walked over to the Republican leader of the assault, Christopher Bond, and had a talk with him. Bond withdrew from the battle, and the bill passed without the damaging modification. Of course, Moseley-Braun and her colleagues had to make certain concessions, but she indicated that she would deal with that later. The old coalition-building, negotiat-

ing, political veteran had obviously landed on her feet.

Still, Moseley-Braun is capable of backing an unpopular, even a losing cause, when it is a cause she believes in. When the Senate approved legislation to alter drastically the country's welfare system, Moseley-Braun stood beside such long-time advocates of the poor as Senators Patrick Moynihan, Ted Kennedy, Bill Bradley, and Paul Simon in opposing the bill. "This bill," she declared, "takes a Pontius Pilate approach to Federal responsibility. We are washing our hands of our responsibility to poor children." She was one of only twelve senators to vote against the bill.

KATHLEEN THOMPSON

Motley, Constance Baker (1921–)

In the 1950s and 1960s, the courts of our country were battlegrounds in the war for civil rights. One of the leaders in the effort was Constance Baker Motley, long-time counsel for the NAACP Legal Defense and Educational Fund, Inc., and later a federal judge.

Constance Baker was born September 14, 1921, in New Haven, Connecticut, to Willoughby Alva and Rachel Huggins Baker, both West Indian emigrants. Her father was chef for a Yale fraternity. She attended the New Haven public schools and learned black history through lectures given in her Sunday school. She became active in community activities while she was still in high school, becoming president of the New Haven Youth Council and secretary of the New Haven Adult Community Council.

After graduation from high school, she went to work for the National Youth Administration because college was financially impossible. Then Clarence Blakeslee, a local businessman, heard Baker speak at a New Haven community center. Blakeslee had built the building and wanted to know why it was not used by black citizens. Baker's answer so impressed him that he wondered why she was not in college. When Baker said she wanted to go to law school but could not afford the tuition, Blakeslee offered to pay for her schooling.

Baker attended Fisk University and then transferred to New York University, graduating from its Washington Square College in 1943 with an A.B. in economics. She went on to Columbia Law School, graduating in 1946. That same year, she married Joel Wilson Motley, an insurance broker. Then she went out to find a job.

"My first job interview," she remembers, "was an accurate sign of the times. . . . When I appeared for my interview, a balding middle-aged white male appeared at a door leading to the reception room where I was standing. The receptionist had not even asked me to have a seat. Even after the door to the reception room quickly closed, she still did not invite me to sit down. She knew as well as I that the interview was over."

Fortunately, Motley heard that there was a vacancy for a law clerk at the NAACP Legal Defense and Educational Fund and she applied for a job there. Thurgood Marshall interviewed Motley for the job and hired her at once. At the interview he told her the first of many stories about successful black women. "Over the years," says Motley, "he told me about every successful African-American woman he encountered."

As a clerk, Motley was responsible for a great deal of research. Marshall suggested

When the distinguished judge Constance Baker Motley applied for a job as law clerk at the NAACP in the late 1940s, she was interviewed by Thurgood Marshall, who hired her on the spot. During the interview, Marshall encouraged Motley with stories of successful black women. During the course of their long friendship, he made it a point to tell her about every successful African-American woman he encountered. (MOORLAND-SPINGARN)

that in order to have access to its library, she should join the New York City Bar Association. Having done so, she went to use the library. "When I got there," she says, "I saw the 'gate keeper' standing at his desk immediately inside the door. He was an elderly white man with snow-white hair who appeared to be one year older than God." After some time, Motley got his attention, only to be told that the library was for members only. She told him she was a member and, recovering from his shock, he asked what her name was. " 'Mrs. Motley,' I said, guarding against what all African-American women guarded against in those days. When he found my name on the membership list, he exclaimed, 'Oh, right this way, *Constance.*' " Respect did not come quickly or easily.

In 1950, Motley became assistant counsel for the Legal Defense and Educational Fund and became involved in trying cases. She helped write the briefs filed in the U.S. Supreme Court in the school desegregation case, *Brown v. Board of Education.* Her reputation as a fine lawyer and a dedicated civil rights proponent grew. "Among the better known cases I personally tried," she says, "were those against the Universities of Mississippi, Georgia, and Alabama, and Clemson College in South Carolina. As a result, James Meredith, the plaintiff in the University of Mississippi case, became a national hero in 1962. Charlayne Hunter-Gault and Hamilton Holmes, the plaintiffs in the University of Georgia case, brought Georgia kicking and screaming into the twentieth century in 1961. George Wallace and Alabama finally gave up massive resistance to desegregation in 1963. And now South Carolina brags about Harvey Gantt, the plaintiff in the Clemson College case in 1962, who became mayor of Charlotte."

In 1963, leaders of the Democratic Party in New York asked her to fill the unexpired term of New York State Senator James Watson. She agreed and was then elected to the New York State Senate in 1964, becoming the first black woman in that legislative body. She resigned to run in a special election to fill a one-year vacancy as president of the Borough of Manhattan. She was then reelected to a full four-year term.

Over the years, Motley argued ten civil rights cases in the Supreme Court, winning nine. During one of those cases, Ramsey Clark, who was then Attorney General of the United States, was in court and heard her. Afterward, he went back to the White House and suggested to President Lyndon Johnson that he appoint Motley to the federal bench. Initially, Johnson submitted her name for a seat on the Court of Appeals for the Second Circuit, but, according to Motley, "the opposition to my appointment was so great, apparently because I was a woman, that Johnson had to withdraw my name. I remember how stunned both Johnson and Marshall were at the strength and intensity of the opposition."

In January 1966, Johnson submitted Motley's name to the U.S. Senate for confirmation of her nomination as a U.S. District Judge. At that time, only two other women were federal district judges. Over fierce opposition from a group headed by James Eastland of Mississippi, Motley was finally confirmed in August.

"When I was introduced as a new judge at a Second Circuit Judicial Conference," relates Motley, "the master of ceremonies said, 'And now I want to introduce Connie Motley who is doing such a good job on the District Court.' In contrast, everyone else was introduced with a full-blown curriculum vitae."

In 1982, Motley became chief judge of the Southern District of New York, serving in that position until October 1, 1995, when she became a senior judge.

KATHLEEN THOMPSON

N

National Organization of Black Elected Legislative Women

The National Organization of Black Elected Legislative Women (NOBEL) was founded in 1985 in Philadelphia, Pennsylvania, by California State Senator **Diane Watson.** NOBEL is an organization of black women state legislators seeking to improve the lives of black women by furthering their education about public policy issues, promoting participation in the development of public policy, and introducing and supporting legislation that improves the lives of black women.

NOBEL's purpose is to train and educate black women and thus increase the number of black women in local, state, and national elected and appointed offices. NOBEL's primary goal is to assess the needs of all women and provide a national voice in policy debates addressing these needs. Another objective is to work with governments to create programs to further legal, social, economic, and educational opportunities for women.

NOBEL has addressed various issues in national forums and has coordinated numerous activities. In 1989 the main issue for the organization was at-risk youth; the organization lobbied successfully for legislation that would help black youth. NOBEL also pressed for the rights of political refugees in South Africa. In 1990 NOBEL's second annual legislative conference in New York featured a symposium, "Women's Health Update," that drew attention to diseases affecting women and the black community.

NOBEL's agenda for the 1990s is geared to policy implementation and programs adopted to meet the basic needs of women, particularly black women. Among concerns are the health crisis in the black community, particularly the impact of tobacco, and the increased occurrence of breast cancer among women of color.

An ongoing activity is the Mother's March for Peace that occurs twice annually, once at the National Black Caucus of State Legislators' Conference. NOBEL members also work with other communities of color.

All black women legislators are considered members of NOBEL; total membership in 1992 comprised 102 black women legislators serving thirty-two state legislatures.

CAROLE ECHOLS/GRETCHEN E. MACLACHLAN

National Political Congress of Black Women

The National Political Congress of Black Women (NPCBW) was founded in 1984 in Washington, D.C., by **Shirley Chisholm,** the first black woman to run for president of the United States, to provide a political forum for black women. The NPCBW primarily targets black women of voting age but also encourages women under eighteen years of age to enter and participate in the political process.

The purpose of the NPCBW is to rally black women to participate in elective politics, to encourage them in public policy formulation, and to educate them about all levels of the political process. The special focus of the NPCBW is to bring masses of black women into political leadership roles at all levels of government. The NPCBW builds on the experience of black women, who historically have been beacons of progressive political change, to empower them for the future. The NPCBW acts as a catalyst for this empowerment.

The mission of the NPCBW is to "develop and advocate public positions, at every level of government, and engage in dialogue with the political parties, to encourage the development of policy, platform and strategy beneficial to the needs and aspirations of the black community."

The organization has addressed many issues since its founding. It has pressed for affirmative action, access to nontraditional jobs, economic development, education, health, leadership development, the legislative process, and housing and urban development. It has documented patterns of housing market discrimination against black men and women by holding hearings in Atlanta, St. Louis, San Francisco, and New York. These hearings stimulated legislative action and informed black women of their rights under the law. The NPCBW also focuses on the social and economic status of the black family and encourages family reunions to reaffirm the importance of family to the black community. The first reunion, held in 1986 in Washington, D.C.,

drew 200,000 people. Besides serving as a social outlet, it offered information on job skills, health issues, and the transmission of historical tradition.

The NPCBW's future agenda concentrates on critical issues of job discrimination, health care, drug abuse, single parenting, lack of education and of daycare facilities, and job training. The organization has already initiated programs in some of these areas, including a Black Parents Drug Prevention Program, Parent Education Teleworkshops, the **Fannie Lou Hamer** Day Care Center in Ruleville, Mississippi, and Education 2000.

The NPCBW is an independent, nonpartisan organization. Its membership, made up primarily of black women, is nationwide. The organization's main office in Rancocas, New Jersey, is staffed by one full-time staff member and five volunteers. Some distinguished members and officers of the NPCBW are **Shirley Chisholm,** former congresswoman (chairperson); **C. DeLores Tucker,** former secretary of state of Pennsylvania (vice chairperson); and Mable Thomas, member of the Georgia Legislature (board of directors).

GRETCHEN E. MACLACHLAN/CAROLE ECHOLS

Norton, Eleanor Holmes (1937–)

Eleanor Holmes Norton was the first female chair of the Equal Employment Opportunity Commission (EEOC). Born on June 13, 1937, in Washington, D.C., she is a fourth-generation Washingtonian. After she received her B.A. from Antioch College in 1960, she attended Yale University, where she earned a master's degree in American history in 1963 and a J.D. in 1965.

From 1965 until 1970, she worked for the American Civil Liberties Union (ACLU) in New York City. In 1968, she received national attention for her representation of former Alabama Governor George Wallace, who had been denied permission to hold an outdoor political rally at Shea Stadium in New York City. This case set a precedent for her staunch stand on legal and constitutional principles. After the Wallace case, she became assistant director of the ACLU in New York City.

In 1970, she became head of the New York City Commission on Human Rights, appointed by Mayor John V. Lindsay. Her appointment was renewed by Mayor Abraham D. Beame in 1974.

In 1977, President Jimmy Carter appointed her chair of the EEOC, a position she held until 1981. When she took the post, she inherited a backlog of 130,000 cases, and the commission had the reputation of being a swamp of bureaucratic mismanagement. After only two years in office, she had transformed the EEOC into a highly productive and efficient agency. For example, she cut the backlog of cases in half and increased the productivity of EEOC area offices by 65 percent. She later became a professor of law at Georgetown University and, in 1990, made a successful bid to become the congressional representative for the District of Columbia. She was reelected in 1992 and has been a strong advocate of statehood for the District of Columbia.

Her lifelong commitment to civil rights began with her membership in the **Student Nonviolent Coordinating Committee** (SNCC) and her participation in the **Mississippi Freedom Democratic Party** (MFDP). In 1963, she was a member of the national staff of the March on Washington.

In addition to her career as an activist and politician, Eleanor Holmes Norton is a recognized legal scholar and coauthor of *Sex Discrimination and the Law: Causes and Remedies* (1975). She and husband Edward Norton and their two children, Katharine and John, reside in the District of Columbia.

MECCA NELSON

Eleanor Holmes Norton's lifelong commitment to the cause of civil rights began with her membership in the Student Nonviolent Coordinating Committee in the 1960s. In addition to her career as an activist and politician, Norton is coauthor of Sex Discrimination and the Law: Causes and Remedies. *(OFFICE OF CONGRESSWOMAN NORTON)*

O

O'Leary, Hazel Rollins (1937–)

No stranger to hard work and controversial assignments, Hazel O'Leary took the helm of the Department of Energy in 1992, becoming the first woman and the first African American to hold that post. Appointed by President Clinton to clean up that troubled agency, she was confronted by decades of mismanagement and appalling secrets. With characteristic tact and determination, she built a team and went to work.

The daughter of two doctors, O'Leary was born on May 17, 1937, and raised in segregated Newport News, Virginia. Her parents were divorced when she was eighteen months old. She was raised by her father, Dr. Russell Reid, and her stepmother, Hazel Palleman Reid. She grew up in an atmosphere of responsibility and service. One grandmother helped found the first public library for African Americans in her community. Another grandmother kept extra boxes of clothes neatly wrapped by sizes to give to those who needed them.

Her parents did everything to protect her from segregation, chauffeuring her and her sister to events and having them spend summers at a camp in Massachusetts. When it was time to enter high school, her parents sent her to live with an aunt in New Jersey, so that she could attend a school without segregation.

After high school, O'Leary entered Fisk University in Nashville, where she majored in history. In 1959 she graduated magna cum laude and earned her Phi Beta Kappa key. She married Carl Rollins and had a son within two years of graduating, but she did not give up on her ambition to become a lawyer. In 1966, she earned her law degree from Rutgers University School of Law. She became an assistant prosecutor in Essex County, New Jersey, then was promoted to assistant attorney general of New Jersey. Next she moved to Washington, D.C., where she became a partner in Coopers & Lybrand, one of the largest accounting firms in the nation.

During the Ford administration O'Leary became director of the Office of Consumer Affairs within the Federal Energy Administration. After developing a reputation as a strong, tough, competent manager, she became general counsel of the Community Services Administration.

Under President Carter, O'Leary was appointed deputy director of the Economic Regulatory Administration, a department under the first secretary of energy. Soon promoted to director of the agency, she oversaw a staff of 2,000 professionals and was a leading figure in the energy crisis of the late 1970s.

In 1980 she married John F. O'Leary, the deputy energy secretary. When Carter lost to Reagan that same year, both left the DOE but stayed in Washington to start their own consulting agency, O'Leary Associates. Hazel O'Leary was vice president and general counsel. Their single largest client was the company which owned the Three Mile Island nuclear power plant. This plant nearly reached meltdown in a widely reported nuclear accident. O'Leary Associates were hired to help the company recover.

John O'Leary died in 1987, and O'Leary disbanded the company. In 1989 she was hired by Northern States Power Company, one of the largest utilities companies in the Midwest. She became executive vice-president for corporate affairs, in charge of environmental policy, public relations and lobbying. She spearheaded conservation programs and also became involved in a controversy about toxic chemicals and the disposal of used nuclear fuel. After this she was promoted to NSP Gas, their new natural gas division. Before she could begin this assignment, she received a call from Bill Clinton, offering her the position of Secretary of Energy.

The Department of Energy was a deeply troubled institution. It was organized under Carter, but it inherited numerous agencies that had been operating since the dawn of the Cold War. Behind cloak-and-dagger secrecy, some of these agencies had shown reckless disregard for ordinary citizens. With the end of the Cold War, these stories were coming to light.

One of the first problems faced by O'Leary was the revelation that five Americans had been injected with plutonium, an extremely radioactive material, as part of a medical experiment in the 1940s. O'Leary caused a controversy by saying that the victims should be compensated.

Further investigations showed careless dumping of radioactive waste and other toxic materials from weapons plants. Per-

Hazel O'Leary made history by becoming the first African American and the first woman to become U.S. Secretary of Energy. One of her first acts was to acknowledge the government's role in controversial medical experiments in the 1940s, and to urge that the victims be compensated. (OFFICE OF SECRETARY O'LEARY)

haps the most troubling revelations were the harassment of "whistle-blowers," employees and others who spoke out against dangerous conditions.

Past DOE secretaries sometimes ended up at war with their own staffs, trying to clean up these problems. The old managers were powerful and deeply entrenched and they did not want these things to come to light. O'Leary took a unique approach. Instead of hiring new bureaucrats, she brought in a group of aides who had previously been DOE's most vocal critics.

They were smart, informed and unafraid to make changes.

A daring manager, a perfectionist and a savvy politician, O'Leary can be both warm and demanding. She plans to retire after this assignment and so she has nothing to lose. It shows in her courage.

ANDRA MEDEA

P

Payton, Carolyn Robertson (1925–)

A psychologist and counselor, Carolyn Robertson Payton has dedicated her life to the development of human potential. As the first black woman to head the Peace Corps, Payton insisted that individuals be enabled to succeed and excel to the best of their abilities.

Born on May 13, 1925, in Norfolk, Virginia, Payton was the child of LeRoy Robertson, a cook and shipboard steward, and Bertha Robertson, a seamstress. Although there were lean times during the Depression, her parents saw to it that the family was well-fed and well-clothed. Payton was descended from remarkable people on both sides. Her grandfather was an escaped slave, and her grandparents saw to it that each of their four children got a good education. Three of them attended college, and this was within fifty years of the Civil War. According to family history, her great-grandfather on her father's side was an African prince who was sent to accompany a band of slaves taken from his village. The group ended up in South Carolina, where the prince bought land and settled.

Payton came of age during the Depression in segregated Virginia. Her family was spared poverty, but the racial discrimination was clearly felt. As Payton put it, "I learned, as all children in public school, that I was an American and as such was guaranteed the pursuit of happiness, equality and justice. I learned that lesson well and have continuously struggled to achieve these rights as a minority and as a woman."

In 1941, Payton went to college at Bennett, a women's college in Greensboro, North Carolina. When she graduated in 1945, she wanted to go on to graduate school, but did not know what field she preferred. Her major was decided by Virginia and segregation. Virginia had been forced to follow a separate-but-equal approach to education. If a field was offered in a white college, but not offered in one of the state's black colleges, Virginia was required to pay all expenses for the black student to study at the school of her choice. Psychology was not offered on the graduate level in any black schools in Virginia, and so Payton had her way paid to the University of Wisconsin at Madison.

Payton arrived at the University of Wisconsin with only a handful of psychology credits and a desire to be a psychologist. Three years later, in 1948, she received her master of social work degree. While a graduate student, one of her research projects was to evaluate the intelligence of black and white students by using the Wechsler-Bellevue Test of Intelligence. She found herself doubting the accuracy of the scale, since many blacks who scored poorly went on to scholastic and career success. Many years later, in 1976, Payton was field supervisor for the 1976 revision of the Wechsler Adult Intelligence Test. This later test was believed to be more accurate for diverse populations.

Once out of college, Payton would have preferred to be a clinical psychologist, but such jobs were scarce for African Americans. Instead, she was hired by Livingston College in Salisbury, North Carolina, to teach psychology. As the only psychologist on staff, she also maintained personnel files and administered psychological tests. She stayed there for a pleasant five years, from 1948 to 1953.

In 1953, Payton wished to move closer to her family in Norfolk, so she became dean of women and psychological instructor at Elizabeth City State Teachers College in North Carolina. Being dean of women at that time included chaperoning dances, giving permission for weekend trips, and generally acting the perfect lady. This was not a natural fit for Payton. As she later noted, "All this was a bit of a strain for me. I was and am a very casual dresser. But, I did not flinch from the charge of my position. I donned hat and gloves and set about to become a model of propriety. Apparently I was successful at curbing my proclivities, as my contract continued to be renewed."

Payton continued at Elizabeth City until 1956, when she was recruited to be associate professor of psychology at Virginia State College in Petersburg. This job, as well, was only a short distance from her family. Summers she studied at Columbia, enjoying the exciting cultural life of New York City. In 1958, she took a year's leave of absence to study at Columbia, surviving on a diet of instant oatmeal and cream cheese sandwiches from the local automat. She finally received her Ed.D. in 1962.

Meanwhile, in 1959, Payton returned from her sabbatical to join **Howard University** as assistant professor. She soon inherited a primate lab from a leaving psychologist. While working in the lab, she received a three-year grant from the National Institute of Mental Health for research on perception in rhesus monkeys.

Payton had plans for further primate research, but before further research could be undertaken, President Kennedy was elected and established the Peace Corps. Payton was hired in 1962 as a field placement officer, in order to psychologically evaluate trainees bound for overseas. She was asked back for another assignment in 1963. In 1964 she resigned her post with Howard to work with the Peace Corps full time.

Payton found the enthusiasm, dedication, and commitment of Peace Corps volunteering exciting and inspirational. Her assigned region was Latin America, so she had the chance to travel to many Latin American countries in her line of work. Only one thing bothered her: in talks with volunteers at the end of their field assignments, Payton often found that her eager young recruits had become bitter, even hostile toward the people they had lived among. Payton wished to discover why this was happening. To look at the matter more closely, she took a field placement herself in Barbados, West Indies. There she became deputy director for the eastern Caribbean. During her tenure, there was only one other female director in the Peace Corps.

In 1970, Payton returned to Washington and Howard University, where she became director of the counseling service. She stayed at this position until 1978. At that time, President Carter asked her to return to the Peace Corps as director, the first black woman to head the agency.

Payton was director of the Peace Corps for only one year, until 1979. Her position was cut short by a dispute with her organizational supervisor. Payton wished the Peace Corps to remain a diverse group of hands-on volunteers. Her new boss wished the Peace Corps to shift to an emphasis on older, more highly trained specialists. After a year of struggle and debate, Payton was removed as director. However, in 1978 she was voted Woman of the Year by the prestigious Capital Press Club. Clearly the nation's reporters thought that Payton was doing the right thing.

After this, Payton was recruited to direct a project for a private agency on drug abuse prevention. She later returned to her previous post of director of counseling and career development services at Howard University.

ANDRA MEDEA

Perry, Carrie Saxon (1931–)

Carrie Saxon Perry went from Hartford's housing projects to its mayor's office. She was born on August 10, 1931, in Hartford, Connecticut, to Mabel Lee Saxon. Reared in the poverty of the Depression, she attended the Hartford public schools and then went on to **Howard University** in Washington, D.C., encouraged and supported by her mother, grandmother, and aunt. At Howard, she studied political science and spent two years in the School of Law.

Returning to Hartford, Saxon married James Perry, whom she later divorced, and bore a son, James Perry, Jr. She also began a career in social work, quickly becoming administrator for the Community Renewal Team of Greater Hartford and then executive director of Amistad House. Her experiences with Hartford's poor moved her to work for broader solutions by going into politics. Her first bid for the Connecticut State General Assembly, in 1976, was so narrowly defeated that only the absentee ballots turned the trick for her opponent. Her second bid, in 1980, was successful. In neither race had she received an endorsement from any newspaper, fellow politician, or political organization.

In her first year in the state house, Perry was appointed assistant majority leader. She was active on a variety of committees and subcommittees, always fighting for human rights. Before going on to other political arenas, Perry served four terms in the state legislature. She also attended two Democratic national conventions. In 1987, Perry, having established wide visibility and credibility, ran for mayor of Hartford. She won the election, becoming the first black woman to serve as mayor of a major American city.

KATHLEEN THOMPSON

Phillips, Velvalea Rogers (1924–)

Velvalea Rogers was born in Milwaukee, Wisconsin, on February 18, 1924. She earned her B.S. in 1946 from **Howard University** and her LL.B. in 1951 from Wisconsin Law School. In 1971, she graduated from the University of Nevada Summer College for Juvenile Court Judges.

Vel Rogers Phillips has been a juvenile court judge; county court judge; Milwaukee alderman; Wisconsin secretary of state (1978); Milwaukee children's court judge (1972–74); and a visiting lecturer in the University of Wisconsin Department of African-American Studies. She also has been active in several organizations, including the American Association of University Women, Women's International League for Peace and Freedom, **Delta Sigma Theta,** the **National Association for the Advancement of Colored People** (NAACP), and the Day Care and Child Development Council, John F. Kennedy School.

Among her many accomplishments, Phillips was the recipient of the Milwaukee Star Award for Service (1967) and the Woman of the Year Award (1968) of Milwaukee University Chapter of Theta Sigma Phi Sorority. She was the first black American elected to the Milwaukee Common Council (1956) and the first black American to serve on the Democratic National Convention Committee on Rules and Order of Business. She served on the committee for six years and in 1960 she cochaired it.

She and her husband, W. Dale Phillips, share a law practice and have two children, Dale and Michael.

JUDY WARWICK

Poe, L. Marian Fleming   (1890–1974)

Lavinia Marian Fleming Poe practiced law in Virginia from the 1920s to the 1970s. Along with Leslie A. Lytle in Tennessee and Estelle A. Henderson in Alabama she was one of the first black women admitted to the bar in any Southern state.

Born August 13, 1890, the second of three children of Archer R. Fleming and Florence M. (Carter) Fleming, she grew up in Newport News, Virginia, with her parents and her brothers, Daniel and Archer, Jr. It was a remarkable family. All three siblings returned to the Newport News area to serve their community after completing graduate study at **Howard University.** Poe's brothers attended medical school there; Daniel Fleming became a dentist and Archer Fleming a doctor.

In the early 1910s, Marian Fleming worked in Newport News as a stenographer for a black banker, notary, and real estate agent, E. C. Brown, president of the Crown Savings Bank. On September 20, 1911, she married a waiter named Abram James Poe, and they had two children, Florence Alice (November 30, 1912), and Abram James, Jr. (January 28, 1918). For a time around 1920, Marian Poe worked in the office of J. Thomas Newsome, a black attorney, and her experience with Newsome convinced her that she wished to become a lawyer.

Success was a long shot. The law schools in Virginia—Washington and Lee University, the University of Virginia, the University of Richmond—excluded all black applicants. Moreover, until 1920, Virginia law did not permit women to be licensed to practice the profession. Poe had two young children; but she went off to Washington, D.C., earned a law degree from Howard University in 1925, and later that year passed the Virginia bar examination.

For nearly a half-century, Marian Poe practiced her profession as a general practitioner in Newport News, one of a handful of black attorneys who served the black community there. Across those years, Poe did what she could, too, to help young black lawyers get started, much as Thomas Newsome had done for her.

She participated in the profession in ways that stretched far from Newport News. A charter member of the (predominantly black) Old Dominion Bar Association, she served throughout the 1940s as its secretary; another pioneer member, Roland D. Ealey, a lawyer in Richmond and later a member of the Virginia legislature, recalled her as "the glue that held it [the ODBA] together." She joined the National Bar Association, served for a time as its assistant secretary, and in 1933 she spoke at its ninth annual meeting on "Women's Contribution to the Bench and Bar." In addition, Poe served once at mid-century and twice in the 1960s as the Virginia delegate to the national convention of the National Association of Women Lawyers, a predominantly white but clearly biracial group. Thus she participated in the support systems that promoted the work of black lawyers, particularly in Virginia, and of female lawyers across the nation.

Still, she emphasized her own community. The focal point of her life remained the building where she lived and had her office in the center of the black business district in Newport News. She owned that building, at 628–630 Twenty-fifth Street, and for a time it also housed Alice's Beauty Shop, which her daughter ran, and her son-in-law's enterprise, Webb's Grill and Guesthouse. She was active in civic organizations and, at the First Baptist Church of Newport News, she taught Sunday school, sang in the choir, and became the first woman on the board of trustees. Following her own advice, she kept busy to the end.

Marian Poe died in a local hospital on March 20, 1974, at the age of eighty-three. After services at the First Baptist Church, she was buried at Pleasant Shade Cemetery in Newport News. By the time she died, the number of black female lawyers in Virginia had risen into double digits, and black men and black women alike could be admitted to any law school in the state.

PETER WALLENSTEIN

Powers, Georgia (1923–)

The soft-gray hair and the sparkling eyes belie the strength and determination that mark the life of Georgia Montgomery Davis Powers. The first black to be elected to the Kentucky State Senate (1967–1989), her life has been characterized by the "breaking of barriers." Born in Springfield, Kentucky, on October 29, 1923, Powers was the only female among nine children. She attended Louisville Municipal College. She says she did not know what she wanted to do until she was thirty-nine. She had held thirty jobs, including owning a business, when she decided that politics was her calling. She ran for and won the senate seat from district thirty-three in Louisville in 1967. However, this was not the beginning of Powers' activism but rather a milestone along the way of a dedicated civil libertarian.

Powers was at the center of the Kentucky civil rights movement in the early 1960s and continued the struggle within the chambers of the state senate. In 1964, she organized a march in Frankfort, Kentucky's capital. The march's success was instrumental in the passage in 1966 of Kentucky's Public Accommodations and Fair Employment Law, and it was a key experience in her decision to run for public office.

Her activities in Kentucky brought her into the inner circle of Dr. Martin Luther King, Jr., and she was one of the organizers of the Kentucky affiliate of the Southern Christian Leadership Conference. She participated in the Selma, Alabama, march in 1965; introduced an open housing bill for Kentucky, which became law in 1968; and, on April 4, 1968, she was in Memphis, Tennessee, at the request of Dr. King, to participate in the sanitation workers' march. From her room in the Lorraine Motel, she heard the shots that killed Dr. King.

During her more than twenty years in the Kentucky State Senate, Powers was a successful advocate for women's issues, as well as civil rights. She sponsored Kentucky's Equal Rights Amendment, Kentucky's Affirmative Action Plan, legislation to eliminate race descriptors from Kentucky drivers' licenses, and legislation on sex and age discrimination. In 1980, she introduced legislation to require that at least one black member be appointed to the Board of Regents at each of Kentucky's public universities. Within the senate, she served as chairperson of the Labor and Industry Committee. Her autobiography, *I Shared the Dream: The Pride, Passion and Politics of the First Black Woman Senator from Kentucky,* was published in 1995.

Powers' political skills were developed from adversarial situations, yet adversary relations have a personal price. Powers has had to work through what she calls "diminishing rage." Each act of racial or sexual discrimination diminishes the spirit of a person, and it must be regained. Nevertheless, her struggles for justice, she believes, have earned her the right, borrowing a phrase from her favorite poem by Jenny Joseph, to say—"When I am an old lady I shall wear purple, with a red hat, which doesn't go and doesn't suit me."

PAULA D. McCLAIN

R

Ralston, Elreta Alexander (1919–)

Elreta Alexander Ralston was the first African-American woman to become a judge by popular election. She was only the second African American to be so chosen and the first African American in this century in the South. Yet these are just the tip of an iceberg of firsts and other distinctions. Once, her skill and fairness as a defense lawyer of Ku Klux Klan members so turned their minds around they renounced the Klan.

Elreta Melton Alexander Ralston was born on March 21, 1919, in Smithfield, North Carolina. She was the youngest of three children whose parents were teacher and Baptist minister Joseph C. Melton and Alian A. Reynolds Melton. She attended elementary school in Danville, Virginia, and at only fifteen graduated James B. Dudley High School in Greensboro, North Carolina. Three years later, in 1937, she got her B.A. from Greensboro's North Carolina Agricultural and Technical College (now University).

Ralston taught history and mathematics and was a music director in North and South Carolina for four years before starting studies in New York at the Columbia University School of Law. She was married to surgeon Girardeau Alexander from 1938 until his death in 1979, and they had one son. After Alexander's death, she married John D. Ralston. In 1945, she became the first black woman to receive an LL.B. from that university. For two years then she was law clerk in the New York firm of Dyer & Stevens.

In 1947, she became North Carolina's first black woman to practice law, which she did in Greensboro until 1968. She also became the first to try a case before the state supreme court. In 1965 she was named senior partner in the state's first integrated law firm, and her clients were both black and white.

Her legal exploits have been described as colorful and her style flamboyant. She won a suit against Greensboro's city council for thwarting a black housing project and in so doing became the first African American elected to that council. She led the establishment of the first city-owned golf course for African Americans and personally integrated, in 1950, an exclusive downtown women's store.

Ralston, a Democrat up to 1968, then switched parties to run for a Guilford County district court judgeship. Winning without campaigning, she was the district's only Republican woman, the state's only African American and the country's first African American to be so elected. Soon the Republican Party appointed more women and African Americans to judgeships and government positions in the state.

From her bench came many judicial reforms. One required public officials and other judges not to demean minority attorneys by addressing them by their first names. Another was the assigning of probation officers to offenders regardless of race or gender. Her 1969 rehabilitation program called "Judgment Day" created support-system alternatives to jail. Despite political attacks on it and on her, much of its substance became law.

She left the bench in 1981, having been elected four consecutive terms, and resumed practice at Alexander Ralston, Pell & Speckhard. Recipient of scores of honors and active in a great variety of regional organizations, she displayed her poetic side in the book *When Is a Man Free* and her rhetorical skills in another volume, *Vital Speeches of Today*.

Ralston was known for her creative sentencing of offenders, such as youths charged with drunk driving, which deterred future offenses so effectively that they were made statute. What others have praised as her innovations she has simply called just.

GARY HOUSTON

Ray, Charlotte (1850–1911)

Charlotte Ray was the first black woman regularly admitted to the practice of law in any jurisdiction in the United States. She was born in New York City on January 13, 1850, one of the seven children of the Reverend Charles Bennett Ray, of African, Indian, and white ancestry, and his second wife, Charlotte Augusta Burroughs, a native of Savannah, Georgia. Charles Ray, editor, later owner, of the *Colored American* and pastor of the Bethesda Congregational Church in New York, was one of the distinguished black leaders of his day, known for his fearless work for the Underground Railroad. His daughter, Charlotte, described in the *Woman's Journal* (May

25, 1872) as "a dusky mulatto," had the benefit of educated parents. In 1869, she was a teacher in the Normal and Preparatory Department of **Howard University.**

Shortly thereafter Charlotte began the study of law at Howard. A classmate years later remembered her as "an apt scholar"; a contemporary visitor to the law school was impressed by "a colored woman who read us a thesis on corporations, not copied from the books but from her brain, a clear incisive analysis of one of the most delicate legal questions." She graduated from the Howard University Law School in February 1872, reading an essay on "Chancery" that was well received. She was the first black woman to receive a law degree from any law school in the country.

Rules for bar admission were set by the Supreme Court of the District of Columbia, a court of general jurisdiction established during the Civil War to replace the circuit court. Charlotte Ray's application caused no debate. As a graduate of Howard University Law School she was not required to take a bar examination. She was admitted to practice in the lower courts of the District of Columbia on March 2, 1872, and to practice in the Supreme Court of the District of Columbia on April 23, 1872. After bar admission Charlotte Ray opened a law office in Washington, where she hoped to practice a specialty within real estate law that did not entail trial appearances. It was the very beginning of women's entry into the legal profession, years before a woman could make a living from the law. Reminiscing in 1897, the Wisconsin lawyer Kate Kane Rossi recalled that "Miss Ray . . . although a lawyer of decided ability, on account of prejudice was not able to obtain sufficient legal business and had to give up . . . active practice." The Panic of 1873 and the ensuing economic depression had further dampened her chances for success.

Charlotte Ray attended the annual convention of the National Woman Suffrage Association in New York City in 1876. By 1879, she had returned to New York to live. For a time, like her two younger sisters, she taught in the Brooklyn public schools. Sometime before 1886, she was married to a man with the surname of Fraim, of whom nothing is known. By 1897, she was living in Woodside, Long Island. Charlotte Ray Fraim died of acute bronchitis at her Woodside home on January 11, 1911, at the age of sixty. She was buried in the Ray family plot in Cypress Hills Cemetery, Brooklyn.

In becoming a lawyer Charlotte Ray justified the dreams of many abolitionists, woman suffragists, and free black Americans. Enabled by the Civil War and Reconstruction to gain a law degree and bar admission, Charlotte Ray, with marked intellectual capacity and family support, took advantage of the opportunity.

DOROTHY THOMAS

S

Sampson, Edith (1901–1979)

Edith Sampson was the first black woman appointed as a judge in Illinois, the first woman to graduate from the Loyola University Law School in Chicago, the first black delegate to the United Nations, and the first black person to hold an appointment with the North Atlantic Treaty Organization (NATO).

Edith Spurlock was born on October 13, 1901, in Pittsburgh, Pennsylvania, one of eight children in the family of Louis and Elizabeth (McGruder) Spurlock. Her father earned $75 a month working in a cleaning and pressing establishment, and Elizabeth worked at home, making hat frames and switches for false hair. Louis and Elizabeth Spurlock owned their home and they lived comfortably.

Spurlock was educated in the Pittsburgh public schools. However, periodically she was forced to leave school to earn her tuition; at one time she worked in a fish market. After graduation she entered the School of Social Work at Columbia University in New York. Three years later she married Rufus Sampson, a field agent for Tuskegee Institute, and moved with him to Chicago. This marriage ended in divorce and she later remarried, to Chicago jurist Joseph Clayton.

During her first few years in Chicago, she was a homemaker, raised her sister's two small children after the sister's death, worked full time as a social worker, and earned an LL.B. in 1925 from the John Marshall Law School in Chicago by attending night classes. Sampson failed the bar examination that year. Then, in 1927, she enrolled in the Loyola University Law School and went on to become the first woman to receive an LL.M. from that school. She passed the Illinois bar in 1927 and was admitted to practice before the Supreme Court in 1934.

Sampson's public service career began in earnest shortly after she completed law school. Between 1934 and 1942, she worked simultaneously as a probation officer, a lawyer with a private law practice, and a referee in the Cook County Family Court. In 1949, she was selected by the **National Council of Negro Women** as their representative to participate in America's Town Meeting of the Air Program, with twenty-five other national, civic, cultural, welfare, and labor leaders. The group traveled to twelve countries, debating political issues of world concern. At the group's banquet in a Washington, D.C., hotel, Sampson was refused service and the activity was moved to another location. Many guests were upset, but when Sampson was asked how she could eat under the circumstances, she smiled, saying, "I've been colored a long time and if I stopped eating every time something like this happened, I'd be thin as a rail."

In 1950, Sampson was appointed by President Harry Truman as an alternate delegate to the United Nations General Assembly, where she was a strong advocate for the world's underprivileged children. Sampson's appointment was made at a time when the United States was being criticized for its treatment of black Americans, and officials of Communist governments charged that her appointment was merely window dressing to divert attention from the oppressive racial policies of the United States. Her response was that the president did not ask her to represent 6 million Negroes, but to represent 150 million Americans. She urged black Americans not to fall prey to Communist propaganda and separate themselves from white American society. She argued that under a democracy, black Americans at least have the freedom and opportunity to improve their situations. While a member of the United Nations General Assembly, Sampson also served as a member-at-large of NATO. Sampson was reappointed to the General Assembly in 1952. Also in 1952, Sampson served as a member-at-large of the United Nations Educational, Scientific, and Cultural Organization (UNESCO). Twelve years later, she was appointed to the U.S. Commission on NATO as a member of its U.S. Citizens Commission.

Sampson was an energetic speaker, urging full citizenship for black Americans. She was in great demand as a lecturer, traveling extensively throughout the Middle East, Scandinavia, Europe, and South America. She was as active in public service in Chicago as she was in national activities, holding the offices of assistant corporation counsel, associate judge of the municipal court, and judge of the Cook County Circuit Court.

Sampson died on October 8, 1979, in Chicago. In her long and distinguished career in public service, Edith Sampson worked tirelessly for equality for black citizens in this country. Her efforts are summed up best in her own words, "When we Negroes achieve first class citizenship in America, we will not drape our mantles over our shoulders and return anywhere; we are already there."

GLORIA V. WARREN

Sears-Collins, Leah (1955–)

She is not only the first black woman to serve on the Georgia Supreme Court, but Leah Sears-Collins is also the youngest person ever to serve on the Georgia Supreme Court. Described as hard-working, intelligent, and politically moderate, Sears-Collins offers refreshing change and new insights to what had been a bastion of established white males.

Born on June 13, 1955, in Heidelberg, Germany, Sears-Collins is the daughter of Colonel Thomas Sears and Onnye Jean Sears. Her father was a career officer in the army, a decorated flyer who served in both the Korean and Vietnam Wars. As such, he was assigned to army bases all over the world. Her mother was an elementary schoolteacher who taught at whatever schools happened to be nearby. Sears-Collins had two brothers, who both became flyers like their father before earning law degrees.

As the daughter of an army officer, Sears-Collins was exposed to many other cultures. She had circled the globe twice by the time she was sixteen and benefited greatly from living in other cultures. As she has said, "When you grow up around people of all different nationalities, you learn to feel at ease with people of every kind." Her family lived in Germany and Japan, returning to the United States when she was four. At that time she can remember driving with her family through Harlem and thinking, "Why do the brown people here live so poorly?" It gave her a great deal to think about in following years.

Sears-Collins' father was next stationed in Northern California, where she began school in Monterey. The school was all white, except for herself and her brothers. Other schools she attended in New York state and Georgia were also mostly white. While in Washington, D.C., she went to an all-black school for a year so that she could experience her own culture.

In 1968, Sears-Collins' family was transferred to Savannah, Georgia, where the schools were newly integrated. Sears-Collins became her high school's first black cheerleader and graduated in 1972.

Since she was a little girl, Sears-Collins had dreamed of being a judge. She won a full-tuition scholarship to Cornell University in Ithaca, New York, where she was involved with black studies and women's studies. She graduated with honors in 1976. Soon after graduation she married Love Collins III, a West Point graduate.

Her husband was stationed in Columbus, Georgia, but Sears-Collins had been accepted at Duke University Law School in North Carolina. When she started school in the fall, the separation proved too much for the young couple, and she returned to Columbus after only five weeks.

For the next year Sears-Collins was a feature writer for the *Columbus Ledger,* but she kept her dream of law school. She enrolled at Emory University Law School, which was located closer to her husband's base, in Atlanta, Georgia. There were few black students and no black faculty at Emory, but Sears-Collins did well and graduated in 1980.

Soon after graduation, Sears-Collins joined Alston and Bird, a large and prestigious law firm in Atlanta. She didn't like it. She made a good salary, but was assigned to business law, which she felt was too far away from the human side of law. She still had her old dream of becoming a judge. In 1982 she took a substantial cut in pay to become a municipal traffic judge. While this was hardly glamorous, the workload taught her the sheer discipline of running an effective courtroom.

In 1988, Sears-Collins ran for election to the Fulton County Superior Court. In a close three-way race, she won. She became the first black woman in the Georgia Supreme Court system and the youngest person in the court. She was only thirty-two. While serving on the court, Sears-Collins put her journalistic experience to good use by writing a series of articles on law for a wide range of newspapers and journals. She believed that legal issues should be discussed in clear language and that ordinary people needed to know about the legal issues that affected everyone.

In 1992, Sears-Collins was appointed to the Georgia Supreme Court by the governor of Georgia. As in her previous position, she was the first black woman to sit on the Georgia Supreme Court, and the youngest at the age of thirty-six.

Sears-Collins believes that one of her primary assets on the court is her age. She is the only judge on the Georgia Supreme Court to have grown up in the post-civil-rights era and the only mother of young children. She can often see a side to the cases that other judges overlook.

Sears-Collins is known for being a remarkably hard worker, regularly putting in ten-hour work days plus weekends. She delivers thoughtful, well-balanced decisions and she refuses to be swayed by politics. She has been given excellent reviews by the press, both in her native Georgia and nationally. After her initial appointment, Sears-Collins had to run for election in 1992 against a popular Superior Court judge, and she won by a narrow margin.

Making her way both as a scholar and a determined worker, Sears-Collins is opening the Georgia Supreme Court to what it should be—a court for all the people.

ANDRA MEDEA

Smythe-Haithe, Mabel Murphy
(1918–)

Ambassador, international educator, and world traveler, Mabel Murphy Smythe-Haithe has led a life that many would envy. From working in voter drives in the deep South as a teenager, Smythe-Haithe has gone on to be an ambassador to developing African nations, with many stops along the way in fascinating parts of the world.

Born on April 3, 1918, in Montgomery, Alabama, Smythe-Haithe was the daughter of Harry Saunders Murphy and Josephine Dibble Murphy. Her father was a creative and critical writer, who taught at Alabama State Normal College. He later owned his own printing company. He also wrote articles for newspapers such as the *Atlanta Daily World*. Both her parents were college educated and active in the **National Association for the Advancement of Colored People** (NAACP). As a teenager, Smythe-Haithe went along with them as they recruited black voters in Alabama—not always a safe occupation in those days.

College was a given for young Smythe-Haithe. She went to a private grammar school attached to Alabama State Normal College, then to high school at the Atlanta University Laboratory School. She attended **Spelman College** from 1933 to 1936, then deferred to her father's wishes that she go to college in New England. Having received a scholarship from Mount Holyoke College in Massachusetts, she moved there in 1937 and graduated with a bachelor's degree the same year.

Smythe-Haithe taught from 1937 to 1939 at Fort Valley Normal and Industrial Institute in Georgia, then married her first husband Hugh H. Smythe. Her husband was enrolled at the University of Wisconsin, and she moved north at this time. She received her M.A. from Northwestern University in 1940, then went on for a Ph.D. from the University of Wisconsin in 1942, with a major in economics and a minor in law.

After her husband finished his degree at the University of Wisconsin, he went into the army to serve in World War II. Until he returned, Smythe-Haithe taught at Lincoln University in Jefferson City, Missouri. She went on to become professor of economics at Tennessee Agricultural and Industrial College from 1945 to 1946. In 1946, she moved to the New York area, where she taught economics at Brooklyn College from 1946 to 1947. She did post-doctoral studies at New York University in 1949.

From 1951 to 1953, Smythe-Haithe took the first of her overseas posts at Shiga University in Japan, teaching English as a second language. Her husband Hugh also taught in Japan, at the University of Janaikechi. This opened her eyes to the exciting possibilities of teaching across languages and cultures.

When Smythe-Haithe returned to the United States in 1953, she went to work for the NAACP Legal Defense and Educational Fund, Inc. in Washington, D.C. She became their deputy director for non-legal research for school desegregation cases. This was 1953, when the NAACP and Thurgood Marshall were preparing their landmark school desegregation suits. Smythe-Haithe kept newspapers informed on developments in the case and wrote articles for the *Amsterdam News.*

In 1954, Smythe-Haithe returned to New York, where she was an instructor at New Lincoln School until 1959. From 1959 to 1969, she served as coordinating principal. She went on to be a lecturer at City College of the City University of New York from 1959 to 1960.

From 1970 to 1972, Smythe-Haithe was director of research and publications at the Phelps-Stokes Fund, serving as vice-president from 1972 to 1977. This project took her back to her interest in international education. Among her duties was overseas travel to facilitate African scholars coming to study in the United States.

In 1973, Smythe-Haithe became a scholar in residence for the United States Commission on Civil Rights, serving until 1974. She spent time with her husband at

his diplomatic posts in Syria and Malta, until his death in 1977. Later that same year Smythe-Haithe was asked to become Ambassador to the United Republic of Cameroon, serving until 1980. She was also named Ambassador to the Republic of Equatorial Guinea from 1979 to 1980.

After her experience as ambassador, Smythe-Haithe worked in the State Department stateside as deputy assistant secretary for African affairs. As such, she took part in many diplomatic missions to Mozambique, Zimbabwe, Liberia, and Botswana, among other countries. She also represented the United States at international conferences and meetings around the world.

In the 1980s, Smythe-Haithe returned to teaching at her alma mater, Northwestern, as the Melville J. Herskovits Professor of African Studies. She served at this post from 1981 to 1983. From 1983 to 1985 she was associate director of the African studies department.

In 1985, she married Robert Haithe and moved back to the East Coast. In 1986, she became a board member of Ralph Bunche Institute on the United Nations at the City University of New York. Later she became a Julius Rosenwald Fellow and a Harriet-Remington Laird Fellow.

Smythe-Haithe has written a number of books within her several areas of expertise. After she taught English in Japan, she co-authored *Intensive English Conversation*, which was published in 1953. Her African studies led her to co-author *The New Nigerian Elite*, published in 1960. Her work as a teacher and principal resulted in her co-authoring *Curriculum for Understanding*, published in 1965. She also wrote *Introduction to a Slaver's Log,* published in

1976, and edited the *American Negro Reference Book* in 1974 and *The Black American Reference Book* in 1976.

Smythe-Haithe has had many academic and civic honors, including honorary degrees from Mount Holyoke and Spelman Colleges. In 1981, after serving as ambassador, she was named grand officer, Order of Valor, in Cameroon. The following year in the United States she was given the **Mary McLeod Bethune** Women of Achievement Award. She has served on dozens of educational, diplomatic, and United Nations boards and committees. At different times she has been particularly active in UNESCO, as a member of the board of trustees of Mount Holyoke College, and the Urban League of New York.

A brilliant woman with a zest for life, Smythe-Haithe notes that she also likes to pilot light airplanes.

ANDRA MEDEA

Stout, Juanita Kidd (1919–)

Juanita Kidd Stout is noteworthy for a career of firsts in the legal profession, being both the first black woman to be elected to a judgeship and the first to serve on a state supreme court. Born in Wewoka, Oklahoma, on March 7, 1919, she was the only child of Henry and Mary Kidd. Both college educated, the Kidds raised their daughter in an environment that was conducive to learning. A very bright child, Juanita was taught to read at the age of two by her mother, who was a schoolteacher. Reading together was a favorite family pastime.

Juanita Kidd was educated in the segregated public schools of Wewoka, where she received an excellent education from the dedicated black teachers. Upon graduating in 1935, she left Oklahoma because the separate black college for African Americans, Langston University, was unaccredited. She enrolled at the University of Iowa, where she earned a B.A. in music in 1939.

In June 1942, Juanita Kidd married Charles Otis Stout, who used his educational benefits from the GI Bill so that he could go to graduate school and Juanita could go to law school. Juanita Kidd Stout earned a J.D. (1948), while Charles Otis Stout earned his Ph.D., both from Indiana University.

In 1948, the Stouts moved to Washington, D.C., where Juanita Kidd Stout became the administrative secretary for the Honorable Charles H. Houston of the law firm of Houston, Houston, and Hastie. In 1949, when William H. Hastie was appointed as a judge for the U.S. Court of Appeals for the Third Circuit in Philadelphia, Juanita Kidd Stout joined him in Philadelphia to serve as his administrative secretary. Between 1953 and 1955, she worked in private practice, specializing in civil and criminal law. In 1955, however, she accepted a post as an assistant district attorney for Philadelphia, while continuing a limited private practice. In November 1959, Juanita Kidd Stout was elected as a Philadelphia county court judge, and became the first African-American woman to be elected to a court of record. She successfully ran for retention in 1969 and in 1979. Remarkably, during these years Judge Stout's decisions were reversed fewer than ten times.

Judge Stout was appointed to the state supreme court in February 1988 and was inducted on March 3, 1988, becoming the first African-American woman to serve on a state supreme court. She was forced to retire in 1989, on her seventieth birthday, due to the mandatory retirement provision of the Pennsylvania constitution. She subsequently served as a senior judge in the Court of Common Pleas in Philadelphia.

During the course of her memorable career, Justice Stout has been awarded ten LL.D. degrees and an L.H.D., has written several articles, and has received over 250 organizational awards. An article in the *Retainer,* a publication of the Philadelphia Bar Association, proclaimed that Justice Stout "possesses all of the qualities that are necessary to be a great jurist—a keen intellect, an appreciation of the issues, compassion where appropriate, an inexhaustible supply of energy and the courage to apply the law fairly and justly regardless of how controversial the issues or powerful the parties."

V. P. FRANKLIN

T

Taylor, Anna Diggs (1932–)

Lawyer, judge, and consistent advocate for civil rights, Anna Johnston Diggs Taylor was born on December 9, 1932, in Washington, D.C. Her parents enrolled her in the Northfield School for Girls in East Northfield, Massachusetts. After graduating from Northfield in 1950, she attended Barnard College and Columbia University and received a bachelor's degree in economics in 1954. She was attracted to Yale Law School by its standards and its offer of scholarship aid. In 1957, she graduated with a degree of LL.B. In spite of her strong scholastic record, her race and gender prevented her from being hired by a law firm. With the help of a high-ranking black official, J. Ernest Wilkins, the assistant secretary of labor, she was hired in 1957 as an assistant solicitor in the Solicitor's Office of the U.S. Department of Labor, where she remained until 1960. From 1960 until 1972, Anna Johnston was married to Charles C. Diggs, Jr., a mortician, politician, and a U.S. congressman serving as a Democrat from Detroit since 1955. Living together in Detroit, they had two children: Douglass Johnston Diggs (1964) and Carla Cecile Diggs (1967). In 1976, she married attorney S. Martin Taylor, an executive with state government and, later, with private organizations.

Anna Diggs Taylor has held several significant positions in her professional life and has been involved in numerous civic activities. She was admitted to practice law in Washington, D.C., in 1957 and in Michigan in 1961. She served as assistant Wayne County prosecutor from 1961 to 1962, as assistant U.S. attorney for the Eastern District of Michigan from 1966 to 1967, and supervising assistant corporation counsel for the City of Detroit's Law Department from 1975 to 1979. In 1964, Taylor and Claudia Shropshire Morcom were the only women attorneys volunteering their legal services in civil rights cases handled by the National Lawyers Guild in the Mississippi "Freedom Summer." Taylor worked as an attorney with a law firm from 1970 to 1975 and also taught law courses in the 1970s. Her considerable political involvement included campaigns to reelect Charles Diggs to Congress, serving as Diggs' legislative assistant and manager of his Detroit office from 1967 to 1970 and, in 1973, aiding in the campaign to elect Coleman Young as Detroit's first black mayor. In addition, she worked as chairperson of Lawyers for Humphrey and Lawyers for McGovern and was also prominent in the effort to elect Jimmy Carter president.

In November 1979, Taylor became a federal judge for life when President Jimmy Carter appointed her to the United States District Court, Eastern District of Michigan. Her work as a judge has attracted considerable attention, much praise, and some criticism. She is known for her fairness to all, though a few lawyers think she tends to favor the plaintiff in civil rights cases and the defendant in criminal cases. Even her critics say that she, like other judges, often produces "very good, sophisticated opinions." Vigilant in trying to sensitize others to the negative quality of their racial views, in 1984 she criticized the chief judge of her own court, John Feikens, for his published remarks to the effect that black people had not yet learned how to run city governments and "some will not understand how to run government . . . [or to provide] leadership." Judge Taylor wrote Judge Feikens a letter that eventually became public, stating that his remarks were "an extraordinary insult to all black professionals and/or administrators, and indicates a total failure to value human individuals on their individual merit: the essence of bigotry." Taylor has received many high honors and distinctions and is frequently cited as a model for young people to emulate.

DE WITT S. DYKES, JR.

Tucker, C. DeLores (1927–)

C. DeLores Tucker was born October 4, 1927, in Philadelphia to the Reverend Whitfield and Captilda Gardiner Nottage. She was the tenth of eleven children. She was educated in the public schools of the city and graduated from the Philadelphia High School for Girls in 1946. C. DeLores Nottage attended Temple University, where she studied finance and real estate. She also attended the North Philadelphia Realty School, and two years after her marriage to William Tucker on July 21, 1951, they established Tucker and Tucker Real Estate Company.

With the coming of the protest and demonstrations associated with the civil rights movement in the early 1960s, C. DeLores Tucker became involved in the campaigns in Philadelphia. She served as vice president of the Philadelphia branch of the **National Association for the Advancement of Colored People** and in 1961 she was a delegate to President John F. Kennedy's White House Conference on Civil Rights. Between 1963 and 1966 the Philadelphia NAACP, under the leadership of Cecil Moore, launched a series of protests and demonstrations to end the discriminatory practices of construction trades unions, post offices, and bus companies in the city and C. DeLores Tucker participated in and led these protests. In March 1965, she headed a Philadelphia delegation that accompanied Martin Luther King, Jr., on the famous march from Selma to Montgomery, Alabama, in support of voting rights legislation. In 1968, she became chair of the Pennsylvania Black Democratic Committee.

A Philadelphia public relations firm, C. DeLores Tucker Associates, was formed in 1967 and the following year Tucker was appointed by Mayor James H. J. Tate to the board of adjustment of the Philadelphia Zoning Commission. This was the first of many major political appointments. In 1970, she was appointed vice-chair of the Pennsylvania Democratic Party, and in January 1971, Governor Milton Shapp appointed Tucker as Pennsylvania's secretary of state. She was the first African American to serve in such a position in the United States. She was reappointed to the office in 1975 and served until 1977.

Secretary of State Tucker was instrumental in the appointment of numerous women and minorities to judgeships and political offices throughout the state. She served on numerous state boards and commissions, including the Pennsylvania Commission on Women and the State Bicentennial Commission, and she headed the governor's Affirmative Action Council. She also headed several national organizations, serving as the vice president of the National Association of Secretaries of State (1976), national president of the Federation of Democratic Women (1977), and chair of the Democratic National Committee's Black Caucus (1984).

Tucker also has served on several community boards and a number of charitable organizations. She has been a member of the board of directors of the Philadelphia branch of the **Young Women's Christian Association,** the New School of Music, the Urban Coalition, the United Fund, Philadelphia Tribune Charities, Inc., the Medical College of Pennsylvania (Commonwealth Board), and Messiah College, and a member of the national board of directors for People United to Save Humanity (PUSH).

Tucker has received numerous honors and awards, including the 1961 NAACP Freedom Fund Award, the National Association of Television and Radio Artists' Woman of the Year Award in 1972, the Martin Luther King Service and Achievement Award, and the Community Service Award from the Philadelphia Chapter of B'nai B'rith. She has been awarded honorary degrees from Villa Maria College in Erie, Pennsylvania, and Morris College in Sumter, South Carolina. She was listed among the 100 most influential black Americans by *Ebony* magazine in 1973, 1974, and 1975.

In 1984, along with **Shirley Chisholm,** she founded the **National Political Congress of Black Women** to assist African-American women who are interested in running for political office, and in 1985, she founded the Bethune-DuBois Fund to assist young black professionals in gaining internships and employment in federal agencies in Washington, D.C. Tucker is still active in Philadelphia politics and was appointed by Mayor W. Wilson Goode to serve as Philadelphia's ambassador to Washington, D.C.

V. P. FRANKLIN

W

Waters, Maxine (1938–)

"I don't have time to be polite," says Maxine Waters. "Too many black politicians want to be in the mainstream. They don't want to talk about affirmative action, crime, or drugs. My power comes from the fact that I am ready to talk about black people." Ready to talk. Ready to argue. Ready to fight. Congresswoman Maxine Waters seems to be ready to do anything it takes to make life better for the people she serves.

Born in the housing projects of St. Louis, Missouri, on August 15, 1938, Waters was one of thirteen children of a "sometimes single" mother. After high school, she married, had two children, and worked in factories and as a waitress in segregated restaurants. She and her husband moved to Los Angeles, where she worked in a garment factory and at the telephone company. In the late 1960s, she went to California State University to study sociology. In 1972, she was divorced and, in 1977, was remarried, to Sidney Williams.

Her political involvement grew out of her experience teaching in Head Start. Her activities increased rapidly, leading to her election, in 1976, to the California Assembly from South Central Los Angeles. In 1984, she was chair of the Democratic caucus. It took eight years, but she managed to push through legislation divesting California state pension funds from companies doing business in South Africa. In her own district, she built a vocational and education center that is an extension of the local high school and, through Project Build, brought social services from downtown Los Angeles to the Watts housing projects.

Waters served as a delegate to the Democratic National Convention in 1980 and has been a key advisor to Jesse Jackson since his presidential campaign in 1984. She was elected in 1990 to represent the twenty-ninth district of California in the U.S. House of Representatives. She evinced no freshman shyness. In 1991, she was a leader in the fight to defeat an attempt to weaken laws that require banks and savings and loans to serve minority communities and low-income areas. Shortly thereafter she attacked the chairman of the House Veterans Affairs Committee for not sufficiently representing black soldiers and veterans of Operation Desert Storm.

In 1992, Waters rose to national prominence following the acquittal of four white Los Angeles policemen charged with the beating of Rodney King, a black man. Amid the ensuing riots protesting both the verdict and ongoing governmental neglect of largely black and Latino inner-city neighborhoods, Waters emerged as one of several spokespersons for the black community of South Central Los Angeles. Her terse, angry condemnations of justice denied to black Americans and her criticism of both the Reagan and Bush adminis-

California Representative Maxine Waters was one of thirteen children of a "sometimes single" mother in the housing projects of St. Louis, Missouri. A tireless community activist, Waters emerged as an eloquent spokesperson for the black community of South Central Los Angeles during the riots that ensued after the Rodney King verdict. (OFFICE OF REPRESENTATIVE WATERS)

trations demonstrated her willingness to take tough stands on behalf of her constituents.

KATHLEEN THOMPSON

Watson, Diane Edith (1933–)

Diane Edith Watson was born on November 12, 1933 in Los Angeles. She is the daughter of William Allen Louis and Dorothy Elizabeth O'Neal Watson. She attended the University of California at Los Angeles (UCLA). She pursued a career in teaching, first in Okinawa and France and then at California State University (CSU) at Los Angeles, where she earned a master's degree in school psychology.

In 1975, Watson became the first black woman ever elected to the Board of Education of the Los Angeles Unified School District. The school busing controversy was raging, and Watson, because of her position, was deeply involved. Drawing on her experience, she wrote a doctoral dissertation analyzing the implementation of school desegregation in Los Angeles. She received the degree in 1987.

In the meantime, however, Watson has moved from the school board to the state senate. In 1979, she was elected from California's twenty-sixth district. She was the first African-American woman to serve as a state senator in California.

Watson's district includes much of Los Angeles, including Culver City and such neighborhoods as Cheviot Hills, Crenshaw, Koreatown, Mar Vista, Miracle Mile, and the area around the University of Southern California (USC). It has a diverse, ethnically and culturally mixed constituency, which Watson has now represented for almost two decades.

For the past ten years, Watson has been chair of the Health and Human Services Committee. It is an ideal position from which to minister to the needs of the low-income residents of her district. She has been a champion of expanding the school breakfast program, for example. "If the stomach hurts," she says, "nothing gets through to the brain." She is also enor-

In 1979 Diane Watson became the first African-American woman to serve as a state senator in California. As chair of the Health and Human Services Committee, Watson has worked hard to expand the school breakfast program and to provide decent health care for children. (OFFICE OF SENATOR WATSON)

mously active in the move to provide adequate health care to children. And, in 1995, she cosponsored a bill that would allow the state of California to sue cigarette companies to recoup the health-care costs of smokers.

Working on the state level, Diane Watson has had a lasting impact on politics and life in this country. It remains to be seen whether her activities will stay on that level.

KATHLEEN THOMPSON

Welcome, Verda Freeman
(1907–1990)

"One day I am going to vote and pay back the insult to my father." Verda Welcome's childhood pledge propelled her into becoming one of the most outstanding legislative trailblazers of the civil rights movement in Maryland for more than twenty-five years. In 1962, Welcome was the first African-American woman elected to a state senate seat anywhere in the United States. She led the fight for legislation to open Maryland's public accommodations to all races and became a powerful and influential member of Maryland's senate finance committee.

Welcome was the third of sixteen children born to James and Docia Freeman in Uree (later Lake Lure) in North Carolina. Her mother died when Verda was young and she assumed responsibility for her family. She migrated to Baltimore, Maryland, in 1929 and soon after enrolled in Coppin State Teachers College, graduating in 1932. After marrying Dr. Henry C. Welcome in 1935, she continued teaching in the public school system as well as studying at Morgan State University, from which she graduated in 1939. In 1943, while caring for her husband and daughter Mary Sue, she received a master's degree from New York University to improve her opportunities to teach.

Welcome's political activism began after she emerged as president of Baltimore's North West Improvement Association, which in the 1950s spearheaded the fight to lower racial barriers in public places. With the assistance of a group of fellow activists (called the Valiant Women), she ran for the Maryland House of Delegates in 1958 and defeated the powerful Jack Pollack political machine in the predominantly black fourth legislative district in Baltimore.

Welcome was elected a Maryland state senator in 1962 and retained her seat for almost twenty years. During these years her legislative accomplishments included legislation for public accommodations, the repealing of Maryland's miscegenation law, and bills that required equal pay for equal work, gun control, and voter registration by mail. She survived an April 1964 assassination attempt. Among her numerous awards were honorary doctorates from the University of Maryland (1970), **Howard University** (1972), and Morgan State University (1976).

Verda Freeman Welcome died in 1990.

GLENN O. PHILLIPS

Williams, Margaret (1954–)

"She's brilliant," says **Marian Wright Edelman,** founder of the Children's Defense Fund. "She has one of the best strategic minds I've ever seen." She is also the most powerful black women ever to serve in the White House. Maggie Williams, Chief of Staff to First Lady Hillary Clinton, is adviser, liaison, manager, and communications firefighter for the powerful and controversial first lady. From working with the press on managed health care to tailoring Hillary Clinton's image to the public, Williams has been astute and quick to handle good news and bad. Refusing to play power broker in a town where power madness is an occupational disease, Williams remains a much-needed voice of sanity.

Born in Kansas City, Missouri, on Christmas Day, 1954, Williams is the daughter of a schoolteacher and a government clerk. Her spiritual values and work ethic came from her mother, Erma Williams. Her father died suddenly when she was still young, and the $100 each month from social security survivor's benefits helped put her through college. Her older

As chief of staff to First Lady Hillary Clinton, Margaret ("Maggie") Williams serves as adviser, liaison, manager and communications firefighter for her controversial boss. She's so good at her job the president once tried to hire her to work for him, but Williams opted to stay with the first lady. (WHITE HOUSE PHOTOGRAPH)

brother, who had already gone to college, sent her spending money.

Williams attended Trinity College in Washington, D.C., graduating with a degree in political science in 1977. She was ill at ease as part of a small black minority at a private school in an overwhelmingly black city. She regularly posted news from nearby **Howard University** in her own college paper.

While still an undergraduate, Williams began her adventures in politics, first as an aide to Congressman Morris Udall of Arizona, then as legislative secretary for Congressman Alan Howe of Utah. She next became deputy press secretary for the Democratic National Committee, writing and editing Democratic communications from 1979 to 1981.

In 1982, Williams became press secretary for Rep. Robert Torricelli, the Democratic congressman from New Jersey. She now was in charge of communications for the congressman, dealing with the press and arranging media events. At the beginning of 1983 Williams became deputy director at the Center on Budget and Policy Priorities, which again emphasized her dealing with the media.

In 1984, Williams moved on to become senior media analyst at the Children's Defense Fund, developing their teenage pregnancy prevention media campaign. She quickly realized that it wouldn't work just to tell teenagers to stop getting pregnant. Instead, pregnancy prevention would have to be sold to teenagers, like fashion. Working with the ad agency Fallon McElligott, Williams developed a multi-media ad campaign that still continues to win awards.

In 1988, Williams was promoted to Director of Media Affairs at the Children's Defense Fund, which put her in charge of a staff of sixteen, with a budget of nearly $1 million. It was at this point that she began to work with Hillary Clinton, who was on the board of directors.

In 1990, after many years of Republican administrations, Williams had had enough of government. She decided to leave Washington with its power plays and go to graduate school at the Annenberg School of Communications at the University of Pennsylvania. She had a standing job offer with Fallon McElligott, where she worked on the pregnancy prevention campaign. She liked the slower pace and smaller egos. She thought she might like to get a Ph.D. Instead she got a call at school from Hillary Clinton. Williams finished her M.A. in 1992 and went to work that August in the Clinton campaign.

Williams' role at the White House includes managing press and media coverage for the first lady, as well as acting as adviser and representing the White House on various occasions. Williams is known for being able to deliver the truth, whether that is easy or not. Williams handled a tigerish press while Hillary Clinton was pursuing pubic health care issues. Williams has handled her staff so well that President Clinton tried to hire her away, to be deputy chief of staff for himself. She declined, staying with Hillary.

Oddly, one of Williams' most controversial roles had little to do with her talent or politics. After answering a beeper message, Williams was one of three White House aides who went to the office of White House Counsel Vincent Foster immediately after he committed suicide. Rumors and innuendo flew, with tales of stolen reports and aides hurriedly hiding files. Williams reports a much more normal response. She sat on the coach and cried. She was relieved to get the matter cleared up finally at a grand jury hearing.

A refreshing dose of normality in a high-pressure position, Williams walks the corridors of power without letting it turn her into a different person. And someday she may get out of Washington yet.

ANDRA MEDEA

Williams, Patricia J. (1951–)

"We may no longer issue scarlet letters," writes Patricia J. Williams, "but from the way we talk we might as well: W for welfare, S for Single, B for black, CC for children having children, WT for white trash."

Patricia J. Williams has confronted stereotyping and "branding" not only in her books but in her life. Born on August 28, 1951, in Boston, Massachusetts, she is the great-great-granddaughter of a slave and a white Southern lawyer. She attended Wellesley College, where she received her B.A., and then went on to Harvard Law School, where she received her J.D., and Dartmouth College, where she was a fellow in the School of Criticism and Theory.

Williams has been an associate professor at the University of Wisconsin School of Law and department of women's studies. She has worked as a consumer advocate in the office of the city attorney in Los Angeles, California, and been a fellow at the Humanities Research Institute in Irvine,

Great-great-granddaughter of a slave and a white Southern lawyer, Patricia Williams is a law professor and an author. Her books, The Alchemy of Race and Rights *and* The Rooster's Egg *have been warmly praised by Henry Louis Gates, Jr. and Cornel West.*
(JON NICKSON)

California. She was also a visiting scholar-in-residence at Duke University.

Among the many articles Williams has published are "Anthony Burns: The Defeat and Triumph of a Fugitive Slave," "On Being the Object of Property," and "The Electronic Transformation of Law."

Of her first book, *The Alchemy of Race and Rights,* Henry Louis Gates, Jr., wrote in the *Nation* that it was "one of the most invitingly personal, even vulnerable, books I've read. . . . the law needs a brain . . . and, even more, a heart and some courage. Certificates won't help. This book just might."

After the publication of her second book, *The Rooster's Egg,* Cornel West wrote, "[She] is a towering public intellectual of our time—she articulates a synoptic vision, synthetic analysis, and moral courage with great power."

Williams is a professor of law at Columbia University. A member of the Federal Court of Appeals, Ninth Circuit, she serves on the Advisory Council for the Medgar Evers Center for Law and Social Justice of the City University of New York.

HILARY MAC AUSTIN

Chronology

1619

The first African women are brought to North America, landing at Jamestown, Virginia.

1641

Massachusetts is the first colony in North America to recognize slavery legally.

1644

Lucie van Angola and Antony d'Angola marry on Manhattan Island, New York—the first recorded marriage of African Americans in the colony.

1646

Governor Theophilus Eaton of the New Haven, Conn., colony frees his slaves John Wham and his wife; this is the earliest account of free blacks in New England, as recorded in the "Public Records of the State of Connecticut."

1650

Connecticut is the second colony in North America to recognize slavery legally.

1661

Virginia legally recognizes slavery.

1662

Virginia passes a law stating that children will be considered slave or free depending on the status of their mother.

1663

Settlers are offered twenty acres for every black male slave and ten acres for every black female slave brought into the Carolina colony.

Maryland legalizes slavery.

1664

New York and New Jersey legally recognize slavery.

1681

A black woman is indicted for burning down a building in Roxbury, Massachusetts; she is later burned at the stake.

1682

South Carolina legally recognizes slavery.

1692

A West Indian slave named Tituba is a defendant in the Salem witchcraft trials.

1700

Rhode Island and Pennsylvania legally recognize slavery.

1708

Black women participate in a slave revolt in Newton, Long Island, New York.

1712

Black women participate in a slave revolt in New York City. A pregnant woman is captured by the authorities but pardoned.

1715

North Carolina legally recognizes slavery.

1735

Georgia bans the importation and use of slaves.

1736

Emanuel Manna Bernoon, a free black, opens the first catering business in Providence, Rhode Island; Bernoon and his wife later establish a highly successful oyster house in Providence.

1749

Georgia repeals its ban on slavery.

1750

Georgia is the last colony to recognize slavery legally.

1765

Jenny Slew sues for her freedom in a Massachusetts court and wins.

1776

Margaret Corbin (or "Captain Molly") takes up arms during the Revolution; she is wounded during an attack on Fort Washington, New York.

1777

Vermont abolishes slavery.

1780

Pennsylvania passes a gradual emancipation law. It is the first of the original colonies to do so.

1781

Elizabeth Freeman sues for her freedom in a Massachusetts court, basing her case on the state's constitution, which declares that all men are born free and equal.

1784

Connecticut and Rhode Island pass gradual emancipation laws.

1787

Mary Butler, the daughter of Mary and William Butler, who sued for their freedom and lost their case in 1771, sues for her freedom and wins, establishing a precedent in Maryland that liberalizes the rule of descent.

The United States Constitution is approved with three clauses protecting slavery.

The Northwest Ordinance prohibits slavery in the territory that will become the states of Michigan, Ohio, Illinois, Indiana, and Wisconsin.

1793

Twenty-three free black men and women from Canada and some white supporters sign a petition protesting the state poll tax on free blacks in South Carolina.

The first fugitive slave law is passed by Congress. The law makes it a criminal offense to help a fugitive slave.

1796

Lucy Terry Prince is the first woman to argue her case before the U.S. Supreme Court; the Court rules in favor of the Prince family in a dispute with a white man who attempts to steal land from them.

1799

New York passes a gradual emancipation law.

1804

New Jersey passes a gradual emancipation law.

The Ohio legislature passes the first of a series of Black Laws enacted throughout the Northern states. These laws restrict the rights and movements of free African Americans.

1826

Frances "Fanny" Wright establishes Nashoba, a colony for free blacks near Memphis, Tennessee; plagued by administrative problems and widespread disease, the colony will fail and the remaining settlers move to Haiti in 1830.

1829

Following a terrible race riot in Cincinnati, Ohio, more than 1,000 black women, men, and children leave the city to immigrate to Canada.

1831

The first Colored Female Society is organized in Philadelphia, Pennsylvania.

Maria W. Stewart, an early feminist, publishes a small pamphlet, *Religion and the Pure Principles of Morality, the Sure Foundation on Which We Must Build.*

1832

Maria W. Stewart begins an unprecedented public speaking tour at Franklin Hall, Boston, Massachusetts; she is the first woman in the United States to engage in public political debates.

The Female Anti-Slavery Society of Salem, Massachusetts, is founded by free black women, including Mary A. and Dorothy C. Battys, Charlotte Bell, and Eleanor C. Harvey.

1833

The interracial **Philadelphia Female Anti-Slavery Society** is organized; Lucretia Mott is elected president; **Sarah M. Douglass,** the Quaker principal of the preparatory department of the **Institute for Colored Youth,** Harriet Purvis, and Sarah and Margaretta Forten—daughters of James Forten, Sr.—are charter members.

1834

The Colored Female Anti-Slavery Society is established in Middletown, Connecticut, and Newark, New Jersey.

1836

A group of black women rush a Boston courtroom and carry away to freedom two fugitive slave women before they can be returned to those claiming to be their masters. Black women in New York perform a similar rescue.

1837

The first Antislavery Convention of American Women meets in New York. At least one-tenth of the members are African Americans.

1843

Sojourner Truth leaves New York and begins abolitionist work; she is one of the first black women abolitionist lecturers.

1848

Benjamin Roberts files suit on behalf of his daughter, Sarah, to integrate a Boston school. The suit is denied in 1849 with the first known use of the "separate but equal" defense.

1849

Harriet Tubman escapes from slavery in Maryland. She will return nineteen times to the South to bring out more than 300 slaves on the Underground Railroad.

The Woman's Association of Philadelphia, Pennsylvania, is organized with the specific purpose of raising money to support Frederick Douglass' newspaper *North Star.*

1850

The Fugitive Slave Law is passed. It gives virtually unlimited authority to any white man claiming a black person as his runaway slave.

Thousands of African Americans flee to Canada in response to the Fugitive Slave Law.

1851

Armed black men and women defend against recapture of four escaped slaves in Christiana, Pennsylvania. Thirty-six of them are accused of treason and later acquitted in court.

1854

In New York City, Elizabeth Jennings sues the Third Avenue Railroad Company. She wins $225 in damages and the ruling that "colored persons, if sober, well-behaved and free from disease" can ride the horsecars without segregation.

1861

The Civil War begins. Thousands of slave women and men begin the process of self-emancipation by running away. Many work with the Union Army.

1862

Congress abolishes slavery in Washington, D.C.

Susie King Taylor becomes the first African-American army nurse at the age of fourteen.

1863

Harriet Tubman leads Union troops in a raid along the Combahee River in South Carolina.

1864

Maryland abolishes slavery.

Mary Ann Shadd Cary receives a commission as a recruiting officer from the governor of Indiana. She is the only woman given official recognition as a recruiter during the Civil War.

1865

The Thirteenth Amendment to the Constitution is adopted. It abolishes slavery.

1868

The Fourteenth Amendment is adopted. It extends the rights of citizenship to African Americans.

1869

The American Equal Rights Association splits over whether to put aside the demand for the vote for women until after it has been gained for black men. The National

Woman Suffrage Association and the American Woman Suffrage Association are formed.

Mary Ann Shadd Cary chairs the Committee on Female Suffrage at the Colored National Labor Union (CNLU) convention and becomes the only woman elected to the CNLU's executive committee.

1870

The Fifteenth Amendment is ratified. It extends the right to vote to black men.

1871

Mary Ann Shadd Cary addresses the House of Representatives' Judiciary Committee, speaking on women's suffrage.

1872

Charlotte E. Ray becomes the first black woman to receive a law degree in the United States when she graduates from Howard University Law School in February. She was admitted to the bar of the District of Columbia in March, making her the first black woman regularly admitted to the practice of law in any jurisdiction in the United States.

1875

The Civil Rights Bill of 1875 guarantees equal access to public accommodations without regard to race.

1876

Harriet Purvis is the first African-American woman to be elected vice president of the National Woman Suffrage Association.

1880

Mary Ann Shadd Cary and other black women form the Colored Women's Pro-gressive Franchise Association in Washington, D.C. Its twin goals are to gain the vote for women and to establish black women in business.

1883

The U.S. Supreme Court declares the Civil Rights Act of 1875 unconstitutional.

Mary Ann Shadd Cary becomes the second black woman to earn a law degree when she graduates from Howard University.

1891

Lucy Parsons begins publishing her newspaper, *Freedom: A Revolutionary Anarchist-Communist Monthly.*

1892

Ida B. Wells (Barnett) begins the anti-lynching movement with articles and editorials in the Memphis *Free Speech,* the *New York Age* and the publication of the book *Southern Horrors.*

1896

In *Plessy* v. *Ferguson,* the U.S. Supreme Court rules that "separate but equal" facilities are constitutional. The ruling supports Jim Crow laws.

The **National Association of Colored Women** is founded with **Mary Church Terrell** as its first president.

1900

At the First Pan-African Conference in London, Anna H. Jones of Missouri and **Anna Julia Cooper** of Washington, D.C., are the only black women to address the gathering. Cooper is an official U.S. delegate and an elected member of the executive committee.

1902

President Theodore Roosevelt suspends postal service to Indianola, Mississippi, after white supremacists displace **Minnie Cox** as postmistress.

1903

Georgia Anderson and other working-class women from Savannah submit a petition to the Georgia legislature requesting 2,000 to immigrate to Africa.

1908

Josephine Leavell Allensworth and her husband, Allen, found the all-black colony of Allensworth, California.

1913

Illinois becomes the first state east of the Mississippi River to give women the right to vote.

The **Alpha Suffrage Club** is founded in Illinois.

Ida B. Wells-Barnett is asked not to march with the white Illinois delegation at the National American Woman Suffrage Association parade in Washington, D.C.

1917

Ten thousand African Americans march down Fifth Avenue in New York City in an NAACP-sponsored silent parade to protest racial discrimination and racial violence.

When women gain the vote in Texas, black women organize Negro Women Voter Leagues.

1918

The Women's Political Association of Harlem is one of the first African-American organizations to advocate birth control.

1919

In Los Angeles, Georgia Hill Robinson becomes the first African-American policewoman in the United States.

1920

The Nineteenth Amendment grants women the right to vote.

Violette N. Anderson becomes the first black woman to practice law in Illinois.

1921

Jessie Fauset is a delegate to the Second Pan-African Congress, representing the National Association of Colored Women.

1922

The Anti-Lynching Crusaders is organized under **Mary Talbert**'s leadership.

1924

The National League of Republican Colored Women is organized.

Mary Montgomery Booze is the first black woman elected to the Republican National Committee.

Mary McLeod Bethune is elected president of the National Association of Colored Women.

1926

The National Bar Association is founded.

Violette N. Anderson is the first black woman lawyer to argue a case before the United States Supreme Court.

1927

Minnie Buckingham-Harper becomes the first black woman to serve in a United States legislative body when she is appointed to fill her husband's unexpired term in the West Virginia legislature after his death.

1931

Jane Mathilda Bolin is the first black woman to graduate from Yale University Law School.

1935

Mary McLeod Bethune is appointed to the Advisory Board of the National Youth Administration (NYA).

Crystal Bird Fauset becomes director of Negro women's activities of the Democratic National Committee.

The National Council of Negro Women is founded, with Mary McLeod Bethune as its president.

1938

Crystal Bird Fauset is the first black woman elected to major public office in the U.S. when she is elected to the Pennsylvania State Assembly.

The National Council of Negro Women sponsors a national Conference on Governmental Cooperation in the Approach to the Problems of Negro Women and Children. The conference is held at the Department of the Interior and at the White House.

1939

Jane Mathilda Bolin is appointed justice of the Domestic Relations Court of the City of New York. She is the first black woman judge in the United States.

Mary McLeod Bethune becomes director of the newly created Negro Division of the National Youth Administration. This is the highest federal position held by a black woman to date.

1942

Charity Adams (Earley) is the first black woman to become a commissioned officer in the Women's Army Auxiliary Corps, later known as the WACs.

1944

Anna Arnold Hedgeman is named executive director of the National Council for the federal Fair Employment Practices Commission.

1946

Interstate traveler Irene Morgan refuses to sit at the back of a Greyhound bus in Virginia. The Supreme Court rules that states cannot require segregation on interstate buses.

Willa Brown (a pioneer black woman aviator) runs for Congress on the Republican ticket from the first district of Illinois, making her one of the first black women ever to run for the House from a major party.

1947

The Journey of Reconciliation project sends a biracial group on a bus ride through the Upper South to test compliance with the 1946 *Morgan* decision.

Rosa Lee Ingram is convicted and sentenced to death, along with two of her sons, for the murder of a neighboring white tenant farmer who, she alleged, had assaulted her. The case spurs a national defense campaign, which results in her pardon in 1959.

1948

In *Ada Lois Sipuel* v. *Board of Regents,* the Supreme Court orders the University of Oklahoma School of Law to admit Sipuel because there is no separate and equal professional school for African Americans.

1949

The **Women's Political Council** is founded in Montgomery, Alabama, by **Mary Fair Burks.**

1950

Attorney **Edith Sampson** is the first African American to be appointed an alternate delegate to the United Nations General Assembly.

Juanita Jackson Mitchell is the first black woman to be admitted to the bar of Maryland.

1951

High school student Barbara Johns initiates a student strike that persuades the NAACP to make a Prince Edward County, Virginia, case one of those eventually decided by the U.S. Supreme Court in its 1954 school desegregation ruling.

1952

Charlotta Bass, a member of the Progressive Party ticket, becomes the first black woman to be nominated for vice president of the U.S. by a major political party.

1954

The Supreme Court declares segregated schools unconstitutional in *Brown v. Board of Education.* **Constance Baker Motley** plays a major role in preparing the case.

1955

Rosa Parks and the **Women's Political Council** are major forces in the Montgomery, Alabama, bus boycott.

1957

The first federal Civil Rights Bill since 1875 is passed.

1959

Juanita Kidd Stout is the first black woman elected to a judgeship in the U.S. when she becomes county court judge in Philadelphia.

1960

The Civil Rights Act of 1960 is passed.

1961

Four Freedom Riders, including **Ruby Doris Smith,** exercise civil disobedience when they refuse to pay trespassing fines. This action establishes the **Student Nonviolent Coordinating Committee's** "jail no bail" policy.

Federal courts order **Charlayne Hunter** and Hamilton Holmes admitted to the University of Georgia.

Helene Hillyer Hale becomes a county chairperson in Hawaii, a position equivalent to mayor.

1962

Verda Freeman Welcome is elected to the state senate in Maryland, the first black woman in the country to be a member of a state senate.

1963

The March on Washington draws 250,000 people to the Lincoln Memorial to lobby Congress for passage of a civil rights bill.

1964

The Twenty-fourth Amendment to the U.S. Constitution eliminates the levying of a poll tax for federal elections.

The Civil Rights Act of 1964 prohibits discrimination in public accommodations and employment.

The **Mississippi Freedom Democratic Party** is founded and sends a delegation to the Democratic National Convention. The delegation includes **Annie Devine, Fannie Lou Hamer,** Anna Mae King, and **Unita Blackwell.**

Constance Baker Motley is the first black woman elected to the New York State Senate.

1965

The Voting Rights Act is passed by Congress.

Patricia Roberts Harris is the first black woman to head a U.S. embassy when she is appointed ambassador to Luxembourg.

Constance Baker Motley is elected president of the borough of Manhattan in New York, the highest elected office held by a black woman in a major U.S. city.

1966

Constance Baker Motley becomes the first black woman on the federal bench when she is appointed a U.S. district court judge.

Barbara Charline Jordan is the first black woman in the Texas Senate.

Physician **Dorothy Lavania Brown** is the first black woman to be elected to the Tennessee State Legislature.

1967

The U.S. Supreme Court rules antimiscegenation laws unconstitutional in *Loving* v. *Virginia.*

1968

Shirley Chisholm is the first black woman elected to the U.S. House of Representa-

tives. She represents New York's twelfth congressional district.

Barbara M. Watson, the first woman assistant secretary of state, becomes the first woman administrator of the Bureau of Security and Consular Affairs of the U.S. State Department.

Attorney **Marian Wright Edelman** is congressional and federal agency liaison for the Poor People's Campaign.

Clothilde Dent Brown is the first African-American woman to be promoted to the rank of colonel in the U.S. Army.

1969

Amalya L. Kearse becomes a partner at Hughes, Hubbard & Reed, the first black woman to become a partner at a major Wall Street firm.

1970

Norma Holloway Johnson is confirmed to a seat on the U.S. District Court in Washington, D.C.

1971

The National Women's Political Caucus is founded.

Aileen C. Hernandez is elected president of the National Organization for Women (NOW), the first African-American woman to hold that position.

1972

Barbara Jordan is elected to Congress from Houston's eighteenth congressional district. She is the first black and the first woman to serve in the House of Representatives from Texas.

The first National Black Political Convention is attended by 3,000 delegates and 5,000 observers in Gary, Indiana.

Yvonne Brathwaite Burke cochairs the Democratic National Convention. It is the first time an African American has chaired a major party's national political convention. Burke is also elected, this year, to the House of Representatives, the first black woman from California chosen for that post.

Shirley Chisholm makes a bid for the Democratic Party's presidential nomination.

Jewel Stradford Lafontant-Mankarious, the first black woman to serve as assistant U.S. attorney, is appointed deputy solicitor general of the United States.

The National Association of Black Women Attorneys is founded and led by attorney Wilhelmina Jackson Rolark.

1973

The U.S. Supreme Court confirms, in *Roe v. Wade,* a woman's constitutional right to an abortion.

The National Black Feminist Organization is founded.

Lelia K. Smith Foley becomes the first African-American woman to be mayor in the continental United States when she is elected mayor of Taft, Oklahoma.

Sara J. Harper is the first woman appointed as a justice for the U.S. Marine Corps.

1975

Cardiss Collins is the first African American and the first woman to be appointed Democratic Party whip-at-large of the U.S. House of Representatives.

In a case that highlighted the sexual abuse of black women and the denial of basic rights to black prisoners, JoAnne Little is acquitted of murdering the guard who raped her in a Beaufort, North Carolina, jail cell.

1976

Barbara Jordan is keynote speaker at the Democratic National Convention.

Yvonne Brathwaite Burke is the first woman to chair the Congressional Black Caucus.

Unita Blackwell, elected major of Mayersville, is the first African-American mayor in Mississippi.

Maxine Waters is elected to the California State Assembly.

1977

Patricia Roberts Harris is appointed Secretary of Housing and Urban Development, making her the first black woman in a U.S. cabinet.

Eleanor Holmes Norton is first woman chair of the Equal Employment Opportunity Commission (EEOC).

Mary Frances Berry becomes assistant secretary for education in the Department of Health, Education, and Welfare.

Jewel Prestage, the first African-American woman to receive a Ph.D. in political science in the U.S., becomes a member of the Judicial Council of the national Democratic Party.

1978

Barbara Jordan retires from public office.

1979

Hazel Johnson becomes the first black woman general in the history of the U.S. military.

Patricia Roberts Harris becomes Secretary of Health, Education, and Welfare.

1980

The National Black Independent Political Party is founded. Its charter requires equal female-male representation in all leadership positions.

Mary Frances Berry is appointed to the U.S. Commission on Civil Rights.

1981

Liz Byrd becomes the first black legislator in Wyoming since statehood when she is elected to the house of representatives of that state.

Attorney Arnetta R. Hubbard is the first woman to be president of the National Bar Association.

1983

Ronald Reagan's attempt to gut the U.S. Civil Rights Commission is thwarted when Mary Frances Berry and Blandina Cardenas Ramirez bring suit.

1984

Shirley Chisholm founds the National Political Caucus of Black Women.

1985

Sheridan Grace Cadoria is the first black woman promoted to brigadier general in the regular U.S. Army.

Sharon Pratt Dixon Kelly is the first woman to serve as treasurer of the national Democratic Party.

The **National Organization of Black Elected Legislative Women** is founded in Philadelphia.

1986

The U.S. Supreme Court rules unanimously that sexual harassment constitutes illegal job discrimination.

1987

Beulah MacDonald, after her son is lynched, sues the United Klans of America. She wins a $7 million judgment, which destroys that unit of the Ku Klux Klan.

Carrie Saxon Perry is elected mayor of Hartford, Connecticut.

1988

Lenora Fulani of the New Alliance Party is the first woman and first African-American presidential candidate to get on the ballot in all fifty states.

Juanita Kidd Stout is appointed to the Pennsylvania Supreme Court, making her the first black woman to serve on a state supreme court.

The **Black Women Mayors' Caucus** is founded at the National Conference of Black Mayors.

1990

Sharon Pratt Dixon Kelly is elected mayor of Washington, D.C., becoming the first woman and the first D.C. native to be elected mayor of the nation's capital.

Marcelite J. Harris is the first black woman to hold the rank of brigadier general in the U.S. Air Force.

Eleanor Holmes Norton is elected U.S. congressional delegate from Washington, D.C.

Maxine Waters is elected to the U.S. Congress from California.

Barbara-Rose Collins is elected to the U.S. Congress from Michigan.

1991

Anita Hill's televised testimony before the U.S. Senate Judiciary Committee during the confirmation hearings of Supreme Court

Justice Clarence Thomas initiates a national discussion on sexual harassment.

1992

For the second time, Barbara Jordan is keynote speaker at the Democratic National Convention.

Carol Moseley-Braun of Illinois is the first black woman to be elected to the U.S. Senate. She is also the first black senator from the Democratic Party.

According to the Joint Center for Political Studies, 50 to 60 percent of Democratic Party state officials are African-American women.

Five new black women are elected to the U.S. House of Representatives. They include **Carrie Meek** of Florida, **Eddie Bernice Johnson** of Texas, **Eva Clayton** of North Carolina, **Corrine Brown** of Florida, and **Cynthia McKinney** of Georgia. There are now ten black women in Congress.

Leah Sears-Collins is the first woman and the youngest person to serve on the Supreme Court of Georgia.

Jacquelyn Barrett is elected sheriff of Fulton County, Georgia, making her the first black woman sheriff in the United States.

Pamela Fanning Carter, of Indiana, becomes the first African-American woman to be elected attorney general of any state.

Yvonne Brathwaite Burke, a former congresswoman, becomes the first African American elected to the Los Angeles County Board of Supervisors.

1993

Hazel O'Leary is the first woman and the first African American to serve as Secretary of Energy.

Joycelyn Elders is confirmed as Surgeon General of the United States.

1994

Joycelyn Elders is fired from her position as Surgeon General after voicing a number of controversial opinions.

1995

The U.S. Supreme Court rules it unconstitutional for political districts to be drawn primarily on racial lines.

1996

Alexis M. Herman is nominated for the post of secretary of labor by President Clinton.

Bibliography

GENERAL BOOKS USEFUL TO THE STUDY OF BLACK WOMEN IN AMERICA

Reference Books

African-Americans: Voices of Triumph. Three volume set: *Perseverance, Leadership,* and *Creative Fire.* By the editors of Time-Life Books, Alexandria, Virginia, 1993.

Estell, Kenneth, ed., *The African-American Almanac.* Detroit, Mich., 1994.

Harley, Sharon. *The Timetables of African-American History: A Chronology of the Most Important People and Events in African-American History.* New York, 1995.

Hine, Darlene Clark. *Hine Sight: Black Women and The Re-Construction of American History.* Brooklyn, New York, 1994.

Hine, Darlene Clark, ed., Elsa Barkley Brown and Rosalyn Terborg-Penn, associate editors. *Black Women in America: An Historical Encyclopedia.* Brooklyn, New York, 1993.

Hornsby, Alton, Jr. *Chronology of African-American History: Significant Events and People from 1619 to the Present.* Detroit, Michigan, 1991.

Kranz, Rachel. *Biographical Dictionary of Black Americans.* New York, 1992.

Lanker, Brian. *I Dream a World: Portraits of Black Women Who Changed America.* New York, 1989.

Logan, Rayford W., and Michael R. Winston, eds. *Dictionary of American Negro Biography,* New York, 1982.

Low, W. Augustus, and Virgil A. Clift, eds. *Encyclopedia of Black America.* New York, 1981.

Salem, Dorothy C., ed. *African American Women: A Biographical Dictionary.* New York, 1993.

Salzman, Jack, David Lionel Smith, and Cornel West. *Encyclopedia of African-American Culture and History.* Five vol. New York, 1996.

Smith, Jessie Carney, ed., *Notable Black American Women.* Two Volumes. Detroit, Mich., Book I, 1993; Book II, 1996.

General Books about Black Women

Giddings, Paula. *When and Where I Enter: The Impact of Black Women on Race and Sex in America,* New York, 1984.

Guy-Sheftall, Beverly. *Words of Fire: An Anthology of African-American Feminist Thought.* New York, 1995.

Hine, Darlene Clark, Wilma King, and Linda Reed, eds. *"We Specialize in the Wholly Impossible": A Reader in Black Women's History.* Brooklyn, N.Y., 1995.

Jones, Jacqueline. *Labor of Love, Labor of Sorrow: Black Women, Work, and the Family from Slavery to the Present.* New York, 1985.

Lerner, Gerda, ed. *Black Women in White America: A Documentary History.* New York, 1972.

BOOKS WHICH INCLUDE INFORMATION ON BLACK WOMEN IN LAW AND GOVERNMENT

Dittmer, John. *Local People: The Struggle For Civil Rights in Mississippi.* Urbana and Chicago, Illinois, 1994.

Egerton, John. *Speak Now Against the Day: The Generation Before the Civil Rights Movement in the South.* Chapel Hill, N.C., 1995.

Elliot, Jeffrey M. *Encyclopedia of African-American Politics.* Santa Barbara, California, 1996.

Kluger, Richard. *Simple Justice: The History of Brown v. Board of Education and Black America's Struggle for Equality.* New York, 1975.

Morello, Karen Berger. *The Invisible Bar: The Woman Lawyer in America 1638 to the Present.* Chapter 6, "Double Impairment: Black Women Lawyers." Boston, 1986.

Payne, Charles M. *I've Got the Light of Freedom: The Organizing Tradition and the Mississippi Freedom Struggle.* Berkeley, Calif., 1995.

Smith, J. Clay, Jr. *Emancipation: The Making of the Black Lawyer, 1844–1944.* Philadelphia, 1993.

Contents of the Set

(ORGANIZED BY VOLUME)

Literature

Angelou, Maya
Ansa, Tina McElroy
Bambara, Toni Cade
Bennett, Gwendolyn
Bonner, Marita
Brooks, Gwendolyn
Brown, Linda Beatrice
Burroughs, Margaret
Butler, Octavia E.
Campbell, Bebe Moore
Cary, Lorene
Chase-Riboud, Barbara
Cleage, Pearl
Cliff, Michelle
Clifton, Lucille
Cooper, J. California
Cortez, Jayne
Danner, Margaret Essie
Davis, Thadious
Davis, Thulani
Delaney Sisters, The
DeVeaux, Alexis
Dove, Rita
Drumgold, Kate
Dunbar-Nelson, Alice
Dunlap, Ethel Trew
Fauset, Jessie Redmon
Giddings, Paula
Giovanni, Nikki
Golden, Marita
Greenfield, Eloise
Guy, Rosa
Hamilton, Virginia Esther
Harper, Frances Ellen Watkins
hooks, bell
Hopkins, Pauline Elizabeth
Hunter, Kristin
Hurston, Zora Neale
Johnson, Georgia Douglas
Jones, Gayl
Jordan, June
Kincaid, Jamaica
Larsen, Nella
Lorde, Audre
Madgett, Naomi Long
Marshall, Paule
McElroy, Colleen J.

McMillan, Terry
Meriwether, Louise
Morrison, Toni
Naylor, Gloria
Petry, Ann Lane
Polite, Carlene
Sanchez, Sonia
Sanders, Dori
Shockley, Ann Allen
Southerland, Ellease
Spencer, Anne
Taylor, Mildred
Thomas, Joyce Carol
Vroman, Mary Elizabeth
Walker, Alice
Walker, Margaret Abigail
Wallace, Michele
West, Dorothy
Williams, Sherley Anne
Wilson, Harriet E.

Dance, Sports, and Visual Arts

Dance

Asante, Kariamu Welsh
Baker, Josephine
Blunden, Jeraldyne
Brown, Joan Myers
Collins, Janet
DeLavallade, Carmen
Dunham, Katherine
Forsyne, Ida
Hinkson, Mary
Jamison, Judith
Johnson, Virginia
Primus, Pearl
Turney, Matt
Waters, Sylvia
Yarborough, Sara
Zollar, Jawole Willa Jo

Sports

Ashford, Evelyn
Bolden, Jeanette
Brisco-Hooks, Valerie
Brown, Alice
Brown, Earlene

Cheeseborough, Chandra
Coachman, Alice
Daniels, Isabel
Dawes, Dominique
DeFrantz, Anita
Devers, Gail
Edwards, Teresa
Faggs, Mae
Ferrell, Barbara
Franke, Nikki
Gallagher, Kim
Garrison, Zina
Gibson, Althea
Glenn, Lula Mae Hymes
Harris-Stewart, Lusia
Hudson, Martha
Hyman, Flora
Jacket, Barbara J.
Jackson, Nell Cecilia
Jones, Barbara
Jones, Leora "Sam"
Joyner, Florence Griffith
Joyner-Kersee, Jackie
Love, Lynette
Matthews, Margaret
McDaniel, Mildred
McGuire, Edith
Miller, Cheryl
Mims, Madeleine Manning
Murray, Lenda
Patterson-Tyler, Audrey
  (Mickey)
Pickett, Tydie
Powell, Renee
Rudolph, Wilma
Stokes, Louise
Stone, Lyle (Toni)
Stringer, C. Vivian
Thomas, Debi
Thomas, Vanessa
Tyus, Wyomia
Washington, Ora
White, Willye B.
Williams, Lucinda
Woodard, Lynette

Visual Arts

Beasley, Phoebe
Blount, Mildred E.

Brandon, Barbara
Burke, Selma
Catlett, Elizabeth
Fuller, Meta
Gafford, Alice
Humphrey, Margo
Hunter, Clementine
Jackson-Jarvis, Martha
Jackson, May Howard
Jones, Lois Mailou
Lewis, Mary Edmonia
Maynard, Valerie
McCullough, Geraldine
Moutoussamy-Ashe, Jeanne
Owens-Hart, Winnie
Pindell, Howardena
Piper, Adrian
Pogue, Stephanie
Powers, Harriet
Prophet, Nancy Elizabeth
Ringgold, Faith
Roberts, Malkia
Saar, Alison
Saar, Betye
Savage, Augusta
Sklarek, Norma Merrick
Thomas, Alma
Waring, Laura Wheeler
Woodard, Beulah Ecton

Business and Professions

Andrews, Rosalyn
Avant, Angela
Baker, Augusta
Beasley, Delilah
Bowen, Ruth
Bowser, Yvette Lee
Bradford, Martina
Bragg, Janet Harmon
Bricktop (Ada Smith)
Britton, Mary E.
Brooks, Hallie
Brown, Willa Beatrice
Brunson, Dorothy
Cadoria, Sheridan Grace
Cardozo Sisters

Clayton, Xernona
Coleman, Bessie
Coston, Julia Ringwood
Day, Carolyn Bond
Delaney, Sara "Sadie"
de Passe, Suzanne
Diggs, Ellen Irene
Dunnigan, Alice
Early, Charity Adams
Fisher, Ruth Anna
Florence, Virginia
Fudge, Ann
Gillespie, Marcia Ann
Gleason, Eliza Atkins
Hare, Maud Cuney
Harris, Marcelite
Harsh, Vivian Gordon
Haynes, Elizabeth Ross
Houston, Drusilla Dunjee
Hunter-Gault, Charlayne
Hutson, Jean Blackwell
Jefferson, Lucy
Jemison, Mae C.
Jenkins, Carol
Johnson, Eunice Walker
Jones, Clara Stanton
Jones, Virginia Lacy
Julian, Anna Johnson
King, Reatha Clark
Latimer, Catherine Allen
Lewis, Ida Elizabeth
Major, Gerri
Malone, Annie Turnbo
Malveaux, Julianne
Matthews, Miriam
McClain, Leanita
Morgan, Rose
Murray, Joan
Nelson, Jill
Oglesby, Mary
Payne, Ethel L.
Phinazee, Alethia
Pleasant, Mary Ellen
Procope, Ernesta G.
Proctor, Barbara Gardner
Quarles, Norma R.
Randolph, Lucille
Rhone, Sylvia
Rollins, Charlemae Hill

Saunders, Doris
Simmons, Judy
Simpson, Carole
Sims, Naomi
Smith, Ida Van
Smith, Jessie Carney
Stewart, Pearl
Taylor, Susan
Thompson, Era Bell
Villarosa, Linda
Walker, Madam C. J.
Washington, Sarah Spencer
Wattleton, Faye
Wesley, Dorothy Porter
White, Eartha Mary
Willis, Gertrude

Music

Addison, Adele
Akers, Doris
Allen, Geri
Anderson, Ernestine
Anderson, Marian
Armstrong, Lillian "Lil"
Arroyo, Martina
Ashby, Dorothy Jeanne
Austin, Lovie
Bailey, Pearl
Baiocchi, Regina Harris
Baker, Anita
Baker, LaVern
Barnett, Etta Moten
Barrett, "Sweet Emma"
Barton, Willene
Battle, Kathleen
Blige, Mary J.
Bonds, Margaret
Braxton, Toni
Brice, Carol
Brown, Anne Wiggins
Brown, Cleo Patra
Brown, Ruth
Bryant, Clora
Bryant, Hazel Joan
Bumbry, Grace
Caesar, Shirley
Calloway, Blanche

Education

Religion and Community

Law and Government

Theater Arts and Entertainment

Social Activism

Science, Health, and Medicine

Contents of the Set

(LISTED ALPHABETICALLY BY ENTRY)

Index

Page numbers in **boldface** indicate main entries. Page numbers in *italics* indicate illustrations.